ARIZONA REAL ESTATE

A Professional's Guide to Law and Practice

K. MICHELLE LIND, ESQ., GENERAL COUNSEL
ARIZONA ASSOCIATION OF REALTORS®

K. Michelle Lind, Esq.
Arizona Association of REALTORS®
255 East Osborn Road, Suite 200
Phoenix, Arizona 85021-2327

Table of Contents

To my family and friends,
who have supported me both personally and professionally,
and in particular my sons, Eric and Ryan,
who in their youth supported my studies
during law school.

DEDICATION

This book is dedicated to the members of the Arizona Association of REALTORS® (AAR) whose participation in the association make this book possible. They are the foundation of the real estate transaction and their dedication is reflected in AAR's vision . . . *the best prepared real estate practitioner with the highest standards.*

ACKNOWLEDGMENTS

There are many who have contributed in one way or another to this undertaking, giving unselfishly of their time and input. AAR's Chief Executive Officer Ty Strout, RCE, CAE, first suggested that I compile a few articles years ago and called them *"Michelle's Musings."* Vice President, Information Management Ron LaMee enthusiastically encouraged me to undertake the project of compiling the articles into a book. I have worked closely over the last 14 years with Alice Martin, RCE, CAE, GRI, AAR's Executive Vice President, and Monica Schulik, AAR's Membership Director, on the many association forms and sincerely appreciate their commitment to the industry. I have learned a great deal about legislative issues from Tom Farley, Vice President, Government Affairs, and professional education from Barbara Freestone, Vice President, Professional Development. I would like to acknowledge and thank my legal assistant Christina Smalls, for all her help editing, proofing, cite checking and organizing this book.

Frank Dickens, Coldwell Banker NARICO, provided frequent advice, support and a "practitioner's view," which was invaluable. My former law partner and the AAR Legal Hotline attorney, Christopher Combs, graciously reviewed the first draft of this book and provided input from his perspective. Holly Eslinger, ABR, GRI, CRS, e-Pro, QSC (quality service certified), Realty Executives and Denny Elmes, Designated Broker, Award Realty, also reviewed the initial draft and provided helpful suggestions for improvement. I owe a debt of gratitude to another former law partner,

Richard Mack, for reviewing the final draft of this book, and for always being available to help me work through various difficult legal issues as they have arisen over the years.

Finally, I would like to acknowledge the 2006 Arizona Association of REALTORS® officers, President Craig W. Sanford, CRS, GRI, Realty Executives; President-elect Frank Dickens, Coldwell Banker Narico; First Vice President John R. Gall, ABR, CRS, GRI, RE/MAX Prestige Properties; Treasurer K. Michael "Mike" Wasmann, ABR, CRS, GRI, MRE, SRES, ePRO, RE/MAX Integrity.

THE PURPOSE OF THIS BOOK

The purpose of this book is to organize and expand on the many articles I have written during my years as Arizona Association of REALTORS® legal counsel. The book is intended to be a reference for REALTORS®, other real estate practitioners and attorneys involved in the industry to help address everyday legal and practical real estate issues. My intention is to answer frequently asked questions about Arizona real estate law and the real estate forms provided by the association, so those in the industry can better serve their clients and customers.

Whether you are entering into an employment agreement, drafting a contract, managing a transaction, or teaching another, this book is intended to be an easy reference for subjects involving the practice of real estate. The many references to case law, statutes and rules are included for the attorneys and others who may want to undertake further research on an issue. If you are new to the industry, my hope is that this book is a helpful resource as you gain experience. If you are a "seasoned" practitioner, my hope is that you can use the book as a reference to answer day-to-day questions.

WHERE TO FIND THE FORMS

There are numerous references to Arizona Association of REALTORS® forms and contracts throughout the book. Sample copies of all of the Arizona Association of REALTORS® forms are available on the Arizona Association of REALTORS® Web site (*AARonline.com*).

INTRODUCTION TO THE TERMS AND LEGAL REFERENCES

There are terms, abbreviations, acronyms and legal references in the text, which are best explained upfront.

Use of the Term "Broker"

For ease of reference and to avoid confusion about agency relationships, I have frequently used the term "broker" to refer to all real estate licensees, brokers and salespersons, although they are commonly referred to as "agents."

Legal References

Cases: The cases cited are "court made" or common law that may be located at a law library or on an online legal service. The first name is the plaintiff and the second name is the defendant. The numbers and abbreviations following the case name indicate where the case can be located and the year the case was decided. For example, in *Hill v. Jones,* 151 Ariz. 81, 725 P.2d 1115 (App. 1986), Hill was the plaintiff who sued Jones, the defendant. The case was decided by the Court of Appeals in 1986 and can be found in the 151st volume of the *Arizona Reports* book at page 81 or in the 725th volume of the *Pacific Reporter* book on page 1115. The term *"Id.,"* means that the sentence is referring to what the court said in the previously cited case.

Statutes: The statutes are laws passed by the legislature. Statutes are indicated by A.R.S., which stands for Arizona Revised Statutes. The statutes can be located at a law library, online at the Arizona legislature Web site, or in many cases in the *Arizona Department of Real Estate Law Book.* For example, the statute A.R.S. §32-2101 can be found in title 32, chapter 21. The term *"et. seq."* means "and the following." For example, a reference to A.R.S. §32-2101 *et.seq.* means that statute and all the following statutes in the chapter.

Rules: The "Commissioner's Rules" are a part of the Arizona Administrative Code at Title 4, Chapter 28. The Arizona Administrative Code is abbreviated as A.A.C., which I have omitted and simply referred to R4-28- . . . throughout the text. The Administrative Code is also available at a law library, in the *Arizona Department of Real Estate Law Book* or on the Arizona Secretary of State's Web site.

ABBREVIATIONS

AAR: Arizona Association of REALTORS®
NAR: NATIONAL ASSOCIATION OF REALTORS®
ADRE: Arizona Department of Real Estate

PLEASE REMEMBER

The information provided herein is of a general nature and may not be the most updated or revised information because statutes, rules, case law and forms can change following the date of first publication. Further, this publication reflects only the opinion of the author, is not intended as definitive legal advice, and you should not act upon it without seeking independent legal counsel. For real estate licensees, you should also remember that this book is a guideline of general information, and you should always comply with the office policies and procedures of your employing broker.

INTRODUCTION

Real Estate In Arizona

The ownership, buying and selling of real estate is the cornerstone of the economy on both a large and small scale and is generally the largest financial investment most people ever make. The importance of insuring that the rights of individuals involved in a real estate transaction are protected cannot be overstated. Property ownership provides long-term financial stability for most Americans and is the foundation of communities. The real estate industry involves thousands of professionals including: real estate brokers and salespeople, title and escrow officers, mortgage brokers and bankers, property inspectors, surveyors, appraisers, engineers, and the numerous individuals, both in the private and public sector, involved in land-use planning.

All real estate transactions share a common legal and procedural foundation. However, there is no "typical" real estate transaction. The process differs depending on the individuals involved and their motivations. Transactions also differ depending on the type of property involved. Therefore, the information contained herein is necessarily general in nature.

The significance of the term REALTOR®

A REALTOR® is a licensed real estate broker or salesperson who is a member of the NATIONAL ASSOCIATION OF REALTORS® (NAR)

...
1

and subscribes to the NAR Code of Ethics, which is set forth at the end of this book. An Arizona REALTOR® also is a member of the Arizona Association of REALTORS® (AAR) and in most cases, a member of a local REALTOR® association or board. The term REALTOR® is a registered collective membership mark that identifies the real estate licensee as a REALTOR® member. Thus, the term REALTOR® is not a generic term and not all real estate licensees are REALTORS®.

REALTORS® in Arizona do much more than assist buyers and sellers with a real estate transaction. They are active participants in building communities and protecting private property rights.

The Role of the Arizona Association of REALTORS® (AAR)

AAR is a professional trade association for real estate brokers, agents and other individuals involved in the real estate industry. AAR has more than 53,000 members and is the largest trade association in Arizona. AAR is a part of NAR, which is headquartered in Chicago and has a membership of more than one million members. AAR is comprised of 21 local associations of REALTORS® and seven affiliated chapters of Institutes, Societies and Councils.

AAR is involved in a variety of aspects of the real estate industry, such as education, governmental, legislative and legal issues, professional standards and disseminating real estate related information to members and the public. AAR develops and produces numerous contracts and forms to assist in the transfer of real estate. AAR also provides assistance to consumers and is a source for a variety of real estate related information.

AAR is governed by its Executive Committee and Board of Directors. AAR's activities are directed by Key Result Areas (KRAs), which are committees comprised of volunteers. These KRAs are:

Governmental KRA (GKRA)

The GKRA works to promote AAR's interests at all levels of government and mobilize members to legislative and political action. The GKRA seeks input from all areas of the real estate industry when formulating or reviewing legislation affecting real estate. The GKRA also reviews the rules and regulations proposed by state agencies affecting the industry.

Industry Issues KRA (IIKRA)

The IIKRA concentrates on providing the best possible standard forms, legal information, risk management information and tools, ethics enforcement, professional standards training, international issues, fair housing and diversity, housing affordability, and more. The IIKRA also identifies issues needing legislative or regulatory attention (and contributes to the development of such legislation or regulation), and participates in effective alliances with other industries on related issues.

Information Management KRA (IMKRA)

The IMKRA coordinates AAR's activities relating to technology and the delivery of information. The IMKRA oversees AAR's Web site, aaronline.com, which contains a wealth of real estate information and resources for both members and consumers, and the *Arizona REALTOR® Digest,* a monthly AAR publication. The IMKRA also works on media relations, surveys and research, and membership records.

Professional Development KRA (PDKRA)

The PDKRA provides tools to assist members to be the best prepared and perform to the highest standards. This group oversees educational programs, researches needs for professional development and publicizes the available professional development resources. The PDKRA also oversees the GRI (Graduate REALTOR® Institute) designation program and specialty seminars such as the winter conference, the leadership conference, and various broker seminars.

CHAPTER I
· · · · · · · · · · · · · · ·

The Arizona Department of Real Estate Licensing and Regulatory Authority

The purpose of the Arizona Department of Real Estate (ADRE) is to protect the public interest through licensure and regulation of the real estate profession. A.R.S. §32-2102. Real estate brokers must be licensed by the ADRE. Brokers and the attorneys that represent them should be familiar with the ADRE statutes, rules and policies since the department directly affects a broker's livelihood and the way a broker conducts business.

Arizona statutes define the scope of the department's authority. A.R.S. §32-2101 *et. seq.* The ADRE also has the authority to promulgate rules, which are often referred to as "Commissioner's Rules," and issue Substantive Policy Statements (SPS).[1] The Commissioner's Rules implement statutes or describe the ADRE's procedure or practice. A.R.S. §41-1001(17). The Substantive Policy Statements describe the ADRE's current approach to or opinion of the requirements of the statutes and rules.

---

[1] The rule-making process is governed by statute and all rules must be approved by the Governor's Regulatory Review Council before they become effective. A.R.S. §41-1021 *et. seq.* The SPS policy-making process is not regulated by statute, but a substantive policy statement that exceeds the ADRE's authority may be challenged. A.R.S. §41-1033. An SPS is advisory only and cannot impose additional requirements. A.R.S. §41-1001(20).

LICENSING

A person must be licensed by the ADRE to engage in the real estate brokerage business. It is unlawful for a person to pay anyone for performing any real estate brokerage activities, who is not licensed by the ADRE at the time the service is rendered. A.R.S. §32-2155(B). In fact, "[a]ny act, in consideration or expectation of compensation, which is included in the definition of a real estate . . .broker, whether the act is an incidental part of a transaction or the entire transaction, constitutes the person offering or attempting to perform the act of a real estate broker." A.R.S. §32-2122(D). The definition of a real estate broker is quite extensive. A.R.S. §32-2101(47). As set forth in the statutes, a person must have a real estate license to be paid to:

- sell, exchange, purchase, rent or lease real estate
- offer to sell, exchange, purchase, rent or lease real estate or time-share interests
- negotiate or offer, attempt or agree to negotiate the sale, exchange, purchase, rental or leasing of real estate
- list or offer, attempt or agree to list real estate for sale, lease or exchange
- auction or offer, attempt or agree to auction real estate
- buy, sell, offer to buy or sell or otherwise deal in options on real estate or improvements to real estate
- collect or offer, attempt or agree to collect rent for the use of real estate
- advertise or hold out as being engaged in the business of buying, selling, exchanging, renting or leasing real estate or counseling or advising regarding real estate
- assist or direct in the procuring of prospects, calculated to result in the sale, exchange, leasing or rental of real estate
- assist or direct in the negotiation of any transaction calculated or intended to result in the sale, exchange, leasing or rental of real estate

- incident to the sale of real estate, negotiate or offer, attempt or agree to negotiate a loan secured or to be secured by any mortgage or other encumbrance upon or transfer of real estate
- engage in the business of assisting or offering to assist another in filing an application for the purchase or lease of, or in locating or entering upon, lands owned by the state or federal government
- claim, demand, charge, receive, collect or contract for the collection of an advance fee in connection with any employment enumerated above, including employment undertaken to promote the sale or lease of real property by advance fee listing, by furnishing rental information to a prospective tenant for a fee paid by the prospective tenant, by advertisement or by any other offering to sell, lease, exchange or rent real property or selling kits connected therewith
- engage in any of the acts listed above for the sale or lease of other than real property if a real property sale or lease is a part of, contingent on or ancillary to the transaction
- perform any of the acts listed above as an employee of, or on behalf of, the owner of real estate, or interest in the real estate, or improvements affixed on the real estate, for compensation

An employing broker may employ and pay only active licensees, and a licensee may accept employment and compensation as a licensee only from the legally licensed broker to whom the licensee is licensed. A.R.S. §32-2155(A). However, if a salesperson has rightfully earned a commission while licensed and in the employ of an employing broker, the broker can pay the salesperson even though the salesperson's license has expired or has transferred to another firm. See, Substantive Policy Statement 2005.08. The other limited exemptions from the real estate licensing requirements are listed in A.R.S. §32-2121.

Obtaining a Salesperson's License

To obtain a real estate license, A.R.S. §32-2124, requires that the individual:

- is a person of honesty, truthfulness, character and competency
- has not had a real estate license denied within one year, or revoked within two years immediately preceding the application
- is at least 18 years of age
- has completed 90 hours of prelicensure education and a school and state examination on the course
- take a six-hour continuing education course in contract law and contract writing

Qualifying for a Broker's License

To obtain a broker's license, a person generally must have at least three years of actual experience as a licensed real estate salesperson or real estate broker during the five years immediately preceding the time of application. A.R.S. §32-2124. The person must pass an examination for a broker's license that is more exacting and stringent and of a broader scope than the examination for a salesperson's license. A.R.S. §32-2124 (I).

Corporations, Limited Liability Companies or Partnerships May Be Licensed

A corporation, limited liability company or partnership may hold a broker's license for the entity to act as an employing broker. The entity must designate a natural person who is licensed as a broker and who is an officer of the corporation, manager or member of the limited liability company if management, or partner of the partnership to act as designated broker. A.R.S. §32-2125(A).

Additionally, a salesperson or associate broker may act through a professional corporation (PC) or professional limited liability company (PLLC) that is licensed by the department. A.R.S. §32-2125(B). A designated broker who acts on behalf of an employing real estate entity is also permitted to become a PC or a PLLC.

Unlicensed Activity — Late License Renewal

Paying compensation to an unlicensed person is a violation of A.R.S. §32-2153(A)(10), (A)(14), (B)(6) and A.R.S. §32-2155(A)(B). Unlicensed real estate activity may result from real estate activities by an individual who has never obtained a license or because a broker failed to renew his or her license in a timely manner. For a broker, the failure to comply with the ADRE licensing regulations can result in consequences varying from a letter of concern to loss of the ability to practice in the real estate profession. The Commissioner's Rule, R4-28-306(C)(D), addresses the penalties for late renewal, i.e., unlawful license activity. The penalties depend on how long the broker's license has been expired and the broker's prior disciplinary history. Because of the possible sanctions, employing brokers, designated brokers and salespersons should post reminders to insure that all the applicable licenses are renewed prior to expiration.

A broker, whose license has expired resulting in unlawful license activity for 30 days or less, has no prior history of engaging in unlawful license activity, and against whom there are no pending complaints may apply to renew the license, and the ADRE will not delay processing the application based on the unlawful licensed activity. However, the ADRE will issue an Advisory Letter of Concern. The ADRE may take disciplinary action against a broker who has engaged in unlawful license activity for longer than 30 days, has previously conducted unlawful license activity, or is the subject of a pending complaint.

If the license of an employing broker expires, the licenses of its designated broker and salespersons are severed. Thus, its designated broker and salespeople are all conducting real estate without a license.

Unlicensed Real Estate Assistants

The ADRE Substantive Policy Statement No. 2005.04 provides guidance in regard to the activities in which an unlicensed real estate assistant may engage. The policy clearly states that if an unlicensed assistant is paid on any basis that relies on the ultimate sale of a property, then that person must be licensed. The policy specifies that [a]n unlicensed assistant in the employ of a licensed real estate broker may:

Perform telephone duties, to include calls to:
- collect demographic information
- solicit interest in engaging the services of a licensee or brokerage

- set or confirm appointments (with no other discussion) for:
    - a licensee to list or show property
    - a buyer with a loan officer
    - a property inspector to inspect a home
    - a repair/maintenance person to perform repairs/maintenance
    - an appraiser to appraise property
    - a mortgage and/or title companies to track the status of a file, check daily interest rates and points, check whether buyer has been qualified, confirm closing appointment for licensee, and so forth
- assist a licensee at an open house
- unlock a home for a licensee so that licensee can show a buyer the property or preview the property (no discussion about the property)
- deliver documents (as a mail or delivery service only)

An unlicensed assistant may not perform the following activities:
- hold/host an open house without an agent being present
- perform a walk-through inspection
- answer questions relating to a transactional document
- give instructions to inspectors, appraisers or maintenance/repair people

Scope of Licensure — Broker Price Opinions

A real estate license also authorizes a broker to prepare an opinion as to the price of real estate for the purpose of prospective listing or sale, if this opinion is not referred to as an appraisal.

To perform an "appraisal," a person must be licensed by the Board of Appraisal, and only a licensed or certified appraiser can be compensated for performing an appraisal A.R.S. §32-3638; A.R.S. §32-3603. An "appraisal" is defined as:

a statement independently and impartially prepared by an individual setting forth an opinion as to the market value of real property as of a specific date and supported by the presentation and analysis of relevant market information. A.R.S. §32-3601(1).

However, licensed real estate brokers are exempted from these statutory appraisal licensing and certification requirements. A.R.S. § 32-3602(1) states that the Board of Appraisal statutes do not apply to:

a real estate broker or salesperson who is licensed in this state and who, when acting as such, gives an opinion as to the price of real estate for the purpose of prospective listing or sale if this opinion is not referred to as an appraisal.

Therefore, there is no prohibition from a real estate licensee, when acting as such, from being compensated for performing a price opinion for the purpose of prospective listing or sale. The issue, which remains unclear, is the definition of "for the purpose of prospective listing or sale."[2]

ADRE REGULATORY ISSUES FOR EMPLOYING AND DESIGNATED BROKERS

The issues involved in running a brokerage firm are numerous and complex. In addition to the broker's business plan, recruiting and profitability issues, the broker must consider:

- Employment Laws
- Internal Dispute Resolution
- Errors & Omissions Insurance

---

[2]Another exemption is "[a]n individual appraising real property only for the purpose of providing an opinion in a judicial proceeding or an individual providing an opinion in a judicial proceeding" provided that the person does not imply that the person is a licensed appraiser. A.R.S. §32-3602(8).

- Broker/Salesperson Relationships
- Risk Management
- Regulatory Issues
- Office Policies

The broker must address all of these issues while complying with the ADRE regulatory requirements.

Records Retention

Brokers are required to retain brokerage records in a chronological log or other systematic manner. A.R.S. §32-2151.01(E) (sales); A.R.S. §32-2151.01(E) and §32-2175(F) (nonresidential leasing); A.R.S. §32-2151.01(E) (residential rental agreements).

Property management agreements must be consecutively numbered or kept with a system that is orderly, easily accessible and consistent with generally accepted professional standards. A.R.S. §32-2175(E).

The records must be retained for the following time frames:
- Five years for transaction records. A.R.S. §32-2151.01, R428-802B.
- One year for transactions that did not close. A.R.S. §32-2151.01C.
- Three years for property management records. A.R.S. §32-2175.

Transaction folders must contain the following:
- Sales: evidence that the earnest and down monies were properly handled, complete copy of sales contract, escrow account receipt, closing or settlement statement, escrow instructions, employment agreement, release of escrow monies. A.R.S. §2151.01(F).
- Property management: evidence that earnest and down monies were properly handled, complete copy of lease, employment agreements. A.R.S. §32-2175(F).

Records may be maintained electronically if:
- the records are maintained in a manner allowing reconstruction in the event of destruction of electronic data
- the records can be produced, at the broker's expense, in legible, written form (hard copy) for auditing, inspection or investigation purposes

- the electronic records are exact duplicates of the original
- the stored records are legible

See, Substantive Policy Statement No. 2005.06.

Broker Review

A designated broker is required to review each listing agreement, purchase or lease agreement or similar instrument within five days of the date the parties executed the document, and to place the broker's initials and date of review on the same page as the parties' signatures.[3] A.R.S. §32-2151.01(G). A broker may use an electronic signature to indicate the broker's approval of contracts and agreements, if the following requirements are met:

- The system must meet the criteria under A.R.S. §44-7031 (the Electronic Transactions Act): A signature is a secure electronic signature if, through the application of a security procedure, it can be demonstrated that the electronic signature at the time the signature was made was:
  - unique to the person using it
  - capable of verification
  - under the sole control of the person using it
  - linked to the electronic record to which it relates in such a manner that if the record were changed the electronic signature would be invalidated
- The brokerage must have and enforce a written internal policy regarding personal computer security and, at a minimum, require that any person with electronic signature authority and capability locks or signs off his/her computer every time the person walks away from their computer.

---

[3] However, the designated broker's failure to review the agreement within five days does not affect the agreement's enforceability between the parties.

- The brokerage must have a back-up system defined for when the computers are down for an extended period of time (i.e., how and when contracts and agreements will be manually reviewed).
- The system must have the ability to create a secure history log of all activity for electronic signatures that can be reviewed by ADRE auditors and investigators.

Substantive Policy Statement No. 2005.10.

Place of Business

A brokerage firm must have a definite location. The brokerage may have a P.O. Box as a mailing address, but it must have a physical location. Additionally, the place of business must have a sign at the entrance that contains the employing broker's name. A.R.S. §32-2126.

Reasonable Supervision

The employing broker and designated broker are responsible for supervising the associate brokers, salespersons and employees of the employing broker within the course of their employment. A broker may be sanctioned for the failure "to exercise reasonable supervision over the activities of salespersons, associate brokers or others under the broker's employ." A.R.S. §32-2153(21). A "designated broker who, upon learning of a violation of real estate statutes or rules by a salesperson or associate broker under the broker's supervision, immediately reports the violation to the ADRE is not subject to disciplinary action by the ADRE for failure to supervise the salesperson or broker." *See,* R4-28-1103(F). Further, the designated broker is responsible for notifying the ADRE within 10 days after a salesperson or broker leaves a broker's employment.

Broker Supervision and Control Audit Declaration

Upon license renewal, a designated broker for an employing broker is obligated to complete and submit a signed Broker Supervision and Control Audit Declaration. The completed declaration in the form prescribed by the ADRE must be submitted to the ADRE no earlier than 90 days before the broker's license expiration date. R4-28-303(A)(2)(f).

Office Policies

An employing broker and a designated broker must exercise reasonable supervision and control over the activities of brokers, salespersons and others in the employ of the broker. R4-28-1103(A). If the employing broker has more than one office or employs more than one salesperson, the broker must establish and enforce written policies, procedures, and systems[4] to:

- Review and manage:
    - transactions requiring a salesperson's or broker's license
    - use of disclosure forms and contracts and, if a real estate broker, real estate employment agreements
- Manage:
    - filing, storing, and maintaining documents pertaining to transactions
    - handling of trust funds
    - use of unlicensed assistants by a salesperson or broker
    - oversee delegation of authority to others to act on behalf of the broker
- Familiarize salespersons and associate brokers with the requirements of federal, state and local laws relating to the practice of real estate.
- Review and inspect:
    - documents that may have a material effect upon the rights or obligations of a party to a transaction
    - advertising and marketing
- Establish a system for monitoring compliance with statutes, rules and the broker's policies, procedures and systems.

The ADRE provides a sample broker office policy model manual that can be useful as a checklist of issues that should be included. A designated

---

[4] If an employing broker maintains one office and employs a designated broker, no more than one other licensed person, and no more than one unlicensed person, the employing broker and designated broker are not required to develop and maintain written policies, procedures, and systems. R4-28-1103(G).

broker may use the services of employees to assist in supervising but may not relinquish overall responsibility for supervision and control of the acts of the employees.

PROHIBITED ACTS

The ADRE actively investigates complaints and takes disciplinary action against licensees on a regular and frequent basis. Thus, a real estate broker must be familiar with and comply with all real estate laws or face the possibility of a department sanction. Numerous other actions and inactions are prohibited by law and may result in a disciplinary action. Pursuant to A.R.S. §32-2153 the ADRE may sanction a licensee, deny a license renewal or deny an original license application if the individual committed any of the following offenses.

Transactional Offenses

- made a misrepresentation
- made a false promise
- acted negligently
- demonstrated a lack of basic knowledge or skill
- failed to deal fairly with any party to a transaction that materially and adversely affected the transaction
- failed to appreciate the probable consequences of an action or inaction
- provided the buyer with a false wood infestation report
- signed the name of another person without express written consent
- acted as a dual agent without the knowledge or consent of all parties
- induced any party to a contract to break a contract or to substitute a new contract for personal gain
- sold a property to a buyer that was different than the property represented

Advertising and Marketing Offenses

- authorized any material false or misleading advertisement
- advertised a property or services in violation of a statute or rule
- offered any property for sale or rent without the written authority of the owner
- solicited prospects through a promotion of a speculative nature involving a game of chance or risk or through conducting prohibited lotteries or contests

Convictions, Judgments and General "Bad Acts"

- been convicted a felony or of any crime of forgery, theft, extortion, conspiracy to defraud, a crime of moral turpitude or any other like offense
- been guilty of fraud or dishonest dealings
- violated the terms of any criminal or administrative order, decree or sentence
- not shown that the licensee or applicant is a person of honesty, truthfulness and good character

Violation of Other Laws

- violated the federal fair housing law, the Arizona civil rights law or similar law
- violated any condition or term of a commissioner's order
- violated any federal or state law, regulation or rule that relates to real estate or securities or that involves forgery, theft, extortion, fraud, substantial misrepresentation, dishonest dealings or violence against another person

Records Offenses

- failed to maintain a complete record of each transaction
- failed to account for, or to remit, another's monies, documents or other valuable property within a reasonable time

- failed to keep an escrow or trust account or other record of funds deposited with the licensee relating to a real estate transaction
- commingled money or other property or converted that money or property to the licensee or another
- failed or refused to produce documents required to be maintained when demanded by the ADRE

Licensing Offenses

- submitted a false or misleading license or license renewal application
- engaged in the real estate business without a license
- employed any unlicensed person
- accepted compensation from any person other than the licensed broker to whom the licensee is licensed
- represented a broker other than the broker to whom the licensee is licensed
- failed to pay the biennial renewal fee

Other Offenses

- failed to respond in the course of an investigation or audit by providing documents or written statements
- violated any real estate statutes or Commissioner's Rules
- used the term "real estate broker" without legal right to do so
- paid or received any prohibited rebate, profit, compensation or commission
- as an employing or designated broker, failed to exercise reasonable supervision over the activities of salespersons, associate brokers or others under the broker's employ
- issued an "appraisal" report on property in which the licensee has an interest, unless the nature and extent of the interest are fully disclosed in the report *(Note: Only a licensed or certified appraiser can be compensated for performing an appraisal. A.R.S. §32-3603.)*

Failure to Notify the ADRE in Writing within 10 Days of Convictions and Adverse Actions (R4-28-301(F))

A broker must report any of the following convictions, judgments or adverse actions to the ADRE within 10 days:

- misdemeanor or felony conviction, deferral of judgment or sentencing
- order, judgment or adverse decision involving fraud or dishonesty, or involving a real estate transaction
- action against any other professional or occupational license in any state
- injunction against any conduct in connection with a real estate transaction or involving consumer fraud or racketeering laws
- payment from a recovery fund or similar fund

REQUIREMENT TO SUBMIT OFFERS AND PROVIDE COPIES

The Commissioner's Rules require a broker to promptly submit to the client all offers during the term of the listing. R4-28-802(B). The duty to submit all offers prior to closing does not end with the client's acceptance of an offer unless the client instructs the salesperson or broker in writing to cease submitting offers or unless otherwise provided in the listing agreement, lease, or purchase contract. A broker may voluntarily submit offers to the seller or lessor regardless of any limitations contained in the listing agreement and may submit offers after the listing agreement is terminated.

If the seller permits, the listing broker may disclose to all buyers or their brokers the existence and terms of all additional offers on the listed property. This may result in "shopping offers," which is discussed in greater detail in Chapter 2.

When signatures are obtained on any transaction document, the broker is obligated to deliver a legible copy of the signed document and final agreement to each party signing the document as soon as practical.

R4-28-802(A). However, REALTORS® should be aware that the NAR Code of Ethics requires a REALTOR® to provide the client with signed copies immediately.

PROPERTY NEGOTIATION REQUIREMENTS

The Commissioner's Rules also provide that except for owner-listed properties, negotiations must be conducted exclusively through the client's broker or broker's representative unless:

1. The client waives this requirement in writing, and
2. No licensed representative of the broker is available for 24 hours

See, R4-28-1102. This rule is an issue in limited or minimum service listings in which the seller and the listing broker have agreed that offers will be submitted directly to the seller. AAR has drafted, with input from the ADRE, the *Disclosure of Buyer Agency and Seller Waiver and Confirmation* (DBA) form for a buyer's broker to utilize in such situations. The DBA form is discussed in detail in Chapter 8 — Residential Contract, Related Forms and Other Addenda.

SANCTIONS

The Commissioner has the authority to "suspend or revoke a license, deny the issuance of a license, issue a letter of concern to a licensee, issue a provisional license or deny the renewal or the right of renewal of a license. A "letter of concern" is "an advisory letter to notify a licensee that, while the conduct or evidence does not warrant other disciplinary action, the Commissioner believes that the licensee should modify or eliminate certain practices and that continuation of the activities may result in further disciplinary action against the licensee". A "provisional license" is "a license that the department issues and that allows a licensee to practice as a salesperson or broker subject to either a consent order or the commissioner's terms, conditions and restrictions." A.R.S. §32-2153(F).

In addition, the Commissioner has authority to assess civil penalties for violations of rules, regulations, orders, unlawful practices or any combination of infractions of a statute, rule or commissioner's order. *See, Brown v. Arizona Dep't of Real Estate,* 181 Ariz. 320, 890 P.2d 615 (App. 1995) *(which addresses various aspects of the Commissioner's regulatory authority).*

KEY POINTS TO REMEMBER

- Timely license renewal is imperative — calendar the date and do not depend on a renewal notice from the ADRE.

- A real estate broker can give an opinion as to the price of real estate for the purpose of prospective listing or sale if the opinion is not called an appraisal.

- Employing brokers must maintain transaction records from one to five years depending on the document.

- Most employing brokers must establish and enforce written office policies.

- All convictions (including misdemeanors), judgments or other adverse actions must be reported to the ADRE within 10 days.

CHAPTER 2

· · · · · · · · · · · · · · · ·

The Standard Of Care and
A Broker's Duties

By understanding their duties and complying with the standard of care, real estate brokers not only diminish the potential of costly and time-consuming claims but also reduce the risk that clients will encounter problems during or after the transaction. Arizona statute requires a broker to have expertise in the general purpose and legal effect of any real estate practices, principles and forms, including real estate contracts, agency forms, deeds, mortgages, deeds of trust, security agreements, bills of sale, land contracts of sale and property management, and any other areas that the Commissioner deems necessary and proper. A.R.S. §32-2124(E)(2). This statute serves as a general statement of the standard of care.

STANDARD OF CARE

The law requires that a real estate broker exercise the degree of care that a reasonable broker would exercise in the same or similar circumstances. A broker must act with the same skill and knowledge normally possessed by other brokers. Therefore, a broker complies with the standard of care by performing the broker's services with reasonable care and skill. A real estate broker provides numerous services to the client, such as:

· · · · ·

- marketing properties for sellers, using such strategies as flyers, ads, open houses and tours, as well as listing the property on the MLS
- locating properties for buyers, which almost always involves driving the buyers to numerous properties and viewing each one until a property is located that meets the buyer's needs
- preparing the purchase contract in accordance with the client's instructions and submitting all offers and counteroffers promptly
- negotiating with the other party to obtain the best price on the best terms for the purchase or sale of the property
- answering the client's questions about the transaction and providing the client with resources for information about all aspects of relocating, from loans to moving companies
- coordinating inspections and walk-throughs of the property and guiding the client to sources of information pertaining to the property and the surrounding area
- keeping the client informed as to the status of the transaction while it is in escrow and assisting in facilitating close of escrow

These services must be performed in a manner consistent with the standard of care. For example, a listing broker must "exercise reasonable due care and diligence to effect a sale to the principal's best advantage." *Haldiman v. Gosnell Development Corp.*, 155 Ariz. 585, 588, 748 P.2d 1209, 1212 (App. 1987). Conduct that falls below the standard of care may result in an unsatisfied client, legal liability and ADRE sanctions.

However, what constitutes reasonable care in a transaction varies depending on the situation. The specific conduct, disclosures, advice and counsel required of a broker depend on the facts of each transaction, the knowledge and the experience of the client, the questions asked by the client, the nature of the property and the terms of sale. *See, Jennings v. Lee*, 105 Ariz. 167, 461 P.2d 161 (1969). Reasonable care may include recommending that a client seek professional or technical advice when the matter is beyond the expertise of the broker. If unsure as to how to handle a situation, consult with the designated broker, manager or more experienced peer.

The Commissioner's Rules Can Prescribe the Standard of Care

The ADRE Commissioner's Rules can form the basis for the standard of care. For example, in *Lombardo v. Albu,* 199 Ariz. 97, 14 P.3d 288 (2000), the court stated that Commissioner's Rule R4-28-1101 prescribed an appropriate standard of care in that case — the duty to disclose any information relating to the buyer's inability to perform. Therefore, a broker should be familiar with the Commissioner's Rules and stay updated on any revisions.

Determining Whether a Broker Fell below the Standard of Care

In a lawsuit, after listening to all the testimony or evidence, the "trier-of-fact" decides whether a broker fell below the standard of care. The "trier-of-fact" is generally a jury, but may be the judge or arbitrator in the case. The standard of care is generally established by expert testimony, unless the conduct required by the particular situation is within the common knowledge of a layperson. Therefore, a plaintiff who alleges that a broker acted negligently usually must present testimony of a qualified expert, i.e., another broker, that the defendant broker acted unreasonably and breached the standard of care. To win such a lawsuit, a plaintiff must prove that the broker's conduct fell below the standard of care by failing to use the skill, prudence and diligence that other real estate brokers commonly exercise. Also, a plaintiff must prove that the broker's conduct caused harm to the plaintiff, usually in the form of money damages.

Liability for Conduct that Falls below the Standard of Care

If a broker's conduct falls below the standard of care, the broker is negligent. Once a broker's negligence is established in a lawsuit, the broker will be held liable to the plaintiff for all damages caused by the broker's negligent conduct. Additionally, any judgment arising from such a case must be reported to the ADRE within ten days. The ADRE may also impose regulatory sanctions.

Instructive Lawsuits in Other States Addressing the Standard of Care

- In *McCarty v. Lincoln Green, Inc.,* 620 P.2d 1221 (Mont. 1980), a broker showed one vacant lot to the buyers but drafted the contract for an adjoining lot. The court found that the broker had a duty "reasonably to establish the location of the parcel by geographical landmarks." The court also found that, "[n]o standard could be countenanced by the real estate brokers' profession, accepting as a reasonable standard of care the showing of the wrong property on behalf of the prospective seller to a prospective purchaser."

- In *Tennant v. Lawton,* 615 P.2d 1305 (Wash. App. 1980), the court held that a broker acted unreasonably by failing to verify a contingency of an approved septic tank site on a six-acre property. The seller gave the broker two septic permit applications, but told the broker she thought that they were expired and asked the broker to "check on them." The broker, confident that the property had an approved septic tank site, disregarded the seller's instructions to verify the septic permit applications. After close of escrow, the buyer discovered that the septic permit applications were actually for two adjoining parcels, which the seller had previously sold. The broker knew of the previous sales and the septic permit applications on their face were for the two-and-a-half-acre parcels previously sold, rather than the six-acre parcel being sold. The court held that the broker failed to take simple steps within the broker's expertise and responsibility, which would have disclosed the information that the parcel had no approved septic tank site. In other words, the broker's conduct fell below the standard of care.

- In *Pacific Northwest Life Ins. Co. v. Turnbull,* 754 P.2d 1262 (Wash. App. 1988), the seller owned property previously operated as a garbage dump and landfill site. The seller listed the property for sale, but did not disclose the prior use of the property. The broker had suspicions about the property, but did not disclose these suspicions to the prospective buyer nor did the broker investigate the type of landfill used on the property. After the close of escrow, the buyer discovered that the property was not suited for development due to soil instability caused by improper landfill. The court found that the broker acted unreasonably in the transaction, not because the broker had a duty to determine the suitability of the site for the buyer, but because the broker repeated and reinforced the seller's statements that the property was suitable for development, without verifying the information. The broker acted unreasonably by relying on the seller's information under the circumstances because the broker had suspicions that the information was incorrect.

- Not every failure to obtain pertinent information by the broker is unreasonable. In *Brock v. Tarrant,* 789 P.2d 112 (Wash. App. 1990), a seller insulated the home with urea formaldehyde foam insulation, which caused health problems. The seller moved out, sued the insulation companies and listed the home for sale. The listing broker knew that there was new insulation in the home, but did not ask what type. The broker was informed that the seller was involved in a lawsuit, but the broker was not told the nature of the lawsuit. However, the broker asked the seller whether the lawsuit would affect a new buyer and the seller replied, "Definitely not." When a contract was presented, the broker again asked the seller if there were any defects in the property and the seller said, "No." In the resulting lawsuit against the broker, the court found that the broker acted reasonably. The court stated that a broker has a duty to take reasonable steps to avoid dissemination of false information. A broker is required to employ a reasonable degree of professional expertise to confirm information from the seller which the broker knows, or should know, is pivotal to the transaction from the buyer's perspective. Although a broker will be held to a standard of "reasonable care," a broker need not guarantee every statement made by the seller. The court found that in this

Brock case, the broker's reliance on the seller's statement that there were no defects, did not fall below the standard of care.

DUTY TO CONFORM TO THE STANDARDS OF PRACTICE FOR THE SPECIFIC REAL ESTATE DISCIPLINE

A broker's services must conform to the standards of the professional community for the specific real estate discipline in which the broker engages. Pursuant to Commissioner's Rule, R4-28-1101(H):

A salesperson or broker shall not undertake to provide professional services concerning a type of property or service that is outside the salesperson's or broker's field of competence:

- without engaging the assistance of a person who is competent to provide those services,
- unless the salesperson's or broker's lack of expertise is first disclosed to the client in writing and the client subsequently employs the salesperson or broker.

Area of Practice

Many professions have different and distinct areas of practice. The real estate profession is no different. The practice of real estate may involve residential, commercial, multifamily, vacant land, or businesses. Each area of practice has its own unique considerations.

Residential real estate involves particular statutory property condition disclosures, such a lead-based paint. Commercial property transactions may involve zoning or return-on-investment calculations. Multifamily transactions involve tenant issues and the transfer of leases and security deposits. Vacant land will likely involve water and wastewater issues. Therefore, until a broker becomes competent in an area of practice, the broker should not represent a client in the area without engaging the assistance of a competent practitioner to assist in the transaction or disclosing the broker's lack of expertise to the client in writing.

Geographical Area

Arizona is a geographically diverse state, from the desert to the mountains, small communities to some of the fastest growing cities in the United States. Each part of the state has unique characteristics, advantages, issues and problems.

Because of Arizona's diversity, different areas of the state have unique conditions or issues. When representing a client in a transaction it is important to know about the characteristics and issues in the communities in which the broker is practicing so that the broker can convey all of the pertinent information, particularly to the buyer.

Some of the Association Executives of the 21 local REALTOR® Associations provided examples of issues they considered unique to their particular area:

- *Phoenix:* Light rail alignment and construction resulting in special transit-oriented development (TOD) zoning overlays
- *Sun City:* HOA issues which are addressed in a community addendum
- *Queen Creek:* Fissures
- *Mesa, Chandler, Gilbert:* County island annexation and fire protection issues
- *Rio Rico:* Possible betterment fees
- *White Mountains:* Legal descriptions with gaps, overlaps and odd easements
- *Sedona/Verde Valley:* Water rights and the adjudication process
- *Sierra Vista area:* Military transfers and governmental contracts
- *Casa Grande:* Implications of litigation between homeowners and a builder

Thus, when representing a client in an unfamiliar area, the broker should investigate the area to identify any unique issues that may affect the client, engage the assistance of a broker who is familiar with the area, or disclose to the client in writing that the broker is unfamiliar with the area. Article 11 of the NAR Code of Ethics imposes similar obligations on REALTORS®.

DUTY OF DISCOVERY AND VERIFICATION OF REPRESENTATIONS

There has been some commentary in the past about whether a broker is obligated to verify all representations and discover adverse facts about a property on behalf of a client, by physical inspection or otherwise. Some of this commentary evidences a lack of understanding of the services that a broker provides to the client.

Consider the adverse effect of imposing an imprecise duty to verify representations and to discover property defects upon real estate agents. For example, the case of *Easton v. Strassburger,* 152 Cal. App. 3d 90 (1984) expanded broker liability in California by imposing an overly broad duty on the listing broker to conduct an inspection of the property to discover property defects, leading to increased litigation. The *Easton* decision also strained the E&O insurance market as insurance companies abandoned California. *See,* 28 Pac. L.J. at 677. As a result, the cost of E&O insurance increased dramatically. In response, the California legislature passed Cal. Civ. Code §2079.12, which states in pertinent part:

> The Legislature hereby finds and declares all of the following:
>
> That the imprecision of terms in the opinion rendered in *Easton v. Strassburger,* 152 Cal. App. 3d 90, and the absence of a comprehensive declaration of duties, standards, and exceptions, has caused insurers to modify professional liability coverage of real estate licensees and has caused confusion among real estate licensees as to the manner of performing the duty ascribed to them by the court.

Thus, a broker's duty to the client in this regard must be narrowly interpreted to avoid similar consequences in Arizona.

As one commentator stated: "[o]ne of the preliminary issues to be addressed is whether a real estate broker has the ability to conduct a diligent search for material defects. Although educated in the basic conveyance of property, real estate brokers are typically far from being experts in assessing the integrity of a residence. What may be a 'red flag' to a plumber or a mason, may be nothing more than a bump or noise to an inspecting broker." 28 Pac. L.J. 671 (1997). Therefore, to protect the public, discovery of defects should be left to professional inspectors, not the real estate broker. In circumstances in which there are no suspicious conditions and no specific inquires by the buyer, the real estate broker should have no duty to discover defects or verify representations. *See, Harkala v. Wildwood Realty,* 558 N.E. 195, 201 (Ill. App. 1990) *("nothing in the record suggests that the brokers should have been looking for termite problems or damage when neither the sellers nor the appearance of the home gave evidence of infestation.")*

This policy is consistent with the obligations imposed by the NAR Code of Ethics, Article 2, which states:

"REALTORS® shall avoid exaggeration, misrepresentation, or concealment of pertinent facts relating to the property or the transaction. REALTORS® shall not, however, be obligated to discover latent defects in the property, to advise on matters outside the scope of their real estate license, or to disclose facts which are confidential under the scope of agency or non-agency relationships as defined by state law." Standard of Practice 2-1 states: "REALTORS® shall only be obligated to discover and disclose adverse factors reasonably apparent to someone with expertise in those areas required by their real estate licensing authority. Article 2 does not impose upon the REALTOR® the obligation of expertise in other professional or technical disciplines."

Verifying Information

When passing along information from a third party to a client, the broker should make sure the client understands that the broker has not verified the veracity of the information. No Arizona case imposes a duty on a broker to independently verify information on behalf of a client. The court in *Aranki v. RKP Investments, Inc.,* 194 Ariz. 206, 979 P.2d 534 (App. 1999) held that the listing broker is not liable to the buyers for passing along information from the seller without proof that the listing broker knew or should have known that the information might be false. Therefore, at common law, the listing broker has no duty to the buyer to verify such information absent a "red flag" indicating the information is inaccurate.

The California courts have also addressed this issue and held that a buyer's agent is not required to verify information if the client understands that the information in unverified. *See, Assilzadeh v. California Federal Bank,* 82 Cal. App. 4th 399 (2000). As the court in *Pangano v. Krohn,* 60 Cal. App. 4th 1 (1997) stated: "[w]hen the buyer's agent transmits material information from the seller or others to the buyer, the agent must either verify the information or disclose to the buyer that it has not been verified." *Citing, Salahutin v. Valley of California, Inc.,* 24 Cal. App. 4th 555, 562-563 (1994). "Accordingly, a buyer's agent is not required to verify information received from the seller and passed on to the buyer if the buyer understands the agent is merely passing on unverified information." *Id.* at 563.

ADRE Rule Regarding Verification of Information

A broker is required to obtain and communicate all information material to the client and relevant to the transaction. R4-28-1101(I). And, if the broker questions the accuracy of information being provided, or if a client asks about an issue or questions the information, the broker should assist the client to verify the information.

R4-28-1101(I) states:

> A salesperson or broker shall exercise reasonable care in ensuring that the salesperson or broker obtains information material to a client's interests and relevant to the contemplated transaction and accurately communicates the information to the client. A salesperson or broker is not required to have expertise in subject areas other than those required to obtain the salesperson's or broker's license. A salesperson or broker shall take reasonable steps to assist a client in confirming the accuracy of information relevant to the transaction.

The related Substantive Policy Statement states:

A licensee is a real estate professional with a fiduciary duty to his or her client to act in the client's best interests as described in R4-28-1101(I). Reasonable care or competence may include recommending that a client seek professional or technical advice when the matter is beyond the expertise of the agent.

Licensees are expected to take reasonable steps to assist their clients in confirming or verifying information under circumstances in which a reasonably prudent real estate professional has reason to question the accuracy of the information being provided in a transaction, or where the client has questioned the accuracy of the information.

These considerations are intended to provide a reasonable standard for licensees to follow in complying with their duties and obligations under statute and rule.

Substantive Policy Statement 2005.13 *(Formerly SPS No. 2, Revised 6-1-2001; revised and renumbered 5/28/04, revised and renumbered 4/8/2005).*

Substantive Policy Statement 2005.13 is consistent with the Restatement (Second) of Torts §552, which provides that:

One who, in the course of his business, profession or employment, or in any other transaction in which he has a pecuniary interest, supplies false information for the guidance of others in their business transactions, is subject to liability for the pecuniary loss caused to them by their justifiable reliance upon the information, if he fails to exercise reasonable care or competence in obtaining or communicating the information.

The Guidance Provided in ADRE Rule and Policy

A broker must exercise reasonable care to obtain information material to a client's interests and relevant to the contemplated transaction and accurately communicate the information to the client. What is reasonable in most cases is dependent upon the circumstances and will vary according to many factors. However, the rule and policy provide some guidance on this issue.

"A salesperson or broker is not required to have expertise in subject areas other than those required to obtain the salesperson's or broker's license." In other words, the real estate agent is not required to have the expertise of a home inspector, appraiser or surveyor when representing a client. Therefore, if the seller states that the roof is in excellent condition and only an inspector would have the expertise to determine otherwise, the broker should have no liability for merely passing along the seller's representation.

"A salesperson or broker shall take reasonable steps to assist a client in confirming the accuracy of information relevant to the transaction. Licensees are expected to take reasonable steps to assist their clients in confirming or verifying information under circumstances in which a reasonably prudent real estate professional has reason to question the accuracy of the information being provided in a transaction, or where the client has questioned the accuracy of the information." In other words, if the seller states the roof is new and in excellent condition, but the agent has reason to believe that the roof is old and in a state of disrepair, evidenced by broken shingles and obvious water leaks, the agent should point out these circumstances to the buyer/client and recommend that the buyer obtain a professional roof inspection. Similarly, if the buyer questions the accuracy of the seller's representations or other information provided during the transaction, the same rule applies: the agent should assist the buyer in obtaining independent verification.

"Reasonable care or competence may include recommending that a client seek professional or technical advice when the matter is beyond the expertise of the agent." In other words, in the above scenario, if the client is concerned about the roof's condition, the agent should advise the client to have the roof inspected by a roofing expert.

In addition to referring the buyer to other professionals to assist in investigating and inspecting the property, the broker may also want to provide the buyer with some tools to encourage the buyer to take an active role in the investigation of the property and the verification of information.

For example, the buyer may be provided with access to the *Buyer Advisory,* which provides the buyer with a wealth of information and resources to assist the buyer in becoming more informed about the property being purchased.

DUTY TO REFER TO COMPETENT PROFESSIONALS — NEGLIGENT REFERRALS

As a general rule, when a broker recommends a competent person to do work for a client and exercises no supervision or control over the work, the broker should have no liability even if the person acts negligently.

If a broker fails to exercise reasonable care in recommending a competent individual, a broker may be held liable for any resulting damages. Although the Arizona courts have yet to specifically address this issue, support for such a negligent referral cause of action can be found in the case law of many states. However, to hold a broker liable for negligent referral, there must be evidence that the broker had knowledge that the individual referred was incompetent or lacked skill. In other words, to prevail in a lawsuit, a buyer must prove that the broker knew the recommended person did not have the requisite skill to competently perform the work.

In *Thomson v. McGinnis,* 465 S.E. 2d 922 (W.Va. 1995), a West Virginia court found that a real estate broker may be liable to a buyer for negligent selection and retention of an inspector. In this case, the broker hired an inspector to inspect the heating system of a house. Unfortunately, the inspector hired by the broker was not certified to work on heating systems. The "inspection" consisted only of listening to the furnace while it was running, after which the inspector signed a certification stating the furnace functioned properly. Having received the certification, the buyer purchased the home. After close of escrow, the buyer discovered that the furnace did not function properly. A certified technician informed the buyer that the furnace had many problems and was unsafe to operate. The buyer then sued the inspector and the broker who had hired the inspector.

The broker argued that she could not be held liable for the actions of the inspector. However, the court stated that the broker may have been negligent in hiring the inspector, who was not certified to inspect heating equipment. The court stated:

> While a real estate broker bears no responsibility to conduct an independent investigation of a latent defect, when such broker volunteers to secure an inspection of the premises, or some part thereof, by retaining on behalf of the buyer a third party to conduct the inspection, then that real estate broker may be held liable to the buyer for civil damages if the broker in retaining said third party is negligent in the selection and retention of the third party and if such negligence proximately causes harm to the buyer.

Clients expect their brokers to refer or recommend competent individuals to assist in connection with a home purchase. In general, a broker should provide the client with more than one recommendation when possible. Additionally, the broker should insist that the buyer determine which individual should be hired. A broker should not undertake to directly hire any person on the buyer's behalf. A broker should also encourage the buyer to inquire as to the qualifications of the individual and, if applicable, to determine whether the individual has errors and omissions liability insurance coverage.

DUTY REGARDING "SHOPPING OFFERS"

Questions have arisen in the past about whether a listing broker is obligated to "shop" offers received from buyers, as part of the listing broker's fiduciary duty to the seller. For example, if the listing broker receives two offers on the same property should the listing broker tell both buyer's brokers about the other's offer and divulge the price and terms of each?

A Listing Broker's Duty to the Seller

A listing broker is obligated to exercise reasonable care to effect a sale to the best advantage of the seller, i.e., secure the best terms at the best price obtainable. *See, e.g., Vivian Arnold Realty Co. v. McCormick,* 19 Ariz.

App. 289, 506 P.2d 1074 (1973); *Morley v. J. Pagel Realty*, 27 Ariz. App. 62, 550 P.2d 1104 (1976) *(broker has duty to effect a sale for seller on best terms possible); Meerdink v. Krieger*, 550 P.2d 42 (Wash. App. 1976) *(broker has a duty to exercise reasonable care, skill, and judgment in securing best bargain possible).*

In an Arizona case, *Marmis v. Solot, Co.*, 117 Ariz. 499, 573 P.2d 899 (App. 1977), an unsuccessful prospective buyer filed a lawsuit against the listing broker for "shopping" his offer. In discussing the prospective buyer's claims against the listing broker, the court stated:

> Any efforts by [the listing broker] to obtain a better price were only in performance of its obligations to the seller and the broker cannot be penalized for fulfillment of those duties. Tortuous interference [with contract/economic relations] does not occur through lawful competition. Id. at 502 (citation omitted).

The court further stated:

> Even if the representative from [the listing broker] who was dealing with [the successful buyer] had intended to "bluff" [the prospective buyer] . . . the result was to obtain, through vigorous competitive bidding, a higher price than [the successful buyer] had bid initially, thereby benefiting the seller.
>
> It is clear that a fiduciary relationship arose between [the listing broker] and [the seller]. Having undertaken to sell the property for its principal, [the listing broker] was obliged to effect a sale to the best advantage of the seller, i.e., on the best terms and at the best price obtainable. Id. (citations omitted).

Similarly, in a New Jersey case, *Melveney v. McCrane*, 351 A.2d 385 (N.J. App. 1976), both the actual buyer and the unsuccessful prospective buyer sued the listing broker for "shopping" the buyer's offers. In this case, the listing broker's "shopping" of the offers resulted in sale of the property well in excess of the listed price. In dismissing both buyers' claims against the listing broker, the court stated:

> *It bespeaks only an agency relationship between her [the listing broker] and her principals, [the sellers], throughout which*

> *she kept them fully informed and, following their instructions,*
> *secured for them a purchaser for their property at the highest price*
> *obtainable through vigorous competitive bidding.*

Id. at 461. The court went on to state:

> *In the circumstances it was [the listing broker's] "duty to obtain*
> *the terms most advantageous to the principal" [the sellers].*
> *(Citations omitted). She was required to transmit to the [sellers]*
> *each of the more favorable offers as they were submitted to her.*
> *(Citations omitted). All of her negotiations with [the prospective*
> *buyer] and all of her negotiations with [the actual buyer] were*
> *directed toward fulfillment of these duties. She cannot be penal-*
> *ized for doing what she was obligated to do.*

Id. at 462.

In a 1928 case, a seller sued a broker for failing to "shop" an offer. In this case, *Smith v. Fidelity & Columbia Trust Co.*, 12 S.W. 2d 276 (Ky. App. 1928) the seller listed the property (a "handsome" house) with the broker for a purchase price of $30,000. A prospective buyer submitted an offer of $22,500, which was declined. Two days later, another buyer submitted an offer of $25,000. When the first buyer was advised of second buyer's offer, he increased his offer to $26,000, which he indicated was his limit. When the broker informed the second buyer of the first buyer's offer, the second buyer advised the broker that he would not "bid against anybody for a piece of property," but would consider a counteroffer from the seller. The broker informed the seller, and the second buyer accepted the seller's counteroffer of $27,500.

A month later, the seller filed a lawsuit against the broker seeking to recover damages, alleging that the broker was negligent for failing to give the first buyer the opportunity to bid a higher price. The court stated:

> The particular breach of duty alleged in the petition is the fail-
> ure of the broker to give [the first buyer] an opportunity to bid
> $30,000 for the property, when he was ready, able, and willing
> to do so.

However, the court found that because the first buyer told the broker that his offer of "$26,000 was as far as he would go" that "it was reasonable and natural for the broker to conclude that [the first buyer] had gone his limit." Therefore, the broker was not negligent for failing to seek a higher bid from the first buyer because the broker "had reached a stalemate in playing one bidder for the place against the other, and the second buyer had flatly refused further to be a party to that game."

Thus, the courts recognize that a listing broker has a duty to follow the seller's instructions, keep the sellers informed, and exercise reasonable efforts to sell the seller's property on the best terms with the highest obtainable price. Depending on the circumstances and the seller's instructions, this duty may require "shopping" the offer and disclosing price and terms.

Representing the Seller Professionally

Despite the obligation to obtain the best price on the best terms for the seller, some believe that shopping offers turns the transaction process into unprofessional "deal-making." However, brokers should always act professionally. There is no reason that "shopping" offers should grant brokers permission to act otherwise. "Shopping" offers can be done in a professional manner without alienating other buyers or other brokers.

In all potential "shopping" situations, the listing broker should discuss the situation with the seller before proceeding. The broker should outline all options and risks, then proceed with seller's instructions. There are some situations where it would clearly be in the seller's best interest to "shop" the price and terms, and there are times when it would not be. Sometimes disclosure could greatly increase the chances of a higher offer and other times disclosure of the price and terms to others could drive away all buyers from the negotiations. Only the seller, with the listing broker's counsel and advice, should make this decision.

Based on the foregoing, a listing broker, as part of the listing broker's fiduciary duty to the seller, has an obligation to follow the seller's instructions and obtain an offer at the best price and terms available. There may be some situations in which the seller requests the listing broker to "shop" an offer and other times when the seller requests that the listing broker keep other offers confidential.

In regard to buyers whose offers may be "shopped," NAR Code of Ethics, Standard of Practice 1-13 requires REALTORS® to advise their buyer clients that their offers may not be confidential. Thus, REALTORS® are required to advise their buyer clients of the possibility that sellers or their representatives may not treat their offers, including the offer's terms and conditions, as confidential. The only exceptions to this obligation would be if the law required such confidentiality (and it does not in Arizona) or that the parties have independently reached some confidentiality agreement. REALTORS® must give this advice when they enter into buyer agreements, which for most, would be when they have the buyer complete the AAR Real Estate Agency Disclosure and Election (READE) form, therefore the form includes this advisory. The advisory in the READE form insures that buyers know up front that their offers and related details may be shared with other potential buyers, for example in a "shopping offers" situation.

THE EFFECT OF ARTICLE 26 OF THE ARIZONA CONSTITUTION ON A BROKER'S DUTIES

Real estate brokers and salespersons in Arizona are unique when compared to the rest of the nation. In Arizona, by constitutional amendment, real estate brokers and salespersons are authorized to engage in the limited practice of law by drafting the purchase contract and other documents incident to the transfer of real property. Although Article 26 does not directly relate to a broker's agency's duties, it does affect a broker's duties in general.

How Article 26 Came to Be

Members of the Arizona Association of REALTORS® (AAR) actually drafted the language of Article 26 of the Arizona Constitution. The demand for Article 26 arose in response to the Arizona Supreme Court decision in *State Bar of Arizona v. Arizona Land Title & Trust Co.*, 90 Ariz. 76, 366 P.2d 1 (1961), *supp.* 91 Ariz. 293, 371 P.2d 1020 (1962). In this case, the Arizona State Bar Association's unauthorized practice of law committee filed a lawsuit alleging that real estate licensees and title companies were practicing law without a license by preparing purchase contracts and other legal documents. *Id.* The Supreme Court agreed with the State Bar, and its decision severely restricted the right of real estate licensees to draft or fill in the blanks on legal documents. The court held that:

> [R]eal estate brokers, agents, and salesmen . . . may not, as agents, draft or prepare any instruments purporting to create legal rights or impose legal responsibilities as between third parties.[5]
>
> 90 Ariz. at 97.

The court also stated that the legislature had no power to authorize real estate licensees to practice law by drafting purchase contracts because the unauthorized practice of law is governed by the court, not by the legislature.

As a result, in March 1962, AAR's directors decided to circulate initiative petitions to put a proposal on the ballot to amend the Arizona Constitution and allow real estate licensees to draft purchase contracts. *See, Robert E. Riggs, Unauthorized Practice and the Public Interest: Arizona's Recent Constitutional Amendment,* 37 So. Ca. L. Rev. 1 (1964). "At the same time the directors took the unprecedented action of calling a resolutions committee meeting a month before their annual convention scheduled for April in order to make sure that an appropriate resolution would be properly prepared in every detail." *Robert E. Riggs, Vox Populi: The Battle of 103,* 19 (1964). "The April convention voiced unanimous approval of the directors' action and empowered them to take whatever steps were necessary to amend the constitution." *Id.* Stewart M. Winter, newly-elected president of the AAR for 1962–63 gave this brief account of the convention proceeding: "[a]t a general session of the REALTORS® during the Yuma convention the resolution was read. It was unanimously adopted by one of the most enthusiastic demonstrations ever to take place at an AAR convention. All present, to the last [person], indicated without any doubt

---

[5] Unfortunately, AAR did not intervene or file an amicus brief in this action until after the Supreme Court issued its initial opinion.

they would support a 'go for broke' effort. This was a moment wherein to be a REALTOR® gave one a warm glow of pride." *Id.* at 19 n.43.

Thus, AAR drafted the language of Article 26 as a proposed amendment to the Arizona Constitution to nullify the court's decision. Article 26 states:

> 1.   Powers of real estate broker or salesman
>
> Section 1. Any person holding a valid license as a real estate broker or a real estate salesman regularly issued by the Arizona State Real Estate Department when acting in such capacity as broker or salesman for the parties, or agent for one of the parties to a sale, exchange, or trade, or the renting and leasing of property, shall have the right to draft or fill out and complete, without charge, any and all instruments incident thereto including, but not limited to, preliminary purchase agreements and earnest money receipts, deeds, mortgages, leases, assignments, releases, contracts for sale of realty, and bills of sale.

In an effort to get the proposition approved by the electorate, AAR undertook an extensive campaign. In the 1962 *Initiative and Referendum Publicity Pamphlet,* AAR wrote:

> Real Estate brokers in Arizona, and throughout the nation, have always prepared the customary documents at no additional cost to buyer or seller. They are qualified by training and examination to do so and are bound by a rigid Code of Ethics. We urge you to vote YES on Amendment 103 to restore the right to draft or fill-in these forms to the brokers or salesmen who have performed this service for so many years.

As a result of AAR's campaign, and despite vigorous opposition by the State Bar, the voters overwhelmingly adopted Article 26 as an amendment to the Arizona Constitution, by a 4 to 1 margin, in the November 6, 1962, election.[6]

---

[6] The title companies and the State Bar entered into a "treaty" regarding document preparation and the unauthorized practice of law in 1977. *See Arizona State Bar Committee on Unauthorized Practice of Law Opinion 76-13.*

The Effect of Article 26

Shortly after the election, the Attorney General issued an opinion regarding the effect of Article 26. *Atty. Gen. Op. 63-66-L (R-257) (May 8, 1963)*. The opinion states in pertinent part:

> The only effect of Article XXVI was to confer the limited right upon brokers and salesmen to prepare instruments incidental to a transaction in which they have been employed without receiving a fee for such preparation. Accordingly, it is the opinion of this office that a real estate broker or salesman who is not an active member of the State Bar is engaged in the unauthorized practice of law . . . when he drafts or fills in and completes instruments relating to a real estate transaction with which transaction he is unconnected as a broker, salesman or agent.

Few court cases have interpreted the provisions of Article 26. However, in *Morley v. J. Pagel Realty & Insurance,* 27 Ariz. App. 62, 550 P.2d 1104 (1976), the Court of Appeals states:

> Having achieved, by virtue of [Article 26 Section 1 of the Arizona Constitution], the right to prepare any and all instruments incident to the sale of real property, including promissory notes, real estate brokers and salesmen also bear the responsibility and duty of explaining to the persons involved the implications of these documents. Failure to do so may constitute real estate malpractice.

Id. at 66. In a subsequent case, *Olson v. Neale,* 116 Ariz. 522, 525, 570 P.2d 209 (App. 1977), the court states:

> [A]rticle 26, §1 of the Arizona constitution . . . authorizes brokers and salesmen to engage in limited law practice involving real property transactions. If a broker can practice law in the area of real property sales, it is reasonable to hold him to a full understanding of the implications and ramifications of the Statute of Frauds.

Id. at 525. These cases, and subsequent clarifications by the Arizona courts, indicate that Article 26 imposes a duty upon brokers and salespersons to give competent advice to their clients and to understand the legal implications of the documents they prepare.

KEY POINTS TO REMEMBER

- Reasonable care in a transaction will vary depending on the circumstances.

- If working in an unfamiliar area or type of property, a broker should engage assistance or disclose the broker's lack of expertise to the client.

- The client should be advised to seek the advice of other professionals for issues beyond the broker's expertise.

- A broker should assist the client in verifying information if the broker or the client questions its accuracy.

- In a potential "shopping offers" situation, a broker should always discuss the pros and cons with the seller.

CHAPTER 3

· · · · · · · · · · · · · ·

Agency Relationships and a Broker's Duties

Clearly defining the agency relationships in a real estate transaction is important for both the clients and the brokers. Clients deserve to know who is representing them and acting in their best interests. Brokers must be clear about who they represent in a transaction to determine what duties are owed to which party. Agency relationships become extremely important if a dispute arises — the first question that a lawyer will ask a broker when a claim is filed is "who did you represent?"

AGENCY RELATIONSHIP BETWEEN BROKER AND CLIENT

Agency is a relationship in which one person (the agent) is authorized to represent the interests of another (the client) in business dealings with third parties. By the early 1900s, the Arizona courts recognized the agency relationship between the broker and client in a real estate transaction. *See, Jenkins v. Irvin,* 20 Ariz. 164, 178 P. 33 (1919). By 1950, the Arizona courts overwhelmingly held that a real estate broker is an agent with fiduciary duties to the principal. *E.g., Haymes v. Rogers,* 70 Ariz. 257, 219 P.2d 339 (1950), *modified on rehearing* 70 Ariz. 408, 222 P.2d 789 *("a real estate broker*

· · · · ·
45

employed to sell property owes the duty of utmost good faith and loyalty to his principal and a fiduciary relationship exists"); Leigh v. Loyd, 74 Ariz. 84, 87, 244 P.2d 356 (1952) ("it is well settled that a confidential relationship exists between agent and his principal"). Therefore, a broker owes the utmost good faith and loyalty to his principal. *Tucker v. Green,* 96 Ariz. 371, 396 P.2d 1 (1964). An agent has fiduciary duties to the client, such as confidentiality, accounting, reasonable care, loyalty, obedience, advocacy, and disclosure.

CREATING AN AGENCY RELATIONSHIP

An agency relationship is created by consent. An agency relationship may be created by express consent or it may be implied by the conduct of the parties; no formal agreement is necessary. A broker simply must agree to represent the interests of the client, who consents to the representation and delegates authority to the broker to act on the client's behalf. For example, the listing broker is generally the agent of the seller, who is the principal.

Compensation alone does not establish an agency relationship. Arizona courts have consistently recognized that a broker may represent one party in a transaction, but be paid by the other. *Alaface v. National Investment Co.,* 181 Ariz. 586, 892 P.2d 1375 (App. 1994) *citing Mead v. Hummel,* 58 Ariz. 462, 121 P.2d 423 (1942); *Norville v. Palant,* 25 Ariz. App. 606, 545 P.2d 454 (1976); *Brean v. North Campbell Professional Bldg.,* 26 Ariz. App. 381, 548 P.2d 1193 (1976). In the *Alaface* case, the court held that because the broker was looking for property on the buyer's behalf and contacted the new home seller on the buyer's behalf, the broker was the buyer's agent, even though the broker was paid by the seller. Thus, the seller in this case was not liable for the broker's misrepresentation to the buyer about water availability.

AGENCY DUTIES

Most states have enacted agency legislation that attempts to specifically list a broker's duties to a client and nonclient. However, Arizona has enacted no such legislation. The ADRE Commissioner's Rules do address a broker's duties. R4-28-1101 requires a broker to:

- protect and promote the client's interests
- disclose any known material defect existing in the property
- expeditiously perform all duties without delay
- provide services that conform to the standards of practice and competence recognized in the professional community for the specific real estate discipline in which the salesperson or broker engages
- exercise reasonable care in ensuring that the salesperson or broker obtains information material to a client's interests and relevant to the contemplated transaction and accurately communicates the information to the client
- take reasonable steps to assist a client in confirming the accuracy of information relevant to the transaction, especially under circumstances in which a reasonably prudent broker would question the accuracy of the information or where the client has questioned the accuracy of the information *(Note: Substantive Policy Statement 2005.13 expands on the Rule)*
- recommend to a client that the client seek appropriate counsel from insurance, legal, tax, and accounting professionals regarding the risks of pre-possession or post-possession of a property

R4-28-1101 prohibits a broker from:

- allowing a controversy with another broker to jeopardize, delay, or interfere with the transaction (However, a broker is not obligated to agree to alter the terms of any compensation agreement or to relinquish the right to maintain an action to resolve a controversy)
- acting in a transaction without disclosing in writing before a contract is signed any present or prospective interest or conflict in the transaction
- accepting compensation from more than one party to a transaction without prior written consent
- acting as a dual agent without prior written consent

- accepting any compensation for any goods or services related to or resulting from the transaction without obtaining prior written acknowledgment
- representing a client concerning a type of property or service that is outside the broker's field of competence without the assistance of a person who is competent to provide those services, unless the broker's lack of expertise is first disclosed to the client in writing
- permitting or facilitating a person's occupancy in a property without prior written authorization from the property owner
- delivering possession prior to close of escrow unless expressly instructed to do so by the seller

Question: During a listing presentation, the seller divulges what could be considered confidential information to the broker. The seller does not enter into a listing agreement with the broker, but lists the property with another brokerage firm. Is an implied agency created?

Answer: Although the concept of agency is one of law, whether an agency relationship exists is a determination that a court makes only after considering all the peculiar circumstances of the particular case, and no single fact is regarded as conclusive or controlling. *Busk v. Hoard,* 396 P.2d 171 (1964 Wash. 1964). In other words, whether an agency relationship exists depends on all the facts. In *Hayward v. Graham,* 104 Ariz. 103, 449 P.2d 31 (1968), the court stated:

> An implied agency must be based on facts such as to imply an intention to create the agency, and the implication must arise from a natural and reasonable, and not from a forced, strained, or distorted, construction of them. They must lead to the reasonable conclusion that mutual assent exists, and be such as naturally lead another to believe in and to rely on the agency.

See also, Walter v. Moore, 700 P.2d 1219 (Wyo. 1985).

When applying these concepts to a listing presentation, a court would likely find no implied agency. Generally, a listing presentation alone does not include the intent to create an agency relationship. Further, the mutual assent necessary to create an agency relationship would generally not occur until the seller agreed to list the property with the broker and an express agency relationship was entered into. Thus, an implied agency is not created in a listing presentation, unless the broker demonstrates an intention to create an agency relationship and the seller consents. To avoid this situation, and any implied agency, a broker could explain to the seller early in the listing presentation that no agency relationship will exist until the seller enters into a listing agreement with the broker. Until that time, no information disclosed by the seller should be considered confidential.

Question: The seller has insisted on listing the property at a list price that is above the listing broker's comparable price opinion because the seller believes that the property is worth the price. Should the listing broker provide the buyer with information that is public knowledge or is a matter of public record, such as comparables, when that information is detrimental to the seller's interest?

Answer: Probably not. A listing broker is an agent with fiduciary duties to the seller. *E.g., Haymes v. Rogers,* 70 Ariz. 257, 219 P.2d 339 (1950) (a real estate broker employed to sell property owes the duty of utmost good faith and loyalty to his principal and a fiduciary relationship exits).

A listing broker is obligated to exercise reasonable care to effect a sale to the best advantage of the seller; i.e., secure the best terms at the best price obtainable. See, e.g., *Vivian Arnold Realty Co. v. McCormick,* 19 Ariz. App. 289, 506 P.2d 1074 (1973); *Morley v. J. Pagel Realty,* 27 Ariz. App. 62, 550 P.2d 1104 (1976) (broker has duty to effect a sale for seller on best terms possible); *Meerdink v. Krieger,* 550 P.2d 42 (Wash. App. 1976) (broker has a duty to exercise reasonable care, skill, and judgment in securing best bargain possible).

Despite this fiduciary duty to the seller, the listing broker is obligated to disclose known information to the buyer that materially and adversely affects the consideration to be paid for the property. *See, Lombardo v.*

Albu, 199 Ariz. 97, 14 P.3d 288 (2000); A.A.C. R4-28-1101(B). However, public information such as comparable price information should not be the type of material and adverse information that the listing broker is legally obligated to disclose to the buyer. See, e.g., *Buffington v. Haas,* 124 Ariz. 36, 601 P.2d 1320 (1979) (absent an agency relationship a broker has no obligation to advise a nonclient as to the advisability of the contract terms); *Fraizer v. Southwest Sav. & Loan Ass'n,* 134 Ariz. 12, 653 P.2d 362 (App. 1983) (representations by the bank as to the value and marketability were mere expressions of opinion and statements of future events that could not support a claim). Disclosure of opinions of value is also excluded in the warranty sections of the AAR contracts.

Therefore, the listing broker should not be legally obligated to disclose the comparables to the buyer. Further, if the disclosure would prevent the listing broker from effecting a sale to the best advantage of the seller, the listing broker would breach a duty to the seller by disclosing the information, unless, of course, the broker obtains the seller's consent.

DUAL REPRESENTATION (DUAL AGENCY)

Dual representation (dual agency) occurs when one broker individually, or two salespeople within the same brokerage firm, represent both the buyer and the seller in a real estate transaction. Dual representation is lawful with prior written consent. The ADRE Commissioner's Rules provide that: "A licensee shall not . . . represent both parties to a transaction without the prior written consent of both parties." *See,* R4-28-1101(F). Consequently, the ADRE may sanction a licensee if the licensee has "[a]cted for more than one party in a transaction without the knowledge or consent of all parties to the transaction." A.R.S. §32-2153(A)(2).

Dual representation involves inherent conflicts. Therefore, in most residential resale transactions in which a broker acts as a dual agent, the broker obtains the consent of the parties on the AAR Consent to Limited Representation (12/02) form. This form is not mandated by statute, but is helpful in explaining dual agency and its consequences to the buyer and the seller prior to obtaining the parties consent to the relationship.

In new home and commercial transactions, there is no standard form for obtaining the parties consent to dual agency. In new home sales, there is no standard form because there is less likelihood that the broker in the transaction will act as a dual agent. Most new home sales agents work directly for the seller who has developed the subdivision. In a commercial setting, the issue of agency may be addressed in the purchase contract or simply in a separate writing.

In general, a dual agent must:

- exercise reasonable skill and care in the performance of the agent's duties
- deal honestly with both buyer and seller
- disclose (in writing) to both buyer and seller:
    - any information that the seller is or may be unable to perform
    - any information that the buyer is or may be unable to perform
    - any material defect existing in the property being transferred and
    - the possible existence of a lien or encumbrance on the property being transferred *See,* R4-28-1101(B)

In general, a dual agent must not:

- advocate or negotiate on behalf of either the buyer or the seller
- disclose any confidential information that would place one party at an advantage over the other party (without the informed consent of the other party), such as:
    - the buyer is willing to pay more than the price offered
    - the seller is willing to accept less than the listing price
    - a party will agree to financing terms other than those offered
    - the repairs or improvements that a seller is willing to make or that the buyer is willing to forego
    - the confidential motivating factors of either party

There are no easy answers when it comes to dual agency. In a dual-agency situation, the broker(s) attempts to serve two clients, both of whom have an interest in completing a real estate transaction on the best terms possible. Therefore, difficult questions often arise.

Note: The following Q&As assume that the buyer and the seller have executed an AAR Consent to Limited Representation form.

Question: *May a dual agent point out to a buyer a negative characteristic of the property?*

Answer: A dual agent may point out a negative characteristic of the property only if that negative characteristic is a material fact that must be disclosed by law. Comments such as, "These large windows are impressive, but they may increase your utility bills," should be avoided.

Question: *May a dual agent advise the non-breaching party of possible remedies if one of the parties is in default?*

Answer: The remedies in the event of a breach are generally addressed in the purchase contract (all AAR contracts address remedies) and a dual agent may point out these provisions in the contract to both parties. The dual agent should also point out the alternative dispute resolution provisions and advise the parties as to the information on dispute resolution available on the AAR Web site. Additionally, a dual agent would be wise to recommend independent legal counsel.

AGENCY DISCLOSURE

There is no statutory or regulatory requirement for a broker to disclose the broker's agency relationship to the parties. The only statutory prohibition is that the broker cannot represent both parties to the transaction without their written consent. Nonetheless, AAR has produced a Real Estate Disclosure and Election (READE) form since the early 1990s that explains and discloses the agency relationship. The READE form is used in the majority of resale transactions and is discussed in detail below.

Again, in new home and commercial transactions there is no standard form that is consistently used for explaining and disclosing the agency relationship between the brokers and the parties to the transaction. Most new home sales agents work exclusively for the developer of the subdivision. However, the fact that the new home salesperson represents only the seller may be lost on an unrepresented buyer. The lack of a standardized consent form is less problematic in a commercial setting where the parties are more likely to be experienced in the purchase and sale of real property.

AAR AGENCY FORMS

The AAR agency forms are designed to assist brokers in defining and disclosing agency relationships. Additionally, the use of these forms will prevent undisclosed dual agency.

Real Estate Agency Disclosure and Election (READE)

The READE form is not an employment agreement, but a disclosure and election of the agency relationship that a buyer or seller will have with the broker in the transaction. As the READE form makes clear, regardless of whom the broker represents in the transaction, the broker will exercise reasonable skill and care in the performance of the broker's duties. Further, the broker is obligated to be honest and truthful to both parties and disclose all known facts that materially and adversely affect the consideration to be paid by any party. Additionally, the stigmatized property notice is included in the READE form to alert buyers that information regarding certain "stigmatized" property is not required to be disclosed.

The READE form explains the fiduciary duties a broker owes when representing a buyer or seller exclusively, such as loyalty, obedience, disclosure, confidentiality and accounting. The form also notifies the buyer or seller that the broker may represent others interested in buying or selling the same or similar properties.

The READE form also introduces the concept of limited dual representation. The form discloses that, in the case of limited dual representation, there will be conflicts and that disclosure of confidential information will be made only with written authorization. In the event of a dual agency situation, the parties' informed consent should be acknowledged on the Consent to Limited Dual Representation form.

Consent to Limited Representation (Consent)

The Consent form is designed to be used when there is an identified buyer, seller, and property in an in-house sale. The Consent should be used even if the parties have consented to dual agency on the READE form. The parties may not be truly informed enough to give consent to limited dual representation until a specific property has been identified.

The Consent authorizes the broker to represent both the seller and the buyer in the transaction. The parties consent to the dual representation with the stated limitations of the broker's duties. For example, the broker will not, without written authorization, disclose to the other party that the seller will accept a price or terms other than those stated in the listing or that the buyer will accept a price or terms other than offered. However, the broker is still obligated to exercise reasonable skill and care in the performance of the broker's duties and is obligated to deal honestly with all parties at all times. The Consent also includes the stigmatized property notice, which is particularly important in a dual agency situation. The Consent terminates if the parties do not enter into a contract, if the transaction fails to close, or by agreement of the parties.

TERMINATION OF AN AGENCY RELATIONSHIP

After termination of an agency relationship, the fiduciary duty is ended. *See, Coldwell Banker Commercial v. Camelback Office Park,* 156 Ariz. 226, 231, 751 P.2d 542, 547 (1988). However, confidential information must remain confidential after the termination.[7] Pursuant to the *Restatement (Second) of Agency:*

---

[7] Arizona courts generally follow the Restatement of Law if its view "is logical, furthers the interests of justice, is consistent with Arizona law and policy, and has been generally acknowledged elsewhere." *Ramirez v. Health Partners of Southern Arizona,* 193 Ariz. 325, 972 P.2d 658 (App. 1998).

§396 Using Confidential Information after Termination of Agency:

Unless otherwise agreed, after the termination of the agency, the agent:

. . .

(b) has a duty to the principal not to use or to disclose to third persons, on his own account or on account of others, in competition with the principal or to his injury, trade secrets, written lists of names, or other similar confidential matters given to him only for the principal's use or acquired by the agent in violation of duty. The agent is entitled to use general information concerning the method of business of the principal and the names of the customers retained in his memory, if not acquired in violation of his duty as agent;

. . .

(d) has a duty to the principal not to take advantage of a still subsisting confidential relation created during the prior agency relationship.

The comment in §396 subsection (d) also states in pertinent part that: "one who customarily buys or sells property through a broker can properly assume that the broker will keep confidential information given him in matters connected with dealings in such property, although not in connection with a transaction in which he is employed." Therefore, the broker's duty of confidentiality to the client would preclude the broker from disclosing the confidential information about the client even after termination of the agency relationship, unless the broker obtains the client's consent. NAR Code of Ethics, Standard of Practice 1-9 imposes a similar obligation.

KEY POINTS TO REMEMBER

• Compensation does not necessarily establish an agency relationship.

• An agent has a fiduciary duty to protect and promote the client's interest.

• Dual agency is lawful with prior written consent.

• The AAR READE form will assist a broker in explaining agency relationships to the client.

• The AAR Consent should be used in an in-house sale.

CHAPTER 4

· · · · · · · · · · · · · · ·

Broker Employment Agreements

Most professionals charge their clients for their services on an hourly basis or pursuant to a fee for service agreement. Not so in the real estate industry. Often times, the buyer's broker is not even paid by the buyer, at least not directly, but is paid by the listing broker. Because the various compensation arrangements in a real estate transaction may be less than straightforward, it is vital for a broker to understand the requirements of a valid listing employment agreement and buyer employment agreement. Even when a broker performs and the transaction closes, a client or competitor may challenge the broker's right to compensation. To respond to such a challenge, a broker must grasp the concept of when a commission is earned under an employment agreement with a seller or buyer and when a commission is earned under a co-brokerage agreement.

EMPLOYMENT AGREEMENTS GENERALLY

Most sellers enter into an employment (listing) agreement with the broker to market the property for sale. Some buyers enter into an employment agreement with a broker, commonly called a buyer broker agreement, to assist them in locating a suitable property. However, a real estate employment agreement is not required for a broker to represent a party in a transaction. A.R.S. §32-2151.02(D).

A broker employment agreement is a personal services contract. As such, it is not assignable. A broker may not assign an employment agreement to another broker without the express written consent of all parties to the agreement at the time of the assignment. *See, Olson v. Neale,* 116 Ariz. 522, 570 P.2d 209 (1977) (listing agreement); *see also,* A.R.S. §32-2151.02(B). However, an employing broker can delegate the broker's obligations pursuant to the employment agreement to a real estate salesperson licensed with the broker.

A broker is prohibited from attempting to procure a real estate employment agreement from a seller or buyer who is already subject to an existing exclusive real estate employment agreement, unless the broker has received written acknowledgment from the party that the execution of an additional real estate employment agreement could expose the party to liability for substantial additional commissions. A.R.S. §32-2151.02(C).

Further, a broker must provide a copy of the employment agreement to the client upon execution. *See,* R4-28-802(A). Upon execution of any transaction document, a salesperson or broker shall, as soon as practical, deliver a legible copy of the signed document and final agreement to each party signing the document. Pursuant to the NAR Code of Ethics, Article 9, a REALTOR® must provide a copy of the employment agreement to the client upon their signing.

REQUIREMENTS FOR ALL REAL ESTATE EMPLOYMENT AGREEMENTS

All real estate employment agreements must: (1) be written in clear and unambiguous language; (2) fully set forth all material terms, including the terms of broker compensation; (3) have a definite duration or expiration date, showing dates of inception and expiration; and (4) be signed by all parties to the agreement. A.R.S. §32-2151.02(A). A written employment agreement is also a prerequisite to a broker's action to collect a commission. The Statute of Frauds states in pertinent part:

> No action shall be brought in any court in the following cases unless the promise or agreement upon which the action is brought, or some memorandum thereof, is in writing and signed by the party to be charged, or by some person by him thereunto lawfully authorized: . . . [u]pon an agreement authorizing or employing an agent or broker to purchase or sell real property, or mines, for compensation or a commission.
>
> A.R.S. §44-101(7).

Thus, the Statute of Frauds prohibits a real estate broker from bringing an action for a commission without a written, signed employment agreement that contains the terms and conditions of the commission agreement. *McAlister v. Cooper*, 91 Ariz. 191, 370 P.2d 767 (1962). In order to satisfy the Statute of Frauds, the listing agreement must be signed by the seller, show the fact of employment, the amount of the commission to be paid, and some description of the property. *Nowell v. Andrew Wright Enters.*, 143 Ariz. 79, 691 P.2d 1107 (App. 1984). Further, the specific amount of commission must be contained in the agreement; the "going rate" as a commission amount is too indefinite. *Broadway Realty & Trust v. Gould*, 136 Ariz. 236, 665 P.2d 580 (App. 1983).

The Statute of Frauds is designed to protect buyers and sellers against unfounded claims of brokers. Therefore, the requirement for broker employment agreements has been strictly enforced in Arizona. Neither partial nor complete performance will take an oral contract between broker and seller out of the Statute of Frauds. *Gibson v. Parker Trust*, 22 Ariz. App. 342, 527 P.2d 301 (App. 1974).

COMMISSION AGREEMENTS SHOULD NOT BE ADDRESSED IN THE PURCHASE CONTRACT

The purchase contract should not be used to address broker compensation or commission issues. The contract is an agreement between the buyer and the seller outlining each party's rights and obligations in the sale of a property. The contract should not be utilized to negotiate or renegotiate the rights and obligations of third parties, including the broker (and salespersons).

The commission due to the listing broker should be addressed in the listing agreement, which is a separate agreement between the listing broker and the seller. The commission due to the buyer's broker should be addressed in a written employment agreement between the buyer's broker and the buyer, or through the MLS offer of compensation, which is an agreement between the listing broker and the buyer's broker. All of these agreements are separate to avoid disputes and liability, and should remain so. The AAR contracts clearly state that any commission due as a result of the transaction will be evidenced by a separate written agreement.

Negotiating the commission in the contract can lead to disputes and increased liability. For example, if upon receipt of an offer from the buyer, the listing broker advises the seller to respond with a counteroffer requesting that the buyer's broker reduce his or her commission, that counteroffer has the same legal effect as rejecting the buyer's offer. The buyer would then have the opportunity to reject the counteroffer and decline to enter into a contract with the seller to purchase the home. If the commission issue subsequently becomes an obstacle to contract formation, the listing broker may have breached the broker's fiduciary duty to the seller by making broker compensation a part of the contract negotiation. The same principal applies if the buyer's broker submits an offer on behalf of the buyer with a provision that the listing commission be reduced.

Further, R4-28-1101(D) states in part that: "[a] licensee shall not allow a controversy with another licensee to jeopardize, delay, or interfere with the initiation, processing, or finalizing of a transaction on behalf of a client." Thus, negotiating the commission in the contract may result in a violation of the ADRE Commissioner's Rules if it results in a controversy with the other broker that interferes with the transaction.

Finally, Standard of Practice 16-16 of Article 16 of the NAR Code of Ethics states:

REALTORS®, acting as subagents or buyer/tenant agents or brokers, shall not use the terms of an offer to purchase/lease to attempt to modify the listing broker's offer of compensation to subagents or buyer's agents or brokers nor make the submission of an executed offer to purchase/lease contingent on the listing broker's agreement to modify the offer of compensation. (Amended 1/98).

Therefore, attempts to negotiate the commission in the contract may also result in a violation of the NAR Code of Ethics.

LISTING AGREEMENTS

The listing agreement is an employment agreement between the seller and the listing broker. This agreement establishes the duties of the broker and seller, including the terms under which the broker will earn a commission. Some of the common issues included in a listing agreement are:

- the agency relationship between the broker and seller
- the amount of compensation and when it is earned
- authorization for the listing broker to cooperate with and compensate cooperating brokers
- permission to disseminate information on the MLS, on the Internet, and in other advertising
- permission to use a lockbox and access the property
- a seller cooperation agreement
- a seller warranty of ability to convey title
- dispute resolution

TYPES OF LISTING AGREEMENTS

There are several different general types of listing agreements, such as open listings, net listings, and exclusive right to sell listings. The most common form of listing agreement in residential transactions is the exclusive right to sell listing. The exclusive right to sell listing is also used in commercial transactions, however, not as commonly as in residential practice.

Exclusive Right to Sell Listings

An exclusive right to sell listing agreement gives a single broker the exclusive right to sell the property for the specified period. An exclusive listing also gives the broker the right to a commission if a sale is made by another broker during the term of the listing. *Galbraith v. Johnston,* 92 Ariz. 77, 81, 373 P.2d 587 (1962). In fact, an exclusive listing generally obligates the seller to pay the broker a commission if the property is transferred in any way during the term of the listing. *But see, Mealey v. Orlich,* 120 Ariz. 321, 585 P.2d 1233 (1978) *("taking" by U.S. government was not a "sale" under listing agreement and listing agreement did not address condemnation).* Additionally, a commission will be due if the seller unilaterally withdraws the property from market and sells it without the assistance of any broker. *Larson-Hegstrom & Associates, Inc. v. Jeffries,* 145 Ariz. 329, 701 P.2d 587 (App. 1985) *(seller obligated to pay brokerage commission under an exclusive listing of a shopping center after seller transferred the property to a church for $10 "and other valuable considerations.")*

Open Listings

An open listing agreement allows the seller to enlist more than one broker to attempt to sell the property and the commission is payable only to the successful broker. *See, Demand v. Foley,* 11 Ariz. App. 267, 463 P.2d 851 (1970). The broker has earned a commission pursuant to an open listing agreement once the broker has procured a buyer ready, willing and able to purchase on the precise terms stipulated by the seller in the listing agreement. Further, an open listing permits the seller to sell the property to anyone not procured by the broker without being obligated to pay a commission. *See, Miller Cattle Co. v. Chambers,* 36 Ariz. 282, 285 P. 277 (1930); *Nash v. Goor,* 94 Ariz. 316, 383 P.2d 871 (1963). If the seller sells the property without a broker's assistance, the seller will owe no commission.

The broker must procure a buyer and/or sale under an open listing agreement. In other words, the broker must be the "procuring cause" to be entitled to a commission. The term "procuring cause" is defined as "[a] cause originating a series of events which, without break in their continuity, result in accomplishment of the prime objective of employment of the broker — producing a purchaser "ready, willing and able" to buy real estate on the owner's terms." *Clark v. Ellsworth*, 66 Ariz. 119, 122, 184 P.2d 821, 822 (1947); *see also, Mohammed v. Robbins*, 23 Ariz. App. 195, 197, 531 P.2d 928 (1975). Whether a broker is the procuring cause of a sale is generally a question of fact. *Id.; See also, Puente v. Lee*, 103 Ariz. 534, 447 P.2d 51 (1968), *(broker found not to be procuring cause)*; *Ornamental and Structural Steel, Inc. v. BBG, Inc.*, 20 Ariz. App. 16, 509 P.2d 1053 (1973).

A broker becomes the procuring cause of a sale by doing something that brings the buyer and the seller together. *49 Am. Jur. Proof of Facts 3d 399.* The determination of whether a broker is the procuring cause of the sale is highly fact-dependent and the courts look at the whole context of the transaction. *Id.* The broker's initial contact with the buyer to inform the buyer of the availability of the property is a material and persuasive factor in determining who is the procuring cause of a sale, however, it is not conclusive.

To be the procuring cause of a sale, the broker must initiate negotiations between the parties without a substantial break in negotiations. *Id. at §18.* What constitutes a substantial break in negotiations depends on the specific facts of the transaction. *Even when negotiations have ceased for some period of time, a broker may still be able to establish that the broker was the procuring cause of the sale.*

Net Listings

A net listing is a listing agreement in which the broker receives all monies in excess of the list price. These types of listings may create a conflict between the seller and the broker because the broker is entitled to no commission if the property sells at the list price. Net listings are seldom utilized due to the danger of fraud in this type of commission arrangement and are even prohibited in some states.

WHEN A COMMISSION IS EARNED UNDER A LISTING AGREEMENT

If the agreement is an exclusive listing and the property is transferred during the term of the listing, the broker is generally entitled to a commission. However, what happens when the broker produces a ready, willing and able buyer, but no sale results? As discussed above, the terms of the listing agreement determine when a commission is earned. The agreement may specify that the broker must only procure a ready, willing and able buyer to earn a commission. Other listing agreements provide that the broker is entitled to a commission only when the broker procures a ready, willing and able buyer who enters into a contract with the seller and completes the transaction by closing escrow. *See generally, Am. Jur. Brokers §223.* Some courts rely heavily on the exact language of the listing agreement and make a sharp distinction between an agreement to produce a ready, willing, and able buyer versus an agreement to produce a sale. *See generally, Am. Jur. Brokers §223.* However, in other cases, no apparent distinction is made between an agreement to produce a ready, willing and able buyer and an agreement to produce a sale. In a case where no distinction is made, a broker whose listing agreement requires the broker to sell the property can be held entitled to a commission upon producing a ready, willing and able buyer to purchase upon the terms specified, even when no sale resulted. *Id.*

In *Bass Investment Co. v. Banner Realty Inc.,* 103 Ariz. 75, 436 P.2d 894 (1968), the Arizona Supreme Court stated two general rules for when a broker is entitled to a commission:

(1) If a broker brings the seller a buyer ready, willing and able to pay the list price for the property listed, regardless of whether the seller sells or refuses to sell.

(2) If the broker brings to the seller a buyer who is ready, willing and able to buy at a price below the listed price, the commission is earned if, but only if, the seller actually sells the property or is willing to sell to that buyer.

Id. at 78, 436 P.2d 897.

As set forth in the *Bass* case, if the listing broker produces a buyer ready, willing and able to buy on the terms specified by the seller, with no material contingencies, or with material contingencies that have been satisfied, the listing broker is entitled to a commission even if the seller refuses to sell. However, the courts can interpret what constitutes a material contingency very broadly. For example, a broker who procured a buyer willing to purchase a property, provided a satisfactory mortgage could be obtained, was held not to be entitled to a commission. *Trimmer v. Ludtke*, 105 Ariz. 260, 462 P.2d 809 (1969). In *Trimmer*, the listing broker produced a "ready, willing and able" buyer, but the contract was contingent upon the buyer procuring satisfactory financing. The *Trimmer* court stated: "[i]t is elementary law that the presentation of a purchaser who is "ready, able and willing to buy on the terms authorized by the seller, entitles a broker to his commission regardless of whether a contract is subsequently executed. But where . . . a broker presents a buyer who executes a conditional contract and is willing to buy only if and when the condition is fulfilled, a commission is not earned." *Id.* at 262, 462 P.2d at 811.

Similarly, in *Management Clearing, Inc. v. Vance*, 106 Ariz. 95, 471 P.2d 707 (1970), the listing broker was not entitled to a commission when the prospective buyer's offer was subject to an inspection and approval of the interiors of a 15-unit apartment complex. The court held that acceptance of the buyer's offer that contained the provision 'this offer is subject to inspection and approval of interiors' was conditional acceptance and since it was not binding on the buyer, it did not meet requirements necessary for broker to recover the commission. *Id.; See also, Blaine v. Stinger*, 79 Ariz. 376, 290 P.2d 732 (1955) *(seller dissatisfied with buyer's financial ability)*.

However, in *Nationwide Resources Corp. v. Ngai*, 129 Ariz. 226, 228, 630 P.2d 49 (1981), the Arizona Court of Appeals held that a listing broker was entitled to a commission, even though there were contingencies in the contract. The court distinguished the cases of *Management Clearing, Inc. v. Vance*, 106 Ariz. 95, 471 P.2d 707 (1970); *Trimmer v. Ludtke*, 105 Ariz. 260, 462 P.2d 809 (1969); *Diamond v. Haydis*, 88 Ariz. 326, 356 P.2d 643 (1960); and *Blaine v. Stinger*, 79 Ariz. 376, 290 P.2d 732 (1955), because the court stated that the contingencies in those cases were of "great impor-tance to either the buyer or seller and went to the ability of one of the par-ties to go forward and complete the transaction or the desirability of com-pleting it." There were three contingencies in the *Nationwide Resources Corp.* case: (i) approval of the title, (ii) approval of the termite inspection, and (iii) execution by the buyer and seller of a more detailed agreement than the purchase contract. The court held that these contingencies where not material to the transaction, and, in any event, were either satisfied or waived by the buyer. Therefore, the listing broker was entitled to a com-mission even though the seller refused to perform on the contract.

Further, if either the seller or the buyer is willing to waive any contin-gency operating in their favor, a commission has been earned if a ready, willing and able buyer has been produced. *Manning v. Blackwelder,* 146 Ariz. 411, 706 P.2d 737 (App. 1985) *(waiver of financing contingency)*. In *Manning,* a commission was earned even though the seller was required to sue the buyer for specific performance.

The Arizona Regional Multiple Listing Service (ARMLS) Exclusive Right to Sell/Rent (Listing Contract Legal Language) (9/04) (ARMLS Listing Agreement) states the seller agrees to compensate the broker:

> If Broker produces a ready, willing and able purchaser or ten-ant in accordance with this listing. . .

Thus, pursuant to the ARMLS listing agreement, and other similarly worded listing agreements, the seller is obligated to pay the broker a com-mission if the broker procures a buyer ready, willing and able to buy on the listed terms with no material contingencies, regardless of whether a contract is subsequently executed. *See, Trimmer v. Ludtke,* 105 Ariz. 260, 462 P.2d 809 (1969). Further, a change made by the seller in the price of the property or the terms of the sale from those specified in the listing agreement cannot of itself impair the right of the broker to the commis-sion. *Bishop v. Norell,* 88 Ariz. 148, 353 P.2d 1022 (Ariz. 1960).

Although the seller's obligation to pay the real estate broker a com-mission pursuant to a listing agreement arises when the broker procures a ready, willing and able buyer to purchase the property in accordance with the listing, the actual payment of the commission generally does not occur until close of escrow. *See, J.D. Land Co. v. Killian,* 158 Ariz. 210, 762 P.2d 124 (App. 1988). Further, if the purchase contract was entered into before the expiration of the listing, a commission is owed, even if the transaction closes after expiration of the listing.

What happens if the broker procures a buyer during the term of the listing agreement, but the contract is not executed until after the listing expires? Again, the language of the listing agreement determines whether a broker is entitled to a commission for locating a buyer during the term of the listing, if the buyer does not enter into a contract with the seller until after the expiration of the listing. In *Hearrold v. Gries,* 115 Ariz. 560, 566 P.2d 1036 (1977), the court held that a broker was not entitled to a commission where a prospective purchaser located by the broker purchased the property after the exclusive listing had expired. The court stated:

"The rule established or inferable from the cases seems to be that in the absence of collusion between the owner and the purchaser, or fraud practiced upon the broker, mere negotiations with a prospective purchaser for a sale not consummated within the listing period into a binding and enforceable contract to sell and to buy, do not amount to a sale within the meaning of such a brokerage contract so as to entitle the broker to his commissions, although such negotiations have eventually resulted in a sale made to such prospective purchaser with a deed executed and transfer made to him after the expiration of the listing period." 12 Am. Jur. 2d, page 961, §220, Brokers. Restatement (2d), Agency, s 446, provides:

"An agent whose compensation is conditional upon his performance of specified services or his accomplishment of a specified result within a specified time is not entitled to the agreed compensation unless he renders the services or achieves the result within such time, unless the principal, in bad faith, has prevented him from doing so."

115 Ariz. at 561, 566 P.2d at 1037.

However, in *Hyde Park-Lake Park, Inc. v. Tucson Realty & Trust Co.,* 18 Ariz. App. 140, 500 P.2d 1128 (App. 1972), the court held where an exclusive listing agreement provided for payment of a commission in the event a sale was made within 90 days after expiration of the listing agreement to the party whose name had been submitted in writing to the seller during term of agreement, seller was liable for commission. Therefore, most listing agreements contain a "tail" period clause providing for payment after expiration of the agreement. For example, the ARMLS Listing Agreement states:

> After expiration of this listing, the same commissions, as appropriate, shall be payable if a sale, rental, exchange or option is made by owner to any person to whom the premises has been shown or with whom owner or any broker has negotiated concerning the premises during the term of this listing, (1) within ＿＿＿ days after the expiration of this Listing, unless the premises has been listed on an exclusive basis with another broker, or (2) during the pendency, including the closing, of any purchase contract or escrow relating to the premises that was executed or opened during the term of this Listing . . .
> *See, ARMLS Listing Agreement at paragraph 6(f).*

A LISTING AGREEMENT IS NOT A BINDING AGREEMENT TO SELL

A listing agreement is not a binding agreement to sell. If the broker produces a "ready, willing and able" buyer (with no material contingencies), the seller will likely owe the broker a commission, but the seller is under no obligation to sell the property to the buyer.

Further, a listing agreement does not authorize a broker to conclude a contract for sale that is binding on the seller. *Solana Land Co. v. National Realty Co.*, 77 Ariz.18, 266 P.2d 739 (1954). In the *Solana Land Co.* case, the listing agreement stated:

> In consideration of your agreement to list in your office and of your efforts to find a purchaser for the same, you are hereby authorized to sell (and are given the exclusive right to sell) at any time within *60* days from the above date, the real estate

described on the reverse side of this sheet for *One Hundred Forty Thousand Dollars ($140,000)* and according to the terms therein set forth.

I agree to pay you for services rendered in effecting a sale, a commission of five per cent (5%), based on the sale price.

Upon sale or exchange being made, I agree to furnish deed covering merchantable title, also to supply abstract of title to date, or title insurance policy, to buyer and to pay for revenue stamps, recording fees and drawing such papers as may be necessary to close sale, and also pay my pro-rata share of the current year's taxes, interest on mortgages and assessments, water rents and any similar charges against the real estate.

266 P.2d at 744, 77 Ariz. at 25. The court held that this language in the listing agreement did not confer on the broker the power to bind the seller to the property. *Id.*

The *Solana Land Co.* court noted that the overwhelming weight of authority is to the effect that a broker has no right to execute a binding contract unless such power is expressly conferred by the use of unequivocal expressions in the listing agreement. *Id.* Further, even though the listing agreement may use the terms 'to sell' or 'to make a sale,' it is understood that the seller reserves the right to conclude the sale. 266 P.2d at 744-745, 77 Ariz. at 25-26.

BUYER-BROKER EMPLOYMENT AGREEMENTS

A buyer-broker employment agreement is used when a buyer employs a broker to locate property and negotiate terms and conditions acceptable to the buyer for the purchase, exchange, option, or lease of the property. Generally, by executing a buyer-broker agreement the buyer agrees to work exclusively with the broker and to compensate the broker. However, oftentimes, the compensation the buyer is obligated to pay to the broker is offset by any compensation the broker receives from the listing agent.

For example, the AAR Buyer-Broker Exclusive Employment Agreement (6/03) states:

Broker Compensation: Unless otherwise stated below, broker's compensation shall be paid at the time of and as a condition of closing, as follows:

    a.   Buyer authorizes broker to accept compensation from seller or seller's broker, which shall be credited against any compensation owed by buyer to broker under this agreement.

    b.   In the event that buyer's actions preclude broker's entitlement to compensation from seller or seller's broker, buyer agrees to compensate broker if the buyer or any other person acting on the buyer's behalf enters into an agreement to purchase, exchange, option, or lease any property.

    c.   The amount of compensation shall be: _____.

    d.   If completion of any transaction is prevented by buyer's default or with the consent of buyer, the total compensation due under this agreement shall be immediately due and payable by buyer.

    e.   Buyer agrees to pay such compensation if buyer, within ___ calendar days after the termination of this agreement, enters into an agreement to purchase, exchange, option or lease any property shown to or negotiated on behalf of the buyer by broker during the term of this agreement, unless buyer enters into a subsequent buyer-broker exclusive employment agreement with another broker.

Termination of the Employment Agreement

A broker employment agreement may be terminated in several ways:

- completion of performance by sale and closing of the property
- expiration of the term of the agreement
- mutual agreement of the parties

A broker generally owes no fiduciary duty to the buyer/seller after termination of the employment agreement and the broker is free to act for him/herself or the opposing party as long as the broker does not hinder, delay or interfere with a transaction which the agreement was intended to bring into being. *Coldwell Banker Commercial*, 156 Ariz. 226, 751 P.2d 542 (1988). Further, as discussed previously, the broker must also maintain the buyer/seller's confidential information.

A BROKER CANNOT BE FORCED TO REDUCE THE AGREED-UPON COMMISSION

R4-28-1101(D) states:

A licensee shall not allow a controversy with another licensee to jeopardize, delay, or interfere with the initiation, processing, or finalizing of a transaction on behalf of a client. This prohibition does not obligate a licensee to agree to alter the terms of any employment or compensation agreement or to relinquish the right to maintain an action to resolve a controversy.

Therefore, even if the buyer or seller refuses to close, unless the brokers agree to reduce their commission, the brokers have no duty to do so. Of note, even if the listing broker agrees to reduce the listing commission, the buyer's broker's commission is not affected by the listing broker's agreement with the seller. Unless otherwise agreed, the listing broker is obligated to pay the buyer's broker the amount of commission offered in the MLS, regardless of any subsequent agreements between the listing broker and the seller.

CO-BROKERAGE AGREEMENTS

The Statute of Frauds does not extend to agreements between brokers to cooperate in making sales for a share of commissions. *Nutter v. Bechtel*, 6 Ariz. App. 501, 433 P.2d 993 (1967). Therefore, a co-brokerage agreement does not have to be in writing to be enforceable.

Arizona courts have held that when a broker enters into a commission-splitting agreement with other brokers, their relationship becomes one of joint venture. *Gibson v. Parker Trust*, 22 Ariz. App. 342, 527 P.2d

301 (1974). However, a joint venture relationship may be applicable only when the cooperating broker is the subagent of the seller, but not when the broker is acting exclusively as a buyer's broker, as is more commonly the case in recent years.

MLS Co-brokerage Commission Agreements Between Brokers

A co-brokerage commission agreement between a listing broker and cooperating broker can be created through the MLS. After a listing broker enters into a listing agreement with the seller, the broker generally enters the listing information in the multiple listing service (MLS) of which the broker is a participant. The MLS is a means by which broker participants make blanket unilateral offers of compensation to other broker participants. The NAR *MLS Handbook* (2004) states at Statement 7.56: "Entitlement to compensation is determined by the cooperating broker's performance as procuring cause of the sale (or lease)." (Amended 11/94). See also, Arizona Regional Multiple Listing Service Inc. Rules and Regulations 12.11 (as amended and restated May 22, 2006).

Therefore, a cooperating broker is entitled to a commission from the listing broker pursuant to the MLS offer of compensation when the cooperating broker is the "procuring cause of the sale." This language implies that a "sale" must occur before a commission is earned.

In regard to what constitutes "procuring cause," the NAR *Code of Ethics and Arbitration Manual*, Appendix II, Part 10 states:

> Procuring cause disputes between sellers and listing brokers are often decided in court. The reasoning relied on by the courts in resolving such claims is articulated in Black's Law Dictionary, Fifth Edition, definition of procuring cause:
>
> *The proximate cause; the cause originating a series of events which, without break in their continuity, result in the accomplishment of the prime object. The inducing cause; the direct or proximate cause. Substantially synonymous with "efficient cause."*

A broker will be regarded as the "procuring cause" of a sale, so as to be entitled to commission, if his efforts are the foundation on which the negotiations resulting in a sale are begun. A cause originating a series of events which, without break in their continuity, result in accomplishment of prime objective of the employment of the broker who is producing a purchaser "ready, willing and able" to buy real estate on the owner's terms. *Mohamed v. Robbins*, 23 Ariz. App. 195, 531 P.2d 928, 930.

However, the *Code of Ethics and Arbitration Manual* distinguishes what constitutes "procuring cause" in seller/listing broker disputes from "procuring cause" in listing broker/cooperating broker disputes. The manual states:

> While guidance can be taken from judicial determinations of disputes between sellers and listing brokers, procuring cause disputes between listing and cooperating brokers, or between two cooperating brokers, can be resolved based on similar though not identical principles. While a number of definitions of procuring cause exist, and a myriad of factors may ultimately enter into any determination of procuring cause, for purposes of arbitration conducted by Boards and Associations of REALTORS®, procuring cause in broker to broker disputes can be readily understood as the uninterrupted series of causal events which results in the successful transaction. Or, in other words, what "caused" the successful transaction to come about. "Successful transaction," as used in these Arbitration Guidelines, is defined as "a sale that closes or a lease that is executed." Arbitration Guidelines (Appendix II to Part Ten).

The NAR *Multiple Listing Service Policy* provides that entitlement to compensation is determined by the cooperating broker's performance as procuring cause of the sale. The NAR *Code of Ethics and Arbitration Manual* states:

> Arbitration Guidelines (Appendix II to Part Ten)
> . . .While a number of definitions of procuring cause exist, and a myriad of factors may ultimately enter into any determination of procuring cause, for purposes of arbitration conducted by Boards and Associations of REALTORS®, procuring

cause in broker to broker disputes can be readily understood as the uninterrupted series of causal events which results in the successful transaction. Or, in other words, what "caused" the successful transaction to come about. "Successful transaction," as used in these Arbitration Guidelines, is defined as "a sale that closes or a lease that is executed."

An Unaccepted Offer as a Basis for a Co-brokerage Commission

There has been some concern in the past about whether a listing broker who has listed property in the MLS could be obligated to pay a commission to a cooperating broker who presents a full price, cash offer on behalf of a ready, willing and able buyer, even if the offer was not accepted and no sale resulted. The answer is "no" in a REALTOR® association arbitration and "probably not" in a civil litigation, assuming the parties were acting in good faith.

REALTORS® must arbitrate most commission disputes with other members. *See, Part 10 of the NAR Code of Ethics and Arbitration Manual and Article 17 of the Code of Ethics.* However, to be an arbitrable issue involving procuring cause there must have been a "successful transaction" and a "successful transaction" is "a sale that closes." *See, Appendix II to Part Ten.* Therefore, a cooperating broker cannot pursue a commission in a REALTOR® association arbitration for an offer that did not result in a closed escrow.

Since such a commission dispute could not be arbitrated, it could be pursued in civil litigation. If litigated, the court would likely first look to the language of the offer of compensation in the commission agreement. As previously discussed, some courts rely heavily on the exact language of the commission agreement and make a sharp distinction between an agreement to produce a ready, willing and able buyer versus an agreement to produce a sale. *See generally, American Jurisprudence, Brokers §223.* However, in other court cases, no distinction is made between an agreement to produce a ready, willing and able buyer and an agreement to produce a sale. In a case where no distinction is made, a broker whose employment agreement requires the broker to sell the property can be held entitled to a commission upon producing a ready, willing and able buyer to purchase upon the terms specified, even when no sale resulted. *Id.*

Research revealed no cases addressing whether a listing broker is obligated to pay a commission to a cooperating broker who submits a full-price offer that is not accepted. However, to establish a right to a commission pursuant to an MLS offer of compensation, a cooperating broker would have to convince a court that submission of the offer constituted "performance as procuring cause of the sale," even though no sale resulted. The court would have to disregard the specific language of the MLS offer of compensation to find a commission due under these circumstances.

A REALTORS® Duty to Arbitrate

One of the duties of membership in the REALTOR® association is the duty to submit to arbitration all disputes specified in Part 10 of the NAR *Code of Ethics and Arbitration Manual* by the procedure therein provided, and to abide by the arbitrator's award. Pursuant to Part 10 of the NAR *Code of Ethics and Arbitration Manual,* REALTOR® brokers are obligated to arbitrate "entitlement to commissions and compensation in cooperative transactions that arise out of the business relationships between REALTORS® and between REALTORS® and their clients and customers. . ."

As explained in NAR's *REALTORS® Guide to Arbitration and Mediation:*

> The duty of REALTORS® to arbitrate is based in the NAR *Code of Ethics,* specifically Article 17 which provides:
>
> > In the event of contractual disputes or specific noncontractual disputes as defined in Standard of Practice 17-4 between REALTORS® associated with different firms, arising out of their relationship as REALTORS®, the REALTORS® shall submit the dispute to arbitration in accordance with the regulations of their Board or Boards rather than litigate the matter.
> >
> > In the event clients of REALTORS® wish to arbitrate contractual disputes arising out of real estate transactions,

REALTORS® shall arbitrate those disputes in accordance with the regulations of their Board provided the clients agree to be bound by the decision. (Amended 1/97)

While many disputes that arise between REALTORS® involve contractual questions, under certain circumstances there also may be related "noncontractual" issues or questions that arise. For that reason, the duty to arbitrate encompasses not only contractual issues, but also a number of specific noncontractual issues enumerated in Standard of Practice 17-4 that provides:

- **Standard of Practice 17-4**

  Specific noncontractual disputes that are subject to arbitration pursuant to Article 17 are:

  1. Where a listing broker has compensated a cooperating broker and another cooperating broker subsequently claims to be the procuring cause of the sale or lease. In such cases the complainant may name the first cooperating broker as respondent and may proceed without the listing broker being named as a respondent. Alternatively, if the complaint is brought against the listing broker, the listing broker may name the first cooperating broker as a third-party respondent. In either instance the decision of the hearing panel as to procuring cause shall be conclusive with respect to all current or subsequent claims of the parties for compensation arising out of the underlying cooperative transaction. (Adopted 1/97)

  2. Where a buyer or tenant representative is compensated by the seller or landlord, and not by the listing broker, and the listing broker, as a result, reduces the commission owed by the seller or landlord and, subsequent to such actions, another cooperating broker claims to be the procuring cause of sale or lease. In such cases the complainant may name the first cooperating broker as respondent and may proceed without the listing broker being named as a respondent. Alternatively, if the complaint is brought against the listing broker, the listing broker may name the first

cooperating broker as a third-party respondent. In either instance the decision of the hearing panel as to procuring cause shall be conclusive with respect to all current or subsequent claims of the parties for compensation arising out of the underlying cooperative transaction. (Adopted 1/97)

3. Where a buyer or tenant representative is compensated by the buyer or tenant and, as a result, the listing broker reduces the commission owed by the seller or landlord and, subsequent to such actions, another cooperating broker claims to be the procuring cause of sale or lease. In such cases the complainant may name the first cooperating broker as respondent and may proceed without the listing broker being named as a respondent. Alternatively, if the complaint is brought against the listing broker, the listing broker may name the first cooperating broker as a third-party respondent. In either instance the decision of the hearing panel as to procuring cause shall be conclusive with respect to all current or subsequent claims of the parties for compensation arising out of the underlying cooperative transaction. (Adopted 1/97)

4. Where two or more listing brokers claim entitlement to compensation pursuant to open listings with a seller or landlord who agrees to participate in (or who requests arbitration) and who agrees to be bound by the decision. In cases where one of the listing brokers has been compensated by the seller or landlord, the other listing broker, as complainant, may name the first listing broker as respondent and arbitration may proceed between the brokers. (Adopted 1/97)

As noted above, the Arbitration Guidelines (Appendix II to Part Ten) further provide that an arbitrable issue involving procuring cause requires that there have been a "successful transaction." A "successful transaction" is defined as "a sale that closes or a lease that is executed." Therefore, although cooperating brokers can take legal action in procuring cause disputes where the sale does not close escrow, cooperating brokers cannot arbitrate the issue at the REALTOR® association.

Some of the factors to be considered in determining whether the broker is the procuring cause of the sale in an arbitration include:

- Who first introduced the purchaser or tenant to that property?
- Was the introduction instrumental in creating the desire to purchase/lease?
- Were there previous dealings between the buyer and the seller?
- Did the broker who made the initial introduction to the property engage in conduct (or fail to take some action) that caused the purchaser or tenant to utilize the services of another broker? (estrangement)
- Did the buyer make the decision to buy independent of the broker's efforts/information?
- Did the seller act in bad faith to deprive the broker of his commission?
- Did the original introduction of the purchaser or tenant to the property start an uninterrupted series of events leading to the sale or lease, or was the series of events hindered or interrupted in any way?
- If there was an interruption or break in the original series of events, how was it caused, and by whom?

See, National Association of REALTORS ® 2003 Procuring Cause/ Arbitration Worksheet.

Another factor considered by REALTOR® arbitration panels, is whether the listing broker should be excused from paying the cooperating broker because the listing broker was not paid by the seller. While offers of compensation made by listing brokers to cooperating brokers through MLS are unconditional, a listing broker's obligation to compensate a cooperating broker who was the procuring cause of sale may be excused if an arbitration panel determines that, the listing broker is without fault and acted in good faith and with reasonable care, but it was impossible or financially unfeasible for the listing broker to collect a commission from the seller pursuant to the listing agreement. *NAR MLS Handbook (2004).*

Many REALTOR® arbitrations are held without the parties being represented by legal counsel. However, either party may be represented by legal counsel in a REALTOR® arbitration. A party who intends to be represented must provide timely notice, as described in the NAR *Code of Ethics and Arbitration Manual.*

INDEPENDENT CONTRACTOR AGREEMENTS BETWEEN AN EMPLOYING BROKER AND THE SALESPERSON

Most real estate salespeople enter into independent contractor agreements with the employing broker. An independent contractor agreement may address:

- Obligations of the salesperson to:
  - Remain licensed
  - Maintain REALTOR® membership
  - Abide by all laws and rules
  - Abide by broker's policies and procedures
  - Pay any amounts due to the broker
  - Work diligently
- Obligations of the broker to:
  - Remain licensed
  - Compensate the salesperson
  - Provide office space
- Independent contractor status
- Errors and Omissions insurance
- Allocation of expenses
- Payment of commissions on pending transactions upon departure of the salesperson
- The files and documents that the salesperson may take upon departure
- Dispute resolution between broker and salesperson as well as between two salespersons within the brokerage
- Liability and indemnification

Salespersons are "Statutory Non-employees" for Tax Purposes[8]

The Internal Revenue Code provides a statutory classification for real estate salespersons as "statutory non-employees" for federal income and employment tax purposes. If the employing broker satisfies all the statutory requirements, the employing broker is not required to withhold federal taxes for the salesperson's compensation. To qualify for "statutory non-employee" status, the real estate salesperson must:

- be licensed as a real estate agent
- receive substantially all compensation based on sales or other output, rather than the number of hours worked
- have a written contract with the brokerage firm that provides that the salesperson will not be treated as an employee for federal tax purposes

I.R.C. §3508

Additionally, real estate brokers are, in effect, exempt from Arizona withholding tax requirements as well. State law provides that employers must withhold an amount from compensation paid to employees based on a percentage of the federal tax withheld under the federal tax code. A.R.S. §43-401 (A). Since the federal tax code does not require withholding of income taxes, the Arizona withholding statute does not require withholding either.

Salespersons are also exempt from Workers' Compensation and Employment tax. The Workers' Compensation Act exempts real estate salespersons from its provisions when: (1) substantially all income received for services is directly related to sales rather than the number of hours worked, (2) the services performed by the salesperson are performed pursuant to a written contract between the salesperson and broker, and (3) the contract specifically provides that the salesperson is not treated as an employee for federal tax purposes or for the purposes of the Workers' Compensation chapter. A.R.S. §23-910. The Employment Security Act exempts from its

---

[8] Thanks to Christopher Combs for his input on this issue in an article we co-authored in 2002.

provisions licensed real estate and cemetery brokers and salespeople if all income is received solely by way of commission. A.R.S. §23-617(14).

Salespersons are "Employees" for Regulatory and Civil Liability Purposes

Salespersons are considered employees for other purposes. The Commissioner's Rules require the broker to maintain close supervision and control over salespeople. R4-28-1103(A) provides: "An employing broker and a designated broker shall exercise reasonable supervision and control over the activities of brokers, salespersons, and others in the employ of the broker. Reasonable supervision and control include the establishment and enforcement of written policies, procedures, and systems . . ." Further R4-28-1103 (D) provides: "An employing broker is responsible for the acts of all associate brokers, salespersons, and other employees acting within the scope of their employment."

In regard to civil liability, the Arizona Supreme Court held that the contract language between two people does not determine the relationship of the parties, rather the "objective nature of the relationship, [is] determined upon analysis of the totality of the facts and circumstances of each case." *Santiago v. Phoenix Newspapers, Inc.,* 164 Ariz. 505, 794 P.2d 138 (1990). Therefore, an agreement stating that the salesperson is an independent contractor does not determine the relationship. The court uses the following factors in determining whether an employer/employee or independent contractor relationship exists.

- The extent of control exercised by the master (the broker) over the details of the work and the degree of supervision. A worker who must comply with another's instructions about when, where and how to work is an employee.
- When a worker's tasks are efforts to promote his own independent enterprise, an employer/employee relationship is less likely than when the efforts further the master's (the broker's) business.
- A court is more likely to find an employer/employee relationship where the work does not require the services of a highly educated or skilled person.

- If the master (the broker) supplies the necessary equipment and the employment is in a specific area or over a fixed route, an employer/employee relationship is indicated.
- A continuous working relationship indicates an employer/employee relationship. An employer's right to terminate indicates control in an employer/employee relationship.
- Employees are generally paid by time expended, not by the job.
- A court is more likely to find that a worker is an employee if the work is part of the employer's regular business.

An independent contractor, on the other hand, is a person who contracts with another to do something, but who is not controlled by the other or subject to the other's right to control with respect to the performance of the undertaking. An independent contractor is not subject to the direction and control of another, but is responsible only for the goal to be achieved, not the means by which the goal is accomplished. *Barker v. General Petroleum Corp.*, 72 Ariz. 187, 192-193, 232 P.2d 390 (1951). Thus, in determining whether a person is an independent contractor, the courts look indicia of the "right to control," that aid the court in determining whether a person is acting as an independent contractor. *Smith v. Goodman*, 6 Ariz. App. 168, 430 P.2d 922 (1967) (citing Restatement (Second) §2, 220).

As a result of the right to control factor, the employing broker is held liable for the acts of salespersons under the doctrine of *"respondeat superior,"* which provides that an employer can be held liable for damages caused by the employee acting within the scope of employment. The broker is generally held liable for damages resulting from the negligent or fraudulent conduct of the broker's salespeople.

Conclusion

Because of statutory exemptions, if there is a properly drafted independent contractor agreement, the broker/salesperson relationship is not treated as an employment relationship for the purposes of federal and state tax withholding, unemployment compensation contributions or workers' compensation insurance. However, for regulatory and civil liability purposes the real estate broker/salesperson relationship is generally one of employer/employee.

KEY POINTS TO REMEMBER

- A written, signed employment agreement is a prerequisite to a broker's action to collect a commission from a buyer or seller.

- Generally, commission issues should not be addressed in the purchase contract.

- A broker is not obligated to reduce the agreed-upon commission — even if a party refuses to close escrow unless the broker agrees to do so.

- The MLS co-brokerage commission agreement entitles a cooperating broker to receive compensation from the listing broker when the cooperating broker is the procuring cause of a sale.

- A salesperson should have a written independent contractor agreement with the employing broker addressing the rights and obligations of both, including the payment of commissions on pending transactions upon departure of the salesperson.

CHAPTER 5
....

Advertising and Marketing

Advertising and other marketing techniques are essential parts of the real estate business. Brokers must advertise and market their brokerage services to prospective clients. Listing brokers must advertise their clients' properties to prospective buyers.

Advertising venues include Internet and Web sites, newspapers, billboards, signs, classified ads, direct mail, faxes, cold calls and knocking on doors. The focus of these advertising techniques is to increase business; however, real estate advertising is highly regulated, and it is imperative not to run afoul of the law.

ADVERTISING REGULATIONS[9]

Advertising is defined as:

"the attempt by publication, dissemination, exhibition, solicitation or circulation; oral or written, or for broadcast on radio

---

[9] I would like to acknowledge the assistance and input of Tom Adams, ADRE Director of Regulation for providing the ADRE's interpretation of the advertising rules in an article we co-authored in 2005.

.....

or television to induce directly or indirectly any person to enter into any obligation or acquire any title or interest in [property] and any photographs, drawings or artist's presentations of physical conditions or facilities existing or to exist on the property." A.R.S. §32-2101(2).

Further, the use of the Internet or a Web site that targets Arizona residents with the offering of a property interest or real estate brokerage services pertaining to property located in Arizona constitutes the dissemination of advertising. A.R.S. §32-2163(D); R4-28-502(L). Thus, almost everything brokers do to circulate their names among people, other than "keep in touch" or "thank-you" items fall under the definition of advertising.

The Commissioner's Rule, R4-28-502, sets forth the following rules for all real estate advertising.

- A broker may not advertise property in a manner that implies that no broker is taking part in the offer for sale, lease or exchange.
- A broker advertising their own property for sale must include the words "owner/agent" in the advertisement.
- All advertising must contain accurate claims and representations, fully state factual material relating to the information advertised, and not misrepresent the facts or create misleading impressions.
- All advertising must identify the employing broker's name in a clear and prominent manner.
- A broker who advertises property that is the subject of another broker's real estate employment agreement must display the name of the listing broker in a clear and prominent manner.
- The designated broker must supervise all advertising.
- The term "acre," either alone or modified may not be used unless referring to an area of land representing 43,560 square feet.
- The property owner's consent must be obtained before placing or erecting a sign giving notice that specific property is being offered for sale, and the sign shall be promptly removed upon request of the property owner.

Additionally, the licensee's name must be set forth in a manner that would enable a consumer to find the licensee's license information on the ADRE's Web site. R4-28-302(I).

THE EMPLOYING BROKER'S NAME MUST BE "CLEAR AND PROMINENT"

All advertising must identify the employing broker's legal name or the licensed doing business as (dba) name in a clear and prominent manner. Although the rules do not specify precisely what constitutes "clear and prominent," a primary guideline to consider when creating an advertisement is that the employing broker represents the client in the transaction, and the salesperson represents the employing broker. This relationship must be indicated in the advertisement; that is, the ad must be clear that the employing broker is involved in the process.

- The employing broker's name must be included in all newspaper advertisements, including classified ads, real estate advertising guides, and other magazine ads.
- In advertising flyers, the employing broker's name may be located on either the top or the bottom of the flyer; however, the employing broker's name must be clearly legible.
- On any other promotional material, the employing broker's name must be on the front page or front of the object.
- The employing broker's name must be spelled out in its entirety. For example, if an employing broker's legal or dba name on a license includes "Southeast Valley," that is what must appear in the ad; simply saying "SE" is not sufficient.
- If the brokerage is an office of a franchise, the office must be identified; simply displaying the franchise name alone is not sufficient.
- The employing broker's name must be visible on the first page of the Web page, without the necessity of scrolling down, regardless of the screen size of the computer. Web sites should also identify the employing broker on each Web page because it is possible to link to a single page on a Web site.

TEAM ADVERTISING

A real estate salesperson or broker may use the term "team" or "group" to advertise and promote real estate services if the team or group is comprised of licensed real estate salespersons or brokers who are employed by the same broker. When advertising as a team, the same advertising rules apply as when advertising as an individual broker or salesperson. All team advertising must identify the employing broker in a clear and prominent manner. For example, placing *"The (Team Name) Team"* at the top of the page in large letters with a much smaller brokerage symbol somewhere below is not sufficient. The ad must be clear that the team is a part of the brokerage.

UNSOLICITED FAXED ADVERTISEMENTS PROHIBITED

Unsolicited Faxed Advertisements Prohibited by Federal Law

The Telephone Consumer Protection Act of 1991 prohibits the transmission of unsolicited advertisements to a telephone facsimile machine. 47 U.S.C. §227. The term 'unsolicited advertisement' means "any material advertising the commercial availability or quality of any property, goods, or services which is transmitted to any person without that person's prior express invitation or permission." 47 C.F.R. §64.1200(f)(5). The Act allows a private citizen to file a lawsuit for violations. A person who has received an unsolicited faxed advertisement may sue for actual monetary loss or $500 in damages, whichever is greater, for each faxed unsolicited advertisement. Additionally, if the court finds that the defendant willfully or knowingly violated the act, the court may increase the amount of the award to three times the amount of damages. 47 U.S.C. §227(b)(3).

The Junk Fax Prevention Act permanently inserted the "established business relationship" exception into the federal laws governing facsimile communications. 47 U.S.C. §227(b)(1)(C). Under this act, a fax can be sent to anyone with whom the sender has an established business relationship, so long as the sender received the fax number voluntarily.

Unsolicited Fax Advertisements Also Prohibited by State Law

Arizona also has a law prohibiting unsolicited commercial fax advertisements. *See*, A.R.S. §44-1482. Any person who receives an unsolicited commercial fax advertisement may contact the vendor who sent the fax and request that no further faxes be sent. On receiving a request that no further faxes be sent, a vendor has three business days to update its records. If the vendor continues to send unsolicited commercial faxes three business days after the person requests not to receive further faxes, the person may charge the vendor five dollars for each faxed page received.

Additionally, the Arizona law requires that every commercial fax advertisement include the name, address, fax number and toll free or local contact telephone number of the vendor that sends the fax. And, the law specifically states that it does not alter or restrict any rights a person has under the act or any other federal law to recover for the sending of an unsolicited commercial fax advertisement.

Enforcement of the Law

There are Web sites that explain exactly how an individual can pursue such claims, and attorneys are willing to file lawsuits to enforce the law. Some individuals simply file a lawsuit in small-claims court. Others retain legal counsel.

NATIONAL DO NOT CALL RULES

The Telemarketing Sales Rule (TSR) gives effect to the Telemarketing and Consumer Fraud and Abuse Prevention Act. This legislation gives the Federal Trade Commission (FTC) and state attorneys general law enforcement tools to combat telemarketing fraud and protect consumer privacy. The National Do Not Call Registry is a list of phone numbers of people who do not want to receive telephone solicitations. The TSR prohibits calling to solicit consumers who have put their phone numbers on the National Do Not Call Registry. The registry is managed by the FTC. The law is enforced by the FTC, the Federal Communications Commission (FCC) and state officials.

Restrictions on Real Estate "Cold Calls"

The TSR defines "telephone solicitation" as a "telephone call or message for the purpose of encouraging the purchase or rental of, or investment in, property, goods, or services, which is transmitted to any person." (*See,* 64 CFR 1200(f)(9)). Cold calling by real estate brokers falls within this definition. Thus, real estate brokers may not make a telephone solicitation call to a person whose number is listed on the National Do Not Call Registry, unless the call is:

- reasonably related to an "established business relationship" (which exists for 18 months after the consumer's last purchase, delivery, or payment)
- made within three months after a consumer makes an inquiry
- made with the consumer's written permission

A buyer's broker may call an unrepresented seller whose number is listed in the National Do Not Call Registry about a client's potential interest in the property, because such a call would not be a telephone solicitation. However, a real estate broker should not call an unrepresented seller who is listed in the National Do Not Call Registry to try to list the property.

Individual Do Not Call Lists and Other Restrictions

A real estate broker must also maintain its own Do Not Call list of persons who have asked the broker not to call or requests to be placed on the broker's Do Not Call list. The TSR requires a Do Not Call request to be honored for five years, but Arizona law requires the request to be honored for 10 years. The broker must have a written policy for maintaining the Do Not Call list and train personnel engaged in telemarketing. A broker must comply with any request to be placed on the broker's Do Not Call list within a reasonable time, which may not exceed 30 days.

Further, no telephone solicitation may be made before 8 a.m. or after 9 p.m. When making such calls, the broker must provide the caller's name, brokerage firm name, and a local telephone number or address where the broker may be contacted.

Noncompliance and Mistakes

The fine for calling someone whose name appears on the National Do Not Call Registry is up to $11,000 per call. There is a "safe harbor" for inadvertent mistakes. To avoid liability for calling a number on the registry, the broker must have a personal relationship with the recipient (family member, friend or acquaintance) or have obtained prior signed written consent to call or show that as a part of its routine business practice. Further, the broker must demonstrate that the brokerage:

- has established and implemented written procedures to comply with the National Do Not Call Registry rules
- trains its personnel in these procedures
- monitors and enforces compliance with these procedures
- maintains a list of telephone numbers that are not to be called
- accesses the national registry no more than three months prior to calling any consumer and maintains records documenting this process
- does not use the registry for any purpose other than compliance with the rules
- made the call in violation of the Do Not Call rules as the result of an error

State Requirements for Telephone Solicitors

Most telephone solicitors in Arizona must register with the Secretary of State's office. However, real estate licensees are generally exempt from the registration requirement due to A.R.S. §44-1273 (A)(3), which provides that:

> A person making telephone solicitations without the intent to complete and who does not complete the sales presentation during the telephone solicitation but completes the sales presentation at a later face-to-face meeting between the solicitor and the consumer provided that the later face-to-face meeting is not for the purpose of collecting the payment or delivering any item purchased [is not required to register].

Although exempted telephone solicitors are not required to register, the Secretary of State provides a Telephone Solicitation Exemption Form that may be filled out and filed at the Office of the Secretary of State, Business Services Division. A copy of the exemption form may be obtained on the Arizona Secretary of State's Web site.

Real estate licensees are also still obligated to comply with A.R.S. §44-1278(B), which provides that it is an unlawful practice for a seller or solicitor, or anyone acting on their behalf, to do any of the following when conducting a telephone solicitation:

- call a person who has previously stated a desire not to receive telephone calls made by or on behalf of the seller whose goods or services are being offered
- intentionally make or cause to be made any unsolicited telephone sales call to any mobile or telephone paging device

However, a seller or solicitor is not liable for the foregoing actions if all of the following apply.

- The seller or solicitor has established and implemented written procedures to comply with these prohibitions.
- The seller or solicitor has trained the seller's or solicitor's personnel about the written procedures to comply with these prohibitions.
- The seller or the solicitor acting on behalf of the seller establishes and maintains a no-call list comprised of all persons who request not to be contacted and keeps all Do Not Call requests for at least 10 years.
- The initial outbound call or any subsequent outbound call made by the seller or solicitor is the result of an error.

It is also unlawful for a seller or solicitor to:

- use telephone equipment that blocks the caller identification function on the telephone so that the telephone number of the caller is not displayed
- make a telephone call to any residential telephone using an artificial or prerecorded voice to deliver a message, unless the call is initiated for emergency purposes or the call is made with the prior express consent of the called party

- use any automatic terminal equipment that uses a random or sequential number generator, unless the equipment excludes calls to the following telephone numbers:
  - emergency telephone numbers, including 911, of any hospital, medical physician, health care facility, poison control center, fire protection facility or law enforcement agency
  - any guest room or patient room of a hospital, health care facility, elderly care home or similar establishment
  - a paging service, a cellular telephone service, a specialized mobile radio service or any service for which the called party is charged for the call
  - the telephone numbers maintained on a no call list established pursuant to this statute
- initiate an outbound call except as allowed by the Telephone Consumer Protection Act (47 Code of Federal Regulations, section 64.1200 or 16 Code of Federal Regulations section 310.4), which:
  - prohibits various abusive telemarketing acts or practices
  - prohibits telemarketing calls before 8 a.m. and after 9 p.m.
  - requires a Do Not Call list to be developed through requests by consumers

Summary of Restrictions on Telemarketing by Arizona Brokers

As a result of the foregoing, when telemarketing, Arizona real estate brokers may not:

- Make a call to a person whose number is listed on the National Do Not Call Registry, unless the call is reasonably related to an "established business relationship" (which exits for 18 months after the consumer's last purchase, delivery, or payment; or three months after a consumer makes an inquiry to the business; or if the consumer has given written permission to call).

- Call a person who has asked the broker not to call or requests to be placed on the broker's Do Not Call list.
- Make any abusive calls; call any mobile or telephone paging device; block a phone's caller identification function; call using an artificial or prerecorded voice without express consent; call using a random or sequential number generator, unless the equipment excludes the required calls; or make calls before 8 a.m. or after 9 p.m.

E-MAIL REGULATIONS

The Controlling the Assault of Non-Solicited Pornography and Marketing Act of 2003, or the "CAN-SPAM Act of 2003" (CAN-SPAM Act) was designed to combat deceptive and fraudulent commercial e-mail. The CAN-SPAM Act does not ban commercial e-mails, but regulates these commercial messages. "Commercial e-mails" are defined as "any electronic mail message the primary purpose of which is the commercial advertisement or promotion of a commercial product or service."

The CAN-SPAM Act generally requires that all commercial e-mails include:

- a legitimate return e-mail and physical postal address
- a clear and conspicuous notice of the recipient's opportunity to "opt-out"
- an e-mail address to which a recipient may request not to receive any future e-mail messages from the sender
- a clear and conspicuous notice that the message is an advertisement
- clear notice in subject heading if messages include pornographic or sexual content

THE REALTOR® TRADEMARK IN ADVERTISING

The term REALTOR® is a federally registered collective membership mark owned exclusively by NAR. The REALTOR® membership mark serves the singular function of identifying and distinguishing members of NAR. The mark is licensed for exclusive use by members as a means of indicating their membership status. Further, the REALTOR® membership mark is entitled to the protection provided to trademarks under federal law. *See,* 15 U.S.C. §1054. Each member board, such as AAR, is responsible for monitoring the use of the mark in its jurisdiction.

The use of the REALTOR® mark is subject to the terms and conditions set forth in NAR's Constitution and Bylaws and in accordance with other policies and guidelines adopted by NAR. The NAR *Membership Marks Manual,* which contains those guidelines, may be viewed on the NAR Web site.

Pursuant to IV (E) of the NAR *Membership Marks Manual,* members are licensed to use the term REALTOR®: "only in forms which are likely to highlight the registered status, significance and special meaning of those Marks in the eyes of the public and distinguish them from words of ordinary use and other marks or symbols. The objective of this form of use limitation is to make the terms REALTOR®, REALTORS® and REALTOR-ASSOCIATE® stand out in relation to adjoining print by: (l) the use of capital letters and, where necessary, boldface print or italics; (2) the use of separating punctuation where appropriate; and (3) the use of the federal registration symbol "®" adjacent to each of the terms." The term REALTOR® must refer to a member or a member's firm, whether used as part of a domain name or in some other fashion.

Examples of some of the prohibited uses of the term REALTOR® are:

- as part of the corporate name or business name with descriptive words or phrases to modify the marks, such as Arizona's Number One REALTOR®
- to differentiate among members, such as The REALTOR® with integrity

- as part of a firm name or without using punctuation to separate the name from the REALTOR® mark, such as Blackacre
  REALTORS®, Inc.

To avoid costly advertising mistakes, make sure to consult the NAR
rules and guidelines regarding the proper use the REALTOR® membership mark.

KEY POINTS TO REMEMBER

- The employing broker's name must be clear and prominent in all
  advertising.

- The salesperson's name must be included in the advertising in such
  a way that a consumer would be able to find the salesperson on the
  ADRE Web site.

- A broker may not send unsolicited fax advertisements.

- A broker may not make telephone solicitations to customers who
  have put their names on the National Do Not Call Registry.

- Brokers must use the REALTOR® trademark properly in all
  advertising.

CHAPTER 6
. . . .

Real Property Contracts

Contracts are the basis of buying and selling real estate. A contract is a legal document that affects the buyer, seller, brokers, and every other person involved in a real estate transaction. The contract in a real estate transaction can prevent problems or cause disputes. If the following basic contract law principles are applied, each transaction will proceed more smoothly, with fewer disputes and less liability for the parties and brokers involved.

GENERAL CONTRACT REQUIREMENTS

For a valid contract to exist there must be an offer, acceptance, consideration and sufficient specificity so that the obligations involved can be ascertained. *K-Line Builders, Inc. v. First Federal Savings and Loan Association,* 139 Ariz. 209, 677 P.2d 1317 (App. 1983) *(Discussing minimum contract requirements in a case involving a financing contract between a builder and a savings and loan).* However, real property contracts must meet certain other requirements and usually contain numerous other important provisions relating to the transaction.

Statute of Frauds

A contract for the sale of real property must be in writing and signed by the party to be charged to be enforceable. A.R.S. §44-101(6). The party to be charged is the party against whom enforcement of the contract is sought. *Jolly v. Kent Realty, Inc.,* 151 Ariz. 506, 729 P.2d 310 (App. 1986). While the contract must be signed by the party against whom it is sought to be enforced, the signature of the party who seeks to enforce it is not necessarily required. *Nationwide Resources Corp. v. Massabni,* 134 Ariz. 557, 658 P.2d 210 (1982). Further, a "signature" may be a "mark, if a person cannot write, with the person's name written near it and witnessed by a person who writes the person's own name as witness." A.R.S. §1-215(37).

The parties sometimes forget that any modification to the contract for the sale of real property must also be in writing and signed by the parties. Many disputes between buyers and sellers could be avoided if all contract modifications were put in writing and signed. For example, in the AAR Resale Contract, if the buyer elects to allow the seller an opportunity to correct a disapproved item and the seller agrees to do so, that agreement is a modification of the contract, which must be in writing and signed by the parties. Unfortunately, disputes arise when a broker obtains only the seller's verbal agreement to correct a disapproved item and conveys that verbal agreement to the buyer. If the seller subsequently refuses to correct the item, the buyer is understandably angry, but has no recourse against the seller because the seller's verbal agreement to modify the contract is not legally enforceable.

Spouses

Both husband and wife must sign a real estate contract for the community property to be obligated. A.R.S. §25-214(C)(1) states, "a conveyance or encumbrance of community property is not valid unless executed and acknowledged by both husband and wife. . ." A.R.S. §33-452. Therefore, both husband and wife must sign all contracts and other agreements relating to the transfer of real property, including modifications of the contract. If this is impossible, one spouse can execute documents on behalf of the other pursuant to a power of attorney. A.R.S. §33-454 provides: "either husband or wife may authorize the other by power of attorney, executed and acknowledged in the manner conveyances of real property are executed and acknowledged, to execute, acknowledge and deliver, in his or her name and behalf, any conveyance, mortgage or other instrument affecting the separate or community property or any interest therein of the spouse executing the power of attorney." AAR and the Arizona Land Title Association have agreed upon a standard power of attorney form, which is available on the AAR Web site. However, it is always advisable to check with the title company for the form of power of attorney that the company requires.

Since signing by both spouses is required in any transaction for the sale of community property, a contract signed by one spouse is not enforceable against the nonsigning spouse. *See, Geronimo Hotel and Lodge v. Putzi,* 151 Ariz. 477, 728, P.2d 1227 (1986). However, depending on the circumstances, the signing spouse's sole and separate property may be held liable for any breach of the contract. *Id.*

Also, both husband and wife buyer should sign the written notice of items disapproved and election as provided in the AAR Resale Contract. Disputes have arisen when one buyer spouse signs the written disapproval notice electing to allow the seller an opportunity to correct the items disapproved, and the notice is delivered to the seller without the other spouse's signature. If the nonsigning, buyer spouse, upon seeing the list of items disapproved, wants to elect to cancel immediately instead of allowing the seller an opportunity to correct the items, a dispute is inevitable. Obviously, this kind of dispute creates not only a strain on the buyers' marriage, but a legal dilemma as well. Similarly, both sellers should sign any agreement to make requested repairs.

Offer

An "offer" is an expression of a willingness to enter into an agreement, so made as to justify another person to believe that assent to the offer will result in a contract. *K-Line Builders, Inc.,* 139 Ariz. 209, 677 P.2d

1317 (App. 1983). In other words, an offer creates a power of acceptance, permitting the offeree to transform the offer into a contract.

When an offer or counteroffer is not supported by independent consideration, it may be withdrawn at any time prior to its acceptance. *Bevins v. Dickson Electronic Corp.,* 16 Ariz. App. 105, 491 P.2d 494 (1971); *Patton v. Paradise Hills Shopping Center, Inc.,* 4 Ariz. App. 11, 18, 417 P.2d 382 (1967); *Butler v. Wehrley,* 5 Ariz. App. 228, 425 P.2d 130 (1967). Any statement clearly implying an unwillingness to enter into a contract according to the terms of the offer, communicated to the offeree prior to unequivocal and unconditional acceptance of the offer, is sufficient to withdraw an offer and prevent contract formation. Although formal notice that the offer is withdrawn is not necessary, written confirmation is advisable. *See, Butler,* 5 Ariz. App at 232, 425 P.2d 130. Further, a written offer can be verbally withdrawn, although again, the verbal withdrawal should be followed by a written confirmation. *See, Executive Towers v. Leonard,* 7 Ariz. App. 331, 439 P.2d 303 (1968).

An offer that has been accepted cannot be withdrawn. *Richards v. Simpson,* 111 Ariz. 415, 531 P.2d 538 (1975). In the *Richards* case, the court held that the actions of the prospective buyer in subsequently signing the offer after the offer had been withdrawn did not constitute acceptance of the offer while the offer was still open and a contract was not formed. *See also, Butler v. Wehrley,* 5 Ariz. App. 228, 425 P.2d 130 (1967).

Acceptance

"Acceptance" is a manifestation of assent to terms of an offer in the manner invited or required by offer. *K-Line Builders, Inc.,* 139 Ariz. 209, 677 P.2d 1317 (App. 1983). Acceptance of an offer must be conveyed to be effective. *Id.; Empire Machinery v. Litton Business Tel. Systems,* 115 Ariz. 568, 573, 566 P.2d 1044 (1977). Silence does not ordinarily establish acceptance. *Farnsworth on Contracts, §3.14 p. 231 (1991) citing Restatement (Second) of Contracts §56 ("it is essential to an acceptance by promise either that the offeree exercise reasonable diligence to notify the offeror of acceptance or that the offeror receive the acceptance reasonably.").* If the offer does not specify the manner for acceptance, any reasonable manner of acceptance will be permitted. If the offer contains no time for acceptance, the seller must accept the offer within a reasonable time. However, if the offer specifies the time and manner for acceptance, that provision will control. Therefore, when drafting an offer, it should specify the manner and time for acceptance. For example, the AAR Resale Contract at Section 8p specifies:

> Terms of Acceptance: This offer will become a binding contract when acceptance is signed by seller and a signed copy delivered in person, by mail, facsimile or electronically, and received by Broker named in Section 8r by _____, _____ at _____ a.m./ p.m., Mountain Standard Time. Buyer may withdraw this offer at any time prior to receipt of seller's signed acceptance. If no signed acceptance is received by this date and time, this offer shall be deemed withdrawn and the buyer's earnest money shall be returned.

Acceptance of an offer must be in the exact terms as the offer, and any attempt to accept in terms materially different from the original offer constitutes a counteroffer, which rejects the offer. A counteroffer can become the basis of a contract only if it is accepted by the person who made the original offer. *Malcoff v. Coyier,* 14 Ariz. App. 524, 526, 484 P.2d 1053, 1055 (1971); *Clark v. Compania Ganadera de Cananea, S.A.,* 94 Ariz. 391, 385 P.2d 691 (1963) *(To create mutual consent and therefore a contract, acceptance of the offer must be unequivocal); Richards v. Simpson,* 111 Ariz. 415, 531 P.2d 538 (1975); *United Cal. Bank v. Prudential Ins. Co.,* 140 Ariz. 238, 681 P.2d 390 (1983). Again, once a counteroffer is made, the original offer has been rejected and cannot be accepted.

Consideration

Although consideration is necessary to a valid contract, consideration is easily demonstrated. Consideration need not be money, but may involve a promise for a promise. *Carroll v. Lee,* 148 Ariz. 10, 13, 712 P.2d 923 (1986). Consideration may also be a benefit to a promisor or a detriment to a promisee. Consideration may be entirely without benefit, if there is a detriment to the promisee. *Grant v. White,* 103 Ariz. 257, 439 P.2d 828 (1968) *citing Cavanaugh v. Kelly,* 80 Ariz. 361, 297 P.2d 1102. *(Sellers agreed to accept a smaller down payment in return for the broker's agreement to make part of commission contingent on buyer's future performance.)* By Arizona statute, "[e]very contract in writing imports a consideration." A.R.S. §44-121. However, many contracts still set forth the consideration by the familiar term "for $10 and other valuable consideration" or by requiring earnest money.

Sufficient Specificity

The contract contains all of the parties' legal rights and obligations regarding the transaction. Therefore, the contract must be clear and contain all of the material terms of the transaction. All critical provisions must be specified and agreed upon. *Savoca Masonry Co. Inc. v. Homes and Son Construction Company, Inc.,* 112 Ariz. 392, 542 P.2d 817 (1975) *("The court's role is not that of contract maker. While custom, usage and implications can be used to prove a contract's existence, they cannot be the basis for providing numerous essential elements of an agreement.").* The mere fact that some terms are not filled in is not fatal to the formation of a contract. *AROK Construction Co. v. Indian Construction Services,* 174 Ariz. 291, 848 P.2d 870 (App. 1993).

Parties

The identity of the buyer and seller should be set forth with specificity. If either party is a corporation, limited liability company or partnership, all pertinent information about the entity should be included, such as the entity's name, address and state of formation. If either party is an entity, the signer's authority to bind the entity should be ascertained. Also, check with the title company for their closing requirements, which may include a certificate of good standing, corporate resolution or other related documentation.

To prevent a voidable contract, both buyer and seller should be adults. "Adult" means a person who has attained the age of 18 years. A.R.S. §1-215(3); A.R.S. §1-215(19). *("Majority" or "age of majority" means the age of 18 years or more).*

The parties to the contract must be competent. Competency may be an issue if dealing with an elderly or infirm buyer or seller, or a party with a mental disability or incapacity. However, in order to invalidate a contract based on incompetency, the owner must have been incompetent at the time of the execution of the contract. *See, Golleher v. Horton,* 148 Ariz. 537, 541, 715 P.2d 1225 (App. 1985). Further, the incompetency of an individual will invalidate a general or special power of attorney, (i.e., for specific property) unless the power of attorney is a "durable power of attorney" that specifically states that the power of attorney will not be affected by the incompetency of the principal. A.R.S. §14-5501.

Despite the competency requirement, the parties need not be literate or able to read the contract. The general rule is, absent misrepresentation, an illiterate person who fails to have a contract he signed read to him cannot thereafter claim that he did not assent to its provisions. *Condos v. United Benefit Life Ins. Co.,* 93 Ariz. 143, 379 p.2d 129 (1963); *Betancourt v. Logia Suprema DeLa Alilanza Hispana-Americana,* 53 Ariz. 151, 86 P.2d 1026, modified, 53 Ariz. 263, 88 P.2d 83 (1939); *Sovereign Camp v. Daniel,* 48 Ariz. 479, 62 P.2d 1144 (1936). When dealing with a buyer or seller who cannot read the contract due to an inability to read or an inability to read English, the party should select his or her own translator. *See, Teran v. Citicorp Person-to-Person Fin. Ctr.,* 146 Ariz. 370, 706 P.2d 382 (Non-English speaking borrower was obligated to secure his own interpretation of the loan documents he signed). AAR provides Spanish translations of its most popular forms; nonetheless, a Spanish speaking client should be advised to select a translator for assistance.

Assignee vs. Nominee

On occasion, an offer will be written in the buyer's name "and/or nominee" or "and/or assignee." The addition of this term is often unnecessary because contracts for the sale of real property are generally assignable unless provided otherwise. Nonetheless, including the term does serve to inform the seller that the buyer may assign the contract. The important point to remember is that even if the buyer assigns the buyer's rights or nominates another buyer, the original buyer generally continues to be obligated to the seller and will be liable if the assignee or nominee fails to perform.

Questions have arisen in the past regarding whether there is a practical difference between a "nominee" and an "assignee." *Black's Law Dictionary* defines an assignee as "a person to whom an assignment is made." An "assignment" is defined as a "transfer or making over to another of the whole of any property . . ." *Black's* defines a "nominee" as "one designated to act for another in his or her place."

The Language of Real Estate (5th Edition), John Reilly, contains similar definitions, but states:

> The term *nominee* is not a synonym for *assignee*. Especially if the purchase is based on seller carryback financing, the real buyer may not be able to get specific performance of the sales contract to the nominee on the grounds that there is no real mutuality of agreement and by reason of indefiniteness. Nominee status is simply a name substitution — no legal rights are transferred. On the other hand, assignee status is a substitution of legal rights. Therefore, in most cases use of the word *assignee* rather that *nominee will better achieve the parties' intended result of effectively transferring legal rights to the ultimate purchaser.*

However, research reveals that many courts use the phrase "assignee or nominee" as if the terms were synonymous. Perhaps the court in *Thompson v. Meyers*, 211 Kan. 26, 505 P.2d 680 (1973) provides the best explanation. The court states:

> The sense in which the term "nominee" is used in a contract is ascertained from the intention of the parties as it may be expressed in the instruments as a whole.
>
> In common parlance the word "nominee" has more than one meaning. Much depends on the frame of reference in which it is used.

The court in the *Thompson* case then determined that the parties to the contract at issue in the case used the term "nominee" not simply in the sense of a straw man or limited agent for [the buyers], but in the larger sense of a person designated by them to purchase the real estate, who would possess all the rights given a buyer in the . . . contract."

Property Description

Identifying the property that is the subject of the contract must be done with specificity. The general rule is that the property must be identified so that it can be ascertained. Ideally, the property should be described by legal description. If the property is identified by legal description, it is best to simply attach the legal description obtained from the title company, rather than to rewrite the description and risk typographical errors. However, listing the property's street address or other method of identifying the property is legally sufficient.

If at all possible, the property should be identified on the ground as well as in the contract, for example by a survey. Identifying the property both in the contract and on the ground is particularly important when dealing with vacant land. For example, in *Hill-Shafer Partnership v. Chilson Family Trust*, 165 Ariz. 469, 799 P.2d 810 (1990), the buyer intended to purchase whatever legal description was identified, regardless of size or location. The seller did not have similar intent, but intended to convey only certain property. The legal description in the contract described property other than that which the seller intended to convey. Therefore, the court held there was no mutual assent and no binding contract.

Fixtures and Personal Property

In addition to identifying the land, the contract should identify all personal property to be conveyed with the real property and any fixtures that could be an issue. When dealing with commercial or income property, all contracts, leases, and service agreements to be assumed by the buyer should be identified as well. A fixture is an item that was once personal property but is affixed to the real estate in such a manner as to become a part of the real property. Arizona employs a three-part test for determining when personal property, also known as chattel, has become a fixture: (1) annexation to the realty; (2) adaptability or application as affixed to the use of the real estate; and (3) an intention of the party to make the object a permanent part of the realty. *Murray v. Zerbel,* 159 Ariz. 99, 101, 764 P.2d 1158 (App. 1988); *Voight v. Ott,* 86 Ariz. 128, 341 P.2d 923 (1959). The buyer purchases the fixtures annexed to the real property, but personal property is not part of the transaction unless specified in the purchase contract. *Id.* To avoid ambiguity, the contract should specifically identify all items that are to be conveyed in the transaction, such as solar devices, satellite dishes, track lighting, appliances, etc., regardless of whether the drafter believes the items to be fixtures.

Purchase Price

The terms of payment and the amount of the purchase price are clearly essential elements of a purchase contract. The purchase price, earnest money, down payment and any financing contingency should be specified. Financing is a common contingency in a real estate transaction. The financing contingency may be drafted to continue until the close of escrow date, or the contract may be drafted to require the buyer to remove the contingency at some time prior to the close of escrow.

Close of Escrow

Contracts are not required to have a specific date for close of escrow. Nonetheless, the close of escrow date is an important date that should be specified in the purchase contract. Both parties will likely make significant plans based upon the close of escrow date and may have simultaneous closings on other properties.

The Arizona Court of Appeals called it "a fundamental principle of contract law" that, if the contract does not have a specific date listed for performance, a reasonable time is implied. *Dutch Inns of America, Inc. v. Horizon Corp.,* 18 Ariz. App. 116, 119, 500 P.2d 901 (1972). The law will imply a reasonable date for performance in order to "save a transaction that might otherwise be invalid," *Kerley v. Nu-West, Inc.,* 158 Ariz. 344, 349, 762 P.2d 631 (App. 1988), and to "carry into effect the parties' intentions, whenever reasonable and possible." *Byke Const. Co. v. Miller,* 140 Ariz. 57, 59, 680 P.2d 193, 195 (App. 1984).

However, despite the importance of the close of escrow date in a contract for the sale of real property, time is usually not regarded as being of the essence for closing. *Miller v. Long Family Partnership*, 151 Ariz. 306, 308, 727 P.2d 359, 361 (App. 1986) *citing, Kresse v. Ryerson*, 64 Ariz. 291, 169 P.2d 850 (1946). When a contract for the sale and purchase of real property does not make time of the essence as it relates to closing, a party can breach the contract only by refusing to perform after demanding that closing take place at a reasonable time and place. *Id., citing, Henry v. Ecker*, 415 So.2d 137 (Fla. App. 1982).

Time should be considered of the essence in a contract when:

1. There is an express recital in the contract that time is of the essence.

2. Where, from the nature of the transaction or fluctuations in the value or from the terms of the agreement, the treatment of time as a nonessential will produce a hardship and delay by one party in completing or in complying with a term would necessarily subject the other party to serious injury or loss.

3. There is an express notice, given by a party who is not in default to the other party who is in default, requiring the contract to be performed within a reasonable stated time.

Therefore, the contract should specify that "time is of the essence" and the reason that any delay would create a hardship should be memorialized in either the contract or a contemporaneous writing if at all possible. The AAR contracts contain a "time is of the essence clause."

The close of escrow date was found to be a material term in the case of *Allan v. Martin*, 117 Ariz. 591, 574 P.2d 457 (1978). In this case, the purchase price was not paid into escrow on the last day agreed upon for closing. Therefore, the court held that the sellers had the legal right to refuse to convey their property and to cancel the contract. The court stated that when time for performance is material to a contract and one party fails to perform by the contract deadline date, the other party may treat the contract as ended. *Citing, Corbin on Contracts* §716 (1960); *Phillips and Colby Construction Co. v. Seymour*, 91 U.S. 646, 23 L.Ed. 341 (1875); *Morris v. Prefabrication Engineering Co.*, 160 F.2d 779 (5th Cir. 1947).

Other Terms

The contract contains all of the parties' legal rights and obligations regarding the transaction. Therefore, the contract must be clear and contain specific terms. The AAR contracts contain such specific terms. However, oftentimes the parties alter the standard terms in the contract or add additional terms and conditions. When drafting such terms, it is important to avoid ambiguity. Contract language is ambiguous when it can be reasonably interpreted in more than one way and the meaning of the contract language cannot be determined within the "four corners" of the contract. A court will interpret an ambiguous contract term by trying to determine the intent of the parties at the time of the contract. To avoid ambiguity, avoid "short-cut" phrases, such as "48-hour first right of refusal"; instead, write out exactly what the parties intend.

Contingencies

A contingency is a clause that requires the completion of a certain act before the parties are obligated to perform their contractual obligations. A contingency clause is also known as a "condition precedent." Contingency clauses are a common source of ambiguity. Contingency clauses must be drafted precisely because contingencies frequently become the subject of dispute.

When an express contingency fails, the contract will not be enforced. *Connor v. Cal-Az Properties, Inc.*, 137 Ariz. 53, 668 P.2d 896 (App. 1983) *citing, Sam Levitz Furniture Co. v. Safeway Stores, Inc.*, 105 Ariz. 329, 332, 464 P.2d 612, 615 (1970). In the *Connor* case, the parties entered into a contract that was contingent on the property appraising for at least the sales price. The contingency failed when the property appraised approximately $30,000 below the purchase price. Although a subsequent appraisal was secured for the purchase price, the court held that the contingency was inserted for the buyer's benefit, who could legitimately conclude that the property did not appraise for the purchase price. The buyers were therefore entitled to a return of their earnest money. *Id.* at

54, 668 P.2d. at 898. Further, a contingency will generally be enforced according to its terms, without regard to harshness of the condition. *Arizona Land Title & Trust Co. v. Safeway Stores, Inc.*, 6 Ariz. App. 52, 429 P.2d 686 (App. 1967).

At a minimum, a contingency clause should specify the terms of the contingency, the exact time in which the contingency must be fulfilled, and the rights and obligations of the parties if the contingency is not met. The following are some important considerations when drafting a contingency:

- what is the contingency
- for whose benefit
- when must the contingency be satisfied
- how is the contingency satisfied
- what happens if the contingency is not satisfied

As a general rule, a party may waive any provision of a contract that is solely intended for that party's benefit. *Pruitt v. Pavelin*, 141, Ariz. 195, 685 P.2d 1347 (App. 1984); *Nelson v. Cannon*, 126 Ariz. 381, 616 P.2d 56 (App. 1980).

The most common contingencies are financing, property condition and condition of title. Additionally, a buyer may negotiate other contingencies such as the closing of the sale of an existing property owned by the buyer.

Boilerplate

Pre-printed contract forms are used in many real estate transactions. For example, the AAR contracts all contain pre-printed or boilerplate language. The forms are often revised or supplemented to address issues unique to the particular transaction. Where handwritten provisions of the contract are inconsistent with the pre-printed or boilerplate provisions, the handwritten provisions will prevail. *Autonumerics, Inc., v. Bayer Industries, Inc.*, 144 Ariz. 181, 696 P.2d 1330 (App. 1984).

ELECTRONIC TRANSACTIONS

Technology is changing the way real estate transactions are conducted. More and more real estate practitioners are utilizing electronic forms routinely to conduct business. Electronic forms are available at no cost as an AAR member benefit. The forms are often completed and e-mailed to those involved in the transaction. The contracts may even be executed electronically.

The issues raised by contracting via computer relate more to method than to substance. *See generally, Dodd, Hernandez, Contracting in Cyberspace, Computer Law Review and Technology Journal* (Summer 1998). The substance of a contract does not change simply because the contract was formed via computer, rather than by a traditional writing. A contract formed via computer still requires an offer, acceptance, consideration and sufficient specification of terms so that the obligations can be ascertained. A contract for the sale of real property formed via computer still must be in writing and signed by the party to be charged. The method of obtaining that signed writing is the only real difference in an electronic transaction.

The Arizona Electronic Transactions Act (the ETA) creates statutory authority for creating contracts electronically, via computer. A.R.S. §44-7001 *et. seq.* As a result of this legislation, a contract formed by an electronic record cannot be denied legal effect and enforceability solely because it was formed electronically. A.R.S. §44-7007(B). Similarly, a signature in electronic form cannot be denied legal effect and enforceability solely because it is in electronic form. A.R.S. §44-7007(A). An electronic record and electronic signature satisfy any law that requires a signed writing, such as the Statute of Frauds requirement that a contract for the sale of real property be evidenced by a signed writing to be enforceable. A.R.S. §44-7007(D).

The Parties Must Agree to Conduct the Transaction Via Computer

The ETA applies only to a "transaction between parties each of which has agreed to conduct the transaction by electronic means." A.R.S. §44-7005(B). "Whether the parties agree to conduct a transaction by electronic means is determined from the context and surrounding circumstances, including the parties' conduct." *Id.*

The Contract May Be Signed Electronically

An electronic signature is defined by the ETA as an "electronic sound, symbol or process that is attached to or logically associated with a record and that is executed or adopted by an individual with the intent to sign the record." A.R.S. §44-7002(8). An electronic signature is attributable to a person if the signature was the act of the person. A.R.S. §44-7009(A). "The act of the person may be shown in any manner, including a showing of the efficacy of any security procedure applied to determine the person to which the electronic . . . signature was attributable." *Id.* Therefore, a party may sign an electronic contract with whatever symbol the party has adopted with the intent that such symbol represents a signature.

The Contract May Be Delivered and Received Electronically

An acceptance of an offer must be delivered and received by the buyer or the buyer's designated agent. Pursuant to the ETA, if a law "requires a person to provide, send or deliver information in writing to another person, the requirement is satisfied if the information is provided, sent or delivered, as the case may be, in an electronic record that is capable of retention by the recipient at the time of receipt." A.R.S. §44-7008(A). The writing is not capable of retention if the recipient is unable to print or store the writing. *Id.* "If the sender inhibits the ability of a recipient to store or print an electronic record, the electronic record is not enforceable against the recipient." A.R.S. §44-7008(C). Therefore, both parties' computers must be capable of saving and/or printing the contract.

Unless otherwise agreed, the contract is sent if the record is: (1) properly addressed or otherwise properly directed to the recipient's designated computer system and from which the recipient is able to retrieve the record; (2) is in a form that is capable of being processed by the recipient's designated computer system; or (3) enters a computer system that is outside the control of the sender or sender's agent, or enters a controlled region of the recipient's designated computer system. A.R.S. §44-7015(A).

Unless otherwise agreed, an electronic record is received if the record: (1) enters a computer system that the recipient has designated or uses for the purpose of receiving such records, and the recipient is able to retrieve the record; or (2) is in a form capable of being processed by the recipient's computer system. The contract will be deemed received even if no individual is aware of its receipt. A.R.S. §44-7015(E).

Secure Transactions

The parties can arrange for a secure transaction. Pursuant to the ETA, "[t]here is a rebuttable presumption that a secure electronic record has not been altered since the specific time to which the secure status relates." A.R.S. §44-7033(A). Similarly, "[t]here is a rebuttable presumption that the secure electronic signature is the electronic signature of the party to whom it relates." A.R.S. §44-7033(B).

A signature is secure if, through the application of a security procedure, it can be demonstrated that the signature is: (1) unique to the person using it; (2) capable of verification; (3) under the sole control of the person using it; or (4) linked to the electronic record to which it relates in such a manner that if the record were changed the electronic signature would be invalidated. A.R.S. §44-7031. A record is secure if "through the ongoing application of a security, it can be demonstrated that an electronic record signed by a secure electronic signature has remained unaltered since a specified time." A.R.S. §44-7032. In the absence of a secure electronic record or secure electronic signature, the ETA does not create any presumption regarding the authenticity and integrity of an electronic record or an electronic signature. A.R.S. §44-44-7032(C).

The Effect of Errors

Mistakes and errors do occur. Pursuant to the ETA, "[i]f the parties have agreed to use a security procedure to detect changes or errors and one party has conformed to the procedure but the other party has not, and the nonconforming party would have detected the change or error had that party also conformed, the conforming party may avoid the effect of the changed or erroneous electronic record." A.R.S. §44-7010(A)(1).

Otherwise, the general law of mistake will govern the effect of any such mistake or error.

"AS IS" CONTRACTS

Many times a seller will want to sell the property "as is" in an effort to avoid liability. The courts often interpret an "as is" clause in a contract to imply that the property could be defective. *See, Universal Inv. Co. v. Sahara Motor Inn, Inc.*, 127 Ariz. 213, 619 P.2d 485 (App. 1980). The use of "as is" is also generally interpreted to be a disclaimer of warranties or representations. In other words, in a clearly defined "as is" contract, the seller is saying that the property will be sold in its existing physical condition, and the buyer is taking the property's condition into account when making an offer.

In a lawsuit, the effect of the "as is" provision varies with the type of claim and the particular circumstances of the case. An "as is" clause can insulate a seller from liability for defects in the property under certain circumstances. For example, in *La Placita Partners v. Northwestern Mutual Life Ins. Co.*, 766 F. Supp. 1454 (N.D. Ohio 1990), a federal court applying Arizona law stated that a seller did not have a duty to disclose certain information regarding possible asbestos in a commercial property, partly because of the existence of the "as is" clause. However, in conjunction with the "as is " clause, the buyer was an experienced real estate developer who thoroughly inspected the commercial property, admitted to seeing the asbestos fireproofing and admitted that he would have purchased the property even if he had known the fireproofing contained asbestos. Given these facts, the court found that the buyer was precluded from claiming that the seller had a duty to warn of the presence of asbestos in the property.

However, a seller may not simply insert an "as is" clause into a contract and assume the seller is safe from claims for property defects. The clause does not negate a seller's common law duty to disclose known latent material defects. *S Development Co. v. Pima Capital Management Co.*, 201 Ariz. 10, 31 P.3d 123 (App. 2001). In *S Development Co.*, the buyers purchased two Phoenix apartment complexes. Both purchase contracts at issue in the case contained substantially similar provisions, which stated:

Disclaimer of Warranties. Buyer acknowledges that except as expressly set forth in this Agreement, seller makes and has made no representations or warranties of any kind whatsoever, including but not limited to warranties concerning the condition of title, physical condition, encroachments, access, zoning, value, future value, income potential, any survey, environmental report or other information prepared by third parties, loan assumability, or the presence on or absence from the Property of any hazardous materials or underground storage tanks. *Buyer is purchasing the Property as a result of its own examination thereof in its "as is" condition, and upon the exercise of its own judgment and investigation.* 201 Ariz. at 13, 31 P.3d at 26.

The contract also allowed the buyer to inspect the property. The buyer employed two engineering firms to perform the inspections, which revealed no substantial problems with the plumbing in the buildings.

However, two years after the close of escrow, the buyers discovered polybutylene pipe had been used in both buildings. Polybutylene pipe is a defective pipe that was the subject of a class action settlement because of its tendency to leak under normal water pressures. The buyer sued the sellers alleging fraud and nondisclosure for failing to disclose the defective plumbing. The sellers argued that the "as is" clause relieved them of any duty to disclose the defective plumbing. The court held that the existence of an "as is" provision in a purchase contract operates only as a waiver of breach of warranty claims, not as a waiver of tort claims. Therefore, the seller was obligated to disclose known latent defects in property, notwithstanding the "as is" clause or disclaimer of warranties. Thus, the Court of Appeals upheld the trial court and the jury's damage award.

"As Is" Contract Drafting Considerations

There are several provisions in the AAR contracts that should be discussed with a seller when drafting a contract to include an "as is" provision. The AAR "As Is" Addendum addresses all the issues in the AAR Resale Contract. However, if the AAR "As Is" Addendum is not utilized, some of the contractual issues in the AAR contracts that should be addressed include:

- Inspection periods: Even though the contract contains an "as is" provision, the buyer is still generally entitled to perform an inspection to determine the value and condition of the property, unless otherwise provided. In fact, there are good reasons for the seller to allow the buyer to inspect the property. Many courts, in analyzing cases where the buyer brings a claim against the seller for property defects in an "as is " sale, place great weight on whether the buyer has inspected the property in determining whether a seller will be held liable for those defects.

- Cancellation Right During Inspection Contingency: The term "as is" alone does not eliminate the buyer's right to cancel the contract pursuant to an inspection period contingency clause unless the contract language is modified. If the seller intends to eliminate the buyer's right to cancel the contract based on the disapproval of items the buyer discovers during the buyers inspection, the buyer's right to cancel should be omitted from the contract.

- Express Seller Warranties and Repair Obligations: If the contract boilerplate provides that the seller warrants and shall maintain and/or repair certain items, some courts have held that, under certain circumstances, an "as is" provision in a contract caused boilerplate express warranties to be waived by the buyer. *See, Craven v. Elmo*, 442 A.2d 526 (D.C.App. 1982). However, to avoid ambiguity, if the seller does not intend to extend any warranties to the buyer or make any repairs to the property, the seller warranty and repair provisions should be omitted from the contract, and all parties should initial the omission. By omitting any conflicting terms in the contract, the buyer and seller (and their respective brokers) should avoid having a court decide what was meant by the "as is " clause.

A seller must be honest and truthful even when selling a property "as is." Further, the clause does not negate a seller's common law duty to disclose known material defects. Therefore, brokers should warn sellers that selling "as is" is not a shield from claims of fraud, misrepresentation and nondisclosure.

If the seller intends to sell the property "as is," the seller should allow the buyer to perform all desired inspections. Further, unless the contract language is modified, the buyer is entitled to cancel the contract based on items disapproved during any inspection period. Finally, the seller's warranty provisions in the contract should be modified as necessary to clarify the parties' agreement.

AAR "As Is" Addendum (10/05)

This addendum is for use when the seller, utilizing the AAR Resale Contract, is selling a home in its existing condition, "as is". The seller makes no warranty to the buyer as to the (1) condition of the premises, including, but not limited to, seller's warranties in lines 163–166 of Section 5a of the AAR Resale Contract; (2) zoning of the premises; or (3) premises' fitness for any particular use or purpose. However, the seller warrants and is obligated to maintain and repair the premises so that, pursuant to lines 167–168 of the AAR Resale Contract, at the earlier of possession or close of escrow, the premises, including all additional existing personal property included in the sale, will be in substantially the same condition as on the date of contract acceptance and all personal property not included in the sale and all debris will be removed from the premises.

The buyer is advised to conduct independent inspection(s) and investigations regarding the premises within the inspection period. The buyer retains the right to cancel the AAR Resale Contract pursuant to the buyer disapproval section of the contract (Section 6J). However, the seller is not obligated to correct any defects that may be discovered during the buyer's inspection(s) and investigations or otherwise.

If an On-Site Wastewater Treatment Facility (conventional septic or alternative system) has been installed on the premises, seller and buyer agree to complete and execute the AAR On-Site Wastewater Treatment Facility Addendum. The seller agrees to pay for the facility inspections, fees or repairs as set forth in the Addendum.

The seller acknowledges that selling the premises "as is" does not relieve the seller of the legal obligation to disclose all known material latent defects to the buyer. The buyer acknowledges that the buyer has been advised to seek appropriate counsel regarding the risks of buying a property in "as is" condition.

KEY POINTS TO REMEMBER

- A contract for the sale of real property, any addenda or modifications must be in writing and signed (by both husband and wife, if applicable) to be enforceable.

- An offer can be withdrawn any time prior to acceptance.

- Any personal property to be conveyed must be listed in the contract.

- The Electronic Transactions Act creates statutory authority for creating a contract via computer.

- An "as is" clause does not negate a seller's duty to disclose all known latent material defects.

. . . .

CHAPTER 7

Interpreting the AAR Residential Resale Contract

The AAR Residential Resale Real Estate Purchase Contract (AAR Resale Contract or contract) is the most common form of contract for the transfer of resale residential real property in Arizona. Therefore, it is vital for everyone involved in a residential transaction to know the terms of the contract and more importantly, how those terms are generally interpreted by those in the industry. Further, the broker should give the client a copy of the contract before an offer is written or submitted, which allows the client the opportunity to become familiar with the form before the client's focus becomes the dream home or purchase price.

The contract is a nine page form with nine major sections and a cover page directed at the buyer. The following is an overview of the major provisions in each of the sections of the AAR Resale Contract and answers to some frequently asked questions about the form.

BUYER ATTACHMENT

The Buyer Attachment is not a part of the contract between the parties. The attachment is designed to alert the buyer to some of the major provisions in the contract of which the buyer should be aware. The attachment should be given to the buyer at the time the offer is written. Of course, the buyer should be advised to read the entire contract.

PROPERTY SECTION

Both the buyer and the seller are identified at the beginning of the contract and the agreement to buy and sell is spelled out. If the buyer's broker does not know the seller's name when writing the offer, the buyer's broker can simply check "as identified in section 9c," which is the acceptance section. The description of the property to be conveyed is defined as the "premises."

Close of Escrow

The Close of Escrow (COE) is defined as when the deed is recorded at the appropriate county recorder's office. In the event that either the escrow company or the recorder's office is closed on the COE Date, COE will occur on the next day that both are open for business. The buyer and seller agree to comply with all terms and conditions, execute and deliver to escrow company all closing documents, and take all other necessary actions in sufficient time to allow COE to occur on the COE Date. The buyer is specifically obligated to deliver to the escrow company a cashier's check, wired funds or other immediately available funds to pay any down payment, additional deposits or buyer's closing costs, and to instruct the lender to deliver immediately available funds to the escrow company, in a sufficient amount and in sufficient time to allow COE to occur on the COE Date.

Question: The parties have executed the contract and the COE Date is Wednesday. The buyer has loan approval, but fails to deliver funds on Wednesday. The seller issues a cure notice (described in Section 7a) on Thursday. The cure period (three days after delivery of the cure notice) ends on Sunday. Is the buyer entitled to close on Monday, since the escrow company and county recorder's office are closed on Sunday?

Answer: Yes. The contract has been interpreted to allow for the extra day under these limited circumstances due to lines 16–17, which state that if the escrow company or recorder's office is closed on the COE Date that COE shall occur on the next day that both are open.

Possession

The seller agrees to deliver possession and keys to the buyer at COE or as otherwise indicated. The advisory required by the ADRE Commissioner's Rule in regard to the risks of pre-possession or post-possession agreements is included in the contract.

Addenda Incorporated

The listed addenda include: the HOA Condominium/Planned Community Addendum (HOA), the On-site Wastewater Treatment Facility Addendum, the Domestic Water Well Addendum, the Additional Compensation Addendum, Assumption and Carryback, Buyer Contingency, HUD forms, Lead-based Paint Disclosure, and Additional Clause Addendum. Each of these addenda should be carefully reviewed prior to use.

Fixtures and Personal Property

The fixtures and personal property to be included in the sale are listed in this section. Additional personal property, such as the refrigerator, washer and dryer, which are commonly included in the sale, are to be included if checked. A line is provided to describe or include the model number of the appliance. The refrigerator, washer, dryer and any other specified additional existing personal property included are not considered part of the premises and are transferred with no monetary value, and are free and clear of all liens or encumbrances. The seller warrants that all additional personal property included in the sale will be in substantially the same condition as on the date of contract acceptance.

Question: *Existing personal property included in the sale will be conveyed in substantially the same condition as on the date of contract acceptance.*

How can the seller establish the condition of the personal property at contract acceptance?

Answer: The seller can document the condition of the personal property in the contract, on the Seller's Property Disclosure Statement (SPDS) or in some other contemporaneous writing. For example, if the refrigerator is included in the sale and the ice maker does not work, the seller can note the nonworking ice maker in the "Other Conditions and Factors" section of the SPDS.

FINANCING SECTION

The financing section obligates the buyer to take specific steps to obtain a loan and to clarify the financing contingency.

Loan Contingency

The buyer's obligation to complete the sale is contingent upon the buyer obtaining loan approval for the loan described in the AAR Loan Status Report without conditions no later than the COE Date.

If the buyer is unable in good faith to obtain loan approval without conditions by the COE Date, the loan contingency is unfulfilled, the contract is cancelled and the earnest money is released to the buyer. In order to give everyone involved in the transaction notice of an unfulfilled loan contingency, the buyer is obligated to deliver a notice of the inability to obtain loan approval to the seller or the escrow company no later than the COE Date. If the buyer fails to deliver this notice by the COE Date, the seller must give the buyer a cure notice and a three-day opportunity to deliver the notice of the unfulfilled contingency. If the buyer fails to deliver the notice, the buyer is in breach (not for the failure to qualify, but for the failure to deliver the notice) and the seller agrees to accept the earnest money as damages (as set forth in Section 7b).

Unfulfilled Loan Contingency

The contract is cancelled for an unfulfilled contingency if, after a diligent and good faith effort, the buyer is unable to obtain loan approval without conditions by the COE Date. The inability to obtain loan approval by the COE Date after a diligent and good faith effort is not a breach of contract; therefore, the cure period does not apply to extend COE. However, the buyer's failure to have the down payment or other funds necessary to obtain loan approval, such as closing costs, at COE is not an unfulfilled loan contingency, but a breach of contract after expiration of the cure period. If the buyer is unable to obtain loan approval and delivers the unfulfilled contingency notice as required, the buyer is entitled to a return of the earnest money.

Question: *The contract is cancelled for an unfulfilled contingency if, after diligent and good faith effort, the buyer is unable to obtain loan approval without conditions by the COE Date. This cancellation has also been described as an automatic termination. Can you further explain this provision?*
Answer: If the loan contingency is not fulfilled, the buyer has no obligation to close escrow. Therefore, the contract can be considered cancelled, terminated or unenforceable against the buyer. Even though the contract is no longer enforceable against the buyer, written mutual cancellation instructions should be executed. And, if the parties agree to allow the buyer additional time to obtain the loan, the parties should execute an amendment to the contract extending COE.

Question: *Why must the seller give the buyer an opportunity to cure the failure to deliver the notice of unfulfilled loan contingency?*
Answer: Because the cure period applies to every noncompliance (potential breach) with the terms of the contract. The contract requires the buyer to deliver a notice of the inability to obtain loan approval to the seller or the escrow company no later than the COE Date. Although the buyer's obligation to close escrow terminates due to the unfulfilled contingency, the seller still has the right to enforce the buyer's obligation to deliver the notice. Therefore, if the buyer fails to deliver this notice by the COE Date, the seller must give the buyer a cure notice and a three-day opportunity to deliver the notice of the unfulfilled contingency. If the buyer fails to deliver the notice, the buyer is in breach for the failure to deliver

the notice, and the seller is entitled to the earnest money as damages. If the buyer delivers the notice within three days, the buyer is entitled to a return of the earnest money.

Question: Is the buyer's notice of the inability to obtain loan approval without conditions conclusive?
Answer: No. If the seller believes that the buyer obtained loan approval or that the buyer failed to make a diligent and good faith effort to obtain loan approval, the seller should contest the notice in writing. If the buyer does not produce evidence of the inability to obtain loan approval after a good faith effort that is satisfactory to the seller, the seller can initiate mediation to resolve the dispute.

Question: What should the seller do if the COE Date arrives and the buyer doesn't close escrow or deliver a notice that the buyer was unable to obtain loan approval? And, who gets the earnest money?
Answer: The seller should deliver a cure period notice to the buyer specifying that the buyer has not complied with the contract by either closing escrow or delivering a notice of the inability to obtain loan approval to the seller or the escrow company. Thereafter:

- *If the buyer is prepared to close escrow within three days the seller must close.*
- *If the buyer delivers notice of the inability to obtain loan approval within three days, the contract is unenforceable against the buyer and the buyer is entitled to a return of the earnest money, assuming that the buyer made a diligent and good faith effort to obtain the loan.*
- *If the buyer does neither, the buyer is in breach of contract and the remedy for the breach depends on the specific noncompliance, therefore:*
  - *if the buyer failed to obtain loan approval and failed to deliver the notice, the buyer is in breach for the failure to deliver the notice, and the seller is entitled to the earnest money.*

> • *if the buyer obtained loan approval or failed to make a diligent and good faith effort to obtain loan approval, the buyer is in breach, and the seller may accept the earnest money as the seller's sole right to damages or pursue the buyer for the actual damages or specific performance.*

Appraisal Contingency

The buyer's obligation to complete the sale is contingent upon an appraisal of the premises by an appraiser acceptable to the lender for at least the sales price. If the premises fail to appraise for the sales price, buyer has five days after notice of the appraised value to cancel the contract or waive the appraisal contingency. The notice of the appraised value may be notice from any source; a complete copy of the appraisal is not required to trigger the five-day time period. If the buyer is unable to obtain the loan and close escrow due to waiving the appraisal contingency, the seller should deliver the cure notice to the buyer. If the buyer fails to close within the cure period, the buyer has breached the contract, and the seller agrees to accept the earnest money as damages (*as set forth in Section 7b*).

Question: *If the appraisal is not performed during the inspection period, does the appraisal contingency expire?*
Answer: No. Although the buyer is instructed to conduct all desired inspections to determine the "value and condition" during the due diligence period (Section 6a), the appraisal contingency is a separate contingency related to financing (Section 2c).

Loan Status Report

The AAR Loan Status Report (LSR) must be attached to every offer and must have, at a minimum, the Buyer's Loan Information section completed, describing the current status of the buyer's proposed loan. The requirement that the LSR be attached and incorporated into every offer does not necessitate that the buyer obtain prequalification from a lender prior to submitting an offer; the buyer can simply indicate on the LSR that the buyer has not yet had the opportunity to visit a lender. Including the LSR information allows the seller to better evaluate the buyer's offer.

The buyer should complete the Buyer's Loan Information section of the LSR, which addresses purchase price, loan amount requested (both first and second, if applicable), loan to value, combined loan to value, term of loan, interest rate, loan program, and occupancy. The buyer must "lock" the interest rate during the inspection period or the maximum interest provision of the loan contingency will be waived. The buyer is also asked to indicate whether the buyer is relying on the sale or lease of a property to qualify for the loan. Finally, and most importantly, the buyer is asked whether the buyer has had the opportunity to consult with a lender.

If the buyer has consulted with a lender, the Lender Prequalification Section of the LSR should be completed by the lender. The lender is asked to answer "yes" or "no" to the following:

- whether the lender has completed a verbal discussion with the buyer for the specified loan strategy, and based on information provided and a Trimerged Residential Credit Report (TMRCR), the buyer is pre-qualified
- whether the lender has received a completed written signed Application/1003, and based on the information provided and a TMRCR, the buyer is pre-qualified
- whether the lender has received and reviewed a written signed Application/1003 with all requested disclosures and supporting documentation, and based on information provided and a TMRCR, the buyer is pre-qualified
- whether the lender has provided the buyer with a Good Faith Estimate

If the answer is "yes" to any of these questions, the lender is asked to indicate the date the action was accomplished.

Question: *Who should complete the Buyer's Loan Information section of the LSR?*

Answer: Since the LSR is a part of the contract, the buyer should complete this section, preferably with the guidance of the buyer's lender, and the buyer should sign the form where indicated. If the buyer has not yet consulted with a lender and does not know how to complete a provision in the LSR, an acceptable response is "don't know."

Question: What should the seller do if the seller receives an offer without the LSR?

Answer: The LSR is an integral part of the contract. First, the listing broker should contact the buyer's broker and request that the LSR be provided. If the LSR is not immediately forthcoming, the listing broker should present the offer, but advise the seller against accepting the offer without it. The buyer's obligation to complete the transaction is contingent upon the buyer obtaining loan approval for the loan described in the LSR. If there is no LSR, no loan terms are included in the contract, which creates an ambiguity in the terms of the loan contingency. Further, the information contained in the LSR will allow the seller to better evaluate the buyer's offer.

Question: What happens if the buyer does not lock the interest rate during the inspection period?

Answer: The LSR requires the buyer to establish the interest rate and "points" by separate written agreement with the lender during the inspection period or the interest rate provision of the loan contingency is waived. If the buyer does not lock the interest rate specified in the LSR during the inspection period, for example at 6%, but can get the other loan terms described in the LSR at, for example 7%, the buyer will be obligated to close escrow or will be in breach of contract (after the expiration of the cure period). However, if the buyer does not lock, but cannot obtain loan approval for some other reason, the loan contingency is unfulfilled, and the buyer is entitled to a return of the earnest money.

Loan Application

Unless the buyer has previously completed the loan application and related actions, the buyer is obligated to:

- complete, sign and deliver to the lender a loan application, with requested disclosures and documentation
- grant the lender permission to access buyer's Trimerged Residential Credit Report
- pay all required loan application fees within five days after contract acceptance

Loan Processing During Escrow

The buyer agrees to diligently work to obtain the loan, to promptly provide the lender with all required documentation, and to authorize the lender to provide loan status updates. A Loan Status Update (LSU) form is available for this purpose, but its use is not mandated by the AAR Resale Contract. The LSU is a companion form to the LSR. The buyer authorizes the lender to provide loan status updates to the seller, and these updates may be provided on the LSU form. The LSU is divided into three subsections: Documentation, Underwriting and Approval, and Closing. The first subsection asks whether the lender has received the contract and whether the appraisal has been ordered or received. The Underwriting and Approval subsection asks whether the lender has obtained loan approval with or without prior to documents conditions. The Closing subsection addresses closing documents and prior to funding conditions.

The buyer is required to sign all loan documents three days prior to the COE Date to allow the funds to be ordered and escrow to close as agreed. If the buyer fails to sign the documents, the seller should give the buyer a cure notice. If documents are not available for signature by the COE Date because the buyer has not obtained loan approval after a diligent and good faith effort, the loan contingency is unfulfilled and the contract is cancelled. If the buyer has obtained loan approval but does not sign the loan documents within three days after receiving the cure notice, the buyer is in breach of contract, and the seller may pursue the remedies for breach.

Question: Does the requirement that the buyer sign all loan documents no later than three days prior to the COE Date apply to all-cash sales (Section 2f)?
Answer: No. If the transaction is an all-cash sale, all terms relating to the loan documents and confirming the buyer's ability to obtain the funds to close escrow must be written into the contract. The AAR Additional Clause Addendum contains a clause for use in all-cash sales.

Question: Does the requirement for the buyer to sign loan documents three days prior to the COE Date conflict with the requirement to obtain approval of the loan without conditions by the COE Date?
Answer: No. Executing the loan documents is a prerequisite to loan approval without conditions. The loan process is set forth in the LSU form, which can be provided to the buyer and seller to use as a checklist.

Type of Financing

The type of financing — conventional, FHA, VA, Assumption or Seller Carryback — is indicated in this section.

Loan Costs

The buyer is responsible for paying any required Private Mortgage Insurance (PMI). The party to be responsible for paying other loan-related costs, such as discount points, lender title insurance policy, origination fee and appraisal fee, is indicated in this section.

Other Loan Costs

This section addresses the additional amount the seller agrees to pay in the event of an FHA or VA loan. All other costs of obtaining the loan are to be paid by the buyer.

Changes

The buyer is obligated to immediately notify the seller of any changes in the loan program, financing terms, or lender described in the LSR. The buyer may not make any changes without the prior written consent of the seller unless the changes do not adversely affect the buyer's ability to obtain loan approval without conditions, increase the seller's closing costs, or delay COE. The notice to the seller of any changes, even if the changes do not affect the buyer's ability to obtain loan approval, delay COE or increase costs, is simply to keep the seller informed as to the buyer's progress in obtaining the loan.

FHA Notice

The HUD home inspection notice is included in the contract.

TITLE AND ESCROW SECTION

This section sets forth the instructions to the escrow company.

Escrow

The contract is to be used as escrow instructions, and the escrow company is identified in this subsection.

Title and Vesting

The buyer will take title as determined before COE. The buyer is advised that taking title may have significant legal, estate planning and tax consequences; therefore, the buyer should obtain legal and tax advice.

Title Commitment and Title Insurance

The escrow company is instructed to deliver a commitment for title insurance together with complete and legible copies of all documents that will remain as exceptions to the title insurance or title commitment to the buyer. The title company is instructed to send the title commitment directly to the buyer and seller, with copies to be sent to broker(s). The buyer has five days after receipt of the title commitment and after receipt of notice of any subsequent exceptions to provide notice to the seller of any items disapproved. The seller agrees to convey title by general warranty deed and provide the buyer with the best title policy available.

Additional Instructions

The additional escrow instructions require the escrow company to:

- furnish a notice of the pending sale that contains the name and address of the buyer to any homeowner's association in which the premises is located
- deliver to the buyer and seller, upon deposit of funds, a closing protection letter from the title insurer indemnifying the parties for any losses due to fraudulent acts or breach of escrow instructions by the escrow company, if the escrow company is also acting as the title agency but is not the title insurer issuing the title insurance policy
- modify its standard documents to the extent necessary to be consistent with the contract
- allocate escrow company fees equally between the seller and buyer, unless otherwise stated
- send copies of all notices and communications pertaining to the transaction to the seller, buyer and broker(s)
- provide the broker(s) access to escrowed materials and information regarding the escrow
- record the Affidavit of Disclosure at COE, if applicable

Tax Prorations

Real property taxes payable by the seller are prorated to COE based upon the latest tax information available.

Release of Earnest Money

In the event of a dispute between the buyer and seller regarding any earnest money deposited with the escrow company, the parties authorize the escrow company to release the earnest money pursuant to the terms and conditions of the contract at its sole and absolute discretion. The parties agree to hold harmless and indemnify the escrow company against any claim or loss arising from the release of the earnest money.

Proration of Assessments and Fees

All assessments and fees that are not a lien as of the COE, including homeowner's association fees, rents, irrigation fees, and, if assumed, insurance premiums, interest on assessments, interest on encumbrances, and service contracts are to be prorated as of COE unless otherwise indicated.

Assessment Liens

The amount of any assessment, other than homeowner's association assessments, which is a lien as of the COE, will be paid as indicated.

IRS and FIRPTA Reporting

The seller agrees to comply with IRS reporting requirements. If applicable, seller agrees to complete, sign and deliver to the escrow company a certificate indicating whether seller is a foreign person or a nonresident alien pursuant to the Foreign Investment in Real Property Tax Act (FIRPTA). Both buyer and seller acknowledge that if the seller is a foreign person, the buyer must withhold a tax equal to 10 percent of the purchase price, unless an exemption applies.

Question: *What does FIRPTA require?*
Answer: FIRPTA, the Foreign Investment in Real Property Tax Act, was enacted in 1980 and provides that if the seller of real property is a foreign person, the buyer must withhold a tax equal to 10% of the gross purchase price, unless an exemption applies. 26 U.S.C.A. §1445(a). The withholding is to ensure that the seller pays U.S. taxes on any taxable gains. A foreign person is a nonresident alien individual, a foreign corporation not treated as a domestic corporation, or a foreign partnership, trust or estate. A resident alien is not considered a foreign person under FIRPTA.

There are numerous exemptions to the FIRPTA withholding requirements. The most common exemption is when the seller furnishes a nonforeign affidavit stating under penalty of perjury that the seller is not a foreign person. 26 U.S.C.A. §1445(b)(2). Another exemption is a transaction involving the transfer of a property acquired for use as the buyer's residence and the amount realized (purchase price) does not exceed $300,000. 26 U.S.C.A. §1445(b)(5). Under certain circumstances, a seller may obtain a "qualifying statement" from the IRS stating that no withholding is required. 26 U.S.C.A. §1445(4).

Although FIRPTA generally provides that 10% of the purchase price must be withheld, the amount withheld should not exceed the seller's maximum tax liability. 26 U.S.C.A. §1445(c). The seller (or buyer) can request the IRS to determine the seller's maximum tax liability with respect to the sale.

A broker for either party can be held liable for the tax that should have been withheld (up to the amount of compensation received), if the broker had actual knowledge that the nonforeign affidavit is false and fails to notify the buyer and the IRS. 26 U.S.C.A. §1446(d). Under certain circumstances, the broker may also be liable for civil or criminal penalties.

Any necessary withholding should be accomplished by requiring the escrow agent to withhold the required funds. The escrow company should be instructed to send the funds to the IRS at COE.

DISCLOSURES SECTION

The disclosure section addresses the disclosures that the seller is obligated to deliver to the buyer.

Seller's Property Disclosure Statement (SPDS)

The AAR SPDS form is specifically required, and the seller is obligated to deliver a completed AAR SPDS form to the buyer within five days after contract acceptance. The issue of late delivery of the SPDS is addressed in that the buyer has the inspection period or five days after receipt of the SPDS, whichever is later, in which to provide notice of items disapproved. See chapter 16 for a more detailed discussion of the SPDS.

Insurance Claims History

The seller is obligated to deliver a written five-year insurance claims history regarding the premises (or a claims history for the length of time the seller has owned the premises if less than five years) from the seller's insurance company, an insurance support organization (such as the Comprehensive Loss Underwriting Exchange or CLUE), a consumer reporting agency, or if unavailable from these sources (for example, if the property is a second home), from the seller, within five days after contract acceptance. The buyer has the inspection period or five days after receipt of the claims history, whichever is later, in which to provide notice of items disapproved.

Lead-based Paint Disclosure

If the premises were constructed prior to 1978, the lead-based paint (LBP) information must be provided, preferably prior to contract acceptance. The buyer is obligated to return a signed copy of the Disclosure of Information on Lead-based Paint and Lead-based Paint Hazards to the seller prior to COE. The buyer must initial this subsection on the appropriate line in every transaction. See chapter 14 for a more detailed discussion of the lead-based disclosure requirements.

Affidavit of Disclosure

If the premises are located in an unincorporated area of the county, and five or fewer parcels of property other than subdivided property are being transferred, the seller must deliver a completed Affidavit of Disclosure in the form required by law to the buyer within five days after contract acceptance. The buyer must provide notice of any Affidavit of Disclosure items disapproved within the inspection period or five days after receipt of the Affidavit of Disclosure, whichever is later. The buyer should deliver the affidavit to the escrow company so that it can be recorded at COE.

Question: Does the Affidavit of Disclosure section comply with Arizona statute?

Answer: Yes. A.R.S. §33-422 requires that the Affidavit of Disclosure be delivered by the seller to the buyer no later than seven days before COE. The contract requires the seller to deliver the affidavit five days after contract acceptance. Five days after contract acceptance is typically "no later than seven days before COE" so the contractual provision does not run afoul of the statute.

See chapter 14 for a more detailed discussion of the Affidavit of Disclosure.

Changes During Escrow

The seller agrees to immediately notify the buyer of any changes in any of the seller's disclosures. Unless the seller is already obligated to correct or repair the changed item, the buyer has five days to provide notice of disapproval.

WARRANTIES SECTION

Seller Warranties

The seller warrants and is obligated to maintain and repair the premises so that, at the earlier of possession or COE:

- all heating, cooling, mechanical, plumbing and electrical systems (including swimming pool and/or spa, motors, filter systems, cleaning systems and heaters, if any), free-standing range/oven, and built-in appliances will be in working condition
- all other agreed upon repairs and corrections will be completed pursuant to Section 6j
- the premises, including all additional existing personal property included in the sale, will be in substantially the same condition as on the date of contract acceptance
- all personal property not included in the sale and all debris will be removed from the premises

Question: *The parties have executed a contract and on the day of COE, the buyer notices that a warranted item has not been fixed by the seller as required. What should the buyer do?*

Answer: The buyer should immediately deliver a cure notice to the seller. The buyer may then delay closing for up to three days to allow the seller the opportunity to cure the noncompliance and repair the warranted item. In the alternative, the buyer may close escrow subject to the potential breach and if the seller fails to make the repair within three days, pursue the seller for the breach and recover the cost of the repair. If the buyer wants to cancel the contract due to the failure of the seller to complete repairs, the buyer should consult independent legal counsel for guidance regarding whether cancellation is the appropriate remedy for the breach.

Warranties that Survive Closing

The seller warrants that:

- the seller has disclosed all material defects and any information, excluding opinions of value, which materially and adversely affect consideration to be paid by the buyer
- payment in full will have been made for all labor, professional services, materials, machinery, fixtures, or tools furnished within the 150 days immediately preceding the COE in connection with the construction, alteration, or repair of any structure on or improvement to the premises
- the information regarding connection to a sewer system or on-site wastewater treatment facility is correct to the best of seller's knowledge

Buyer Warranties

The buyer warrants that the buyer has disclosed any information that may materially and adversely affect the buyer's ability to close escrow and that the buyer has conducted all desired independent inspections and investigations and accepts the premises at the earlier of possession of the premises or COE. The buyer also warrants that the buyer is not relying on any verbal representations concerning the premises except as disclosed on the line in this subsection. If the buyer is relying on verbal representations in drafting the offer, the buyer would be well advised not to complete or submit the offer until the buyer has verified or investigated any verbal representations.

DUE DILIGENCE SECTION

The inspections section is titled "Due Diligence" to reflect the fact that both inspections and investigations of the home should be performed.

Inspection Period

The buyer's inspection period is 10 days unless otherwise indicated. During the inspection period, the contract obligates the buyer to:

- conduct all desired physical, environmental and other types of inspections and investigations to determine the value and condition of the premises
- make inquiries and consult government agencies, lenders, insurance agents, architects and other appropriate persons and entities concerning the suitability of the premises and the surrounding area
- investigate applicable building, zoning, fire, health and safety codes to determine any potential hazards or defects in the premises
- verify any material multiple listing service (MLS) information
- investigate the presence of sex offenders in the vicinity or the occurrence of a disease, natural death, suicide, homicide or other crime on or in the vicinity, if material

The buyer is advised to consult the *ADRE Buyer Advisory* provided by AAR to assist in the due diligence inspections and investigations. (See chapter 8 for a more detailed discussion of the *Advisory*.) The buyer remains obligated to keep the premises free and clear of liens, indemnify and hold the seller harmless from all liability and repair all damages arising from the inspections. The buyer is also obligated to provide the seller and broker(s), at no cost, copies of all inspection reports concerning the premises upon receipt.

Square Footage

The buyer is advised that any reference to square footage is approximate and must be investigated during the inspection period, if material.

Wood-destroying Organism or Insect Inspection

If current or past wood-destroying organisms or insects are a material matter, the buyer must investigate the issue during the inspection period at buyer's expense. If the lender requires an updated Wood-destroying Insect Inspection Report prior to COE, it will be performed at buyer's expense. If wood infestation is found during the updated inspection and the lender requires it to be treated before approving the buyer's loan, the buyer and seller will be required to negotiate whether the treatment will be performed and if so, at whose expense. If the treatment is not performed and the lender will not approve the buyer's loan, the unfulfilled loan contingency provisions will apply.

Question: When representing a buyer should any additional language be included in the contract to protect the buyer in the event that the home has termites?
Answer: No. If the Wood Infestation Report indicates the home has termites, this clause gives the buyer the right to provide written notice of disapproval during the inspection period and either cancel the contract or request specific termite treatment. Further, this clause will enable the buyer to cancel the contract if the buyer discovers past wood infestation of the home during the inspection period.

Despite this language, some buyer's brokers believe that the buyer's offer should contain an additional contingency clause making the seller responsible for providing a "clean" Wood Infestation Report on the house or for performing any necessary termite treatment. However, adding such language may not be in the buyer's best interests. A buyer may want to cancel the contract even if the seller is required to treat the home for termites, especially if the home has been treated for termites repeatedly. Such a clause could be interpreted to eliminate the buyer's right to cancel the contract if termites or past termite infestation is discovered.

Flood Hazard

The buyer is obligated to determine flood hazard designations or the cost of flood hazard insurance during the inspection period. The buyer is advised that if the home is in a special flood hazard area, the lender may require the purchase of flood hazard insurance and it may also affect the ability to encumber or improve the premises.

Insurance

If homeowner's insurance is material, the buyer is obligated to apply for and obtain written confirmation of the availability and cost of homeowner's insurance. The buyer is still advised that any desired insurance should be in place at COE.

Sewer or On-site Wastewater Treatment System

This paragraph indicates whether the premises is connected to a sewer system, septic system, or alternative system and must be initialed in every transaction. If a sewer connection is a material matter to the buyer, it must be investigated during the inspection period. If the premises are served by a septic or alternative system, the AAR On-site Wastewater Treatment Facility Addendum should be completed and incorporated into the contract. This addendum addresses permits, inspections, repair costs, transfer documents and transfer fees. Pursuant to ADEQ Rule, all on-site wastewater treatment systems must be inspected prior to transfer.

Question: *What does the ADEQ on-site wastewater treatment system pretransfer rule require?*
Answer: R18-9-A316 requires that within six months before COE, the seller must retain a qualified inspector to perform a transfer of ownership inspection of the on-site wastewater treatment facility. The inspector must complete a Report of Inspection on a form approved by the ADEQ,

sign it, and provide it to the seller. The Report must address the physical and operational condition of the on-site wastewater treatment facility and describe observed deficiencies and repairs completed, if any. Before COE, the seller must provide the buyer with the completed Report of Inspection and documents in the seller's possession relating to permitting, operation, and maintenance of the on-site wastewater treatment facility. The buyer must complete a Notice of Transfer on a form approved by the ADEQ and send the form with the applicable fee within 15 calendar days after the property transfer to the ADEQ if the facility was completed before January 1, 2001 or the appropriate county agency if the facility was constructed on or after January 1, 2001.

Swimming Pool Barrier Regulations

The buyer agrees to investigate all applicable state, county and municipal swimming pool barrier regulations and agrees to comply with and pay all costs of compliance prior to occupying the premises unless otherwise agreed. If the home contains a swimming pool, the buyer acknowledges receipt of the Arizona Department of Health Services approved private pool safety notice. Because of the importance of educating all buyers about pool safety, the buyer should initial this paragraph in every transaction.

Buyer Acknowledgment

The buyer recognizes, acknowledges and agrees that the broker(s) is not qualified, nor licensed, to conduct due diligence with respect to the premises or the surrounding area. The buyer is instructed to consult with qualified licensed professionals to assist in the buyer's due diligence efforts. Because conducting due diligence with respect to the premises and the surrounding area is beyond the scope of the broker's expertise and licensing, the buyer releases and holds harmless broker(s) from liability for any defects or conditions that could have been discovered by inspection or investigation. This provision should be initialed in every transaction.

Inspection Period Notice

Prior to expiration of the inspection period, the buyer may deliver a signed notice of any items disapproved and cancel the contract or provide the seller the opportunity to correct the item. AAR's Buyer's Inspection Notice and Seller's Response form (BINSR) is available for this notice. The BINSR contains provisions for the buyer's notice, the seller's response, and the buyer's election, as well as a space for notice of nonworking warranted items. The contract specifically states that all desired inspection period inspections and investigations must be conducted prior to delivering the notice and all due diligence items disapproved are to be provided in a single notice.

Question: *The contract requires in Section 6i that all inspection period items be disapproved in a single notice. Does this provision also apply to the notice of disapproval of the SPDS and other disclosures in Section 4?*

Answer: Yes, all inspection period items, including the disapproval of the disclosure items such as the SPDS, must be disapproved in a single notice. However, if the seller fails to deliver the SPDS or other disclosures required within five days after contract acceptance, the disapproval period for those items is no longer the inspection period, but five days after delivery. In such a case, the buyer should submit the BINSR form for all items disapproved within the inspection period prior to expiration of the inspection period and notice of any SPDS or other Section 4 Disclosures within 5 days after delivery.

Buyer Disapproval

This subsection applies to the inspection period notice and all other provisions in which the buyer is allowed an opportunity to disapprove of items. If the buyer, in the buyer's sole discretion, disapproves of items as provided in the contract, the buyer must deliver a notice of the items disapproved and state in the notice that the buyer elects to either:

- immediately cancel the contract and all earnest money shall be released, or

- provide the seller an opportunity to correct the items disapproved, in which case:
  - The seller must respond within five days or as otherwise provided. The seller's failure to respond within the specified time period is deemed to be a refusal to correct any of the items disapproved.
  - If the seller agrees in writing to correct any items disapproved, the corrections must be made, any repairs completed in a workmanlike manner and any paid receipts evidencing the corrections and repairs delivered to buyer within three days or an otherwise specified number of days prior to the COE Date.
  - If the seller is unwilling or unable to correct any of the items disapproved, the buyer may cancel the contract within five days. If the buyer does not cancel the contract, the buyer is obligated to close escrow without correction of those items that the seller has not agreed in writing to correct.

The parties are advised that verbal discussions will not extend these time periods and only a written agreement signed by both parties will extend response times or cancellation rights. The buyer is further advised that the failure to give notice of disapproval of items or cancellation within the specified time period shall be deemed the buyer's election to close escrow without correction of any disapproved items.

If the seller fails to complete the repairs three days prior to the COE Date and the buyer immediately delivers the cure notice, the seller will be liable for breach of contract and breach of warranty if the repairs are not complete by COE.

Question: *If the buyer elects to cancel the contract during the inspection period, must the buyer state the reason for cancellation?*
Answer: Yes. The buyer must deliver to the seller notice of the items disapproved (Section 6j). There are two reasons why the buyer is required to specify the reason for cancellation. First, the seller should be informed of the reason for the cancellation. Second, although the buyer is entitled to cancel at the buyer's sole discretion, this right must be exercised in

good faith; thus stating the reason for cancellation gives some evidence of whether the buyer is acting in good faith.

Question: Is the buyer entitled to disapprove of cosmetic items?
Answer: Yes. The buyer may disapprove of items in the buyer's sole discretion (Section 6j, Line 234). Of course, both parties are always obligated to act in good faith and the buyer's disapproval rights are no exception to that rule. If the buyer elects to cancel the contract, list all the items of which the buyer disapproves in the Inspection Period Notice.

Question: Does the contract give the buyer the option to demand a reduction in the purchase price in lieu of providing the seller an opportunity to correct the item disapproved?
Answer: No. The contract provides that the buyer may either elect to immediately cancel the contract or provide the seller an opportunity to correct the items disapproved. If the buyer wants to negotiate a reduction in purchase price in lieu of repairs, the buyer should obtain several bids to determine the cost of the repairs, negotiate the reduction, reduce the agreement to writing and obtain the seller's signature on the amendment prior to delivering the Inspection Period Notice. If the seller refuses to agree to reduce the purchase price, the buyer can then deliver the Inspection Period Notice and elect to cancel the contract or provide the seller an opportunity to make the repairs.

Question: What if the seller agrees to correct some, but not all, of the items disapproved?
Answer: The buyer has two options: cancel the contract within five days after receiving the seller's responses or accept the premises with the correction of only those items the seller agreed in writing to correct. If the buyer wishes to continue to negotiate the items past the five day time period, the buyer must get a written agreement extending the time periods for cancellation, or the buyer will be obligated to close escrow without correction of the items that the seller has not agreed to in writing, even if the parties continue "negotiating" (Section 6j, lines 249–250).

Question: *What if the parties need more time to negotiate the items disapproved?*

Answer: Any agreement to extend the Buyer Disapproval time periods must be agreed upon in writing and signed by all parties. For example, these time periods may be extended with the following agreement: "Buyer received seller's response on (*date*). Seller is currently unwilling to correct the following items disapproved by buyer: (*list items*). Pursuant to the contract, buyer is entitled to cancel this contract on or before (*date*). Buyer and seller hereby agree to modify the contract and extend the buyer's right to cancel this contract and receive the return of all earnest money until (*date*) to allow the parties additional time to address the items disapproved."

Question: *What if the buyer does not give written notice of items disapproved to the seller during the inspection period?*

Answer: The buyer's failure to give the seller written notice of items disapproved during the inspection period is deemed to be the buyer's election to proceed with the transaction and close escrow without the correction of any disapproved items (except for warranted items) (Section 6j, lines 251–253).

Question: *What happens if the seller fails to respond to the buyer's written notice of items disapproved?*

Answer: The seller's failure to respond is deemed a refusal to correct any of the items disapproved (Section 6j, lines 239-240). In such case, the buyer has five days after the expiration of the time period for seller's response to elect to cancel the contract or proceed with the transaction without the correction of the items disapproved, except for warranted items (Section 6j, lines 244–246).

Question: *Can the buyer change the buyer's election once the election has been made?*

Answer: Probably not. If the buyer disapproves of items, the buyer must state in the notice that the buyer elects to either immediately cancel the contract or provide the seller an opportunity to correct the items. If the buyer gives the seller an opportunity to correct the items, the buyer has made the election and can no longer "immediately cancel" the contract. To avoid this dilemma, make sure the buyer has taken the time allotted to perform all inspections and investigations and has thoroughly considered the options before making an election.

Question: *What happens if the seller fails to make the agreed upon repairs?*
Answer: If the seller fails to complete the repairs three days prior to the COE Date and the buyer immediately delivers the cure notice, the seller will be liable for breach of contract and breach of warranty if the repairs are not complete by COE. The remedy for such a breach may vary depending upon the circumstances, therefore, the buyer may need to consult legal counsel.

Question: *Is a buyer entitled to enter into multiple contracts, with the intent to buy only one, without disclosing this fact to the seller, since the buyer can cancel the contracts during the inspection period in the buyer's sole discretion?*
Answer: No. A buyer and seller have legal duties to each other arising out of their contractual relationship, which include the covenant of good faith and fair dealing. *Lombardo v. Albu,* 14 P.3d 288 (Ariz. 2000). An implied covenant of good faith forbids arbitrary action by one party that disadvantages the other. *See, W.P. Harlin Construction Co. v. Utah State Road Commission,* 431 P.2d 792, 793 (Utah 1967). In short, buyers and sellers must deal fairly with each other.

Although the contract provides that if the buyer, in the buyer's sole discretion, disapproves of items as allowed in the contract, the buyer may cancel the contract, the buyer must exercise that discretion in good faith. *See, Smith v. Grand Canyon Expeditions Co.,* 84 P.3d 1154 (UT 2003) ("where one party has discretion over another according to the terms of a contract, that party must act with good faith and fair dealing"). As the court in *Resource Management Co. v. Weston Ranch & Livestock Co.,* 706 P.2d 1028 (UT 1985) explained, notwithstanding the breadth of the power of exercising a contractual right at a party's "sole discretion," that right may not be exercised capriciously or in bad faith. *See also, Midwest Management Corp. v. Stephens,* 291 N.W.2d 896, (Iowa 1980); *Miller v. O.B. McClintock Co.,* 210 Minn. 152, 297 N.W. 724, 729 (1941); *Fulcher v. Nelson,* 273 N.C. 221, 159 S.E.2d 519, 522 (1968); 1 S. *Williston, The Law of Contracts* §105, at 418-19 (3d ed. 1957); *17 Am. Jur. 2d Contracts* §496 (1964).

Notice of Non-working Warranted Items

The buyer is obligated to provide the seller with notice of any non-working warranted item(s) of which the buyer becomes aware during the inspection period or the seller's warranty for that item(s) will be waived. The buyer may provide this notice on the BINSR form. However, the notice does not affect the seller's obligation to maintain or repair the warranted item(s).

Question: If the buyer gives notice to the seller of a nonworking warranted item, is the seller entitled to refuse to repair the item?
Answer: No. When the buyer and seller enter into the contract, the seller agrees that the warranted items will be in working condition at COE (Section 5a). The buyer's notice that one of these items is not working does not change the seller's obligation to repair the item and deliver it in working condition at COE (Section 6k).

Question: What happens if the buyer discovers a nonworking warranted item during the inspection period but does not notify the seller?
Answer: The seller warranty for that item is waived. In other words, the seller will not be obligated to repair the item.

Question: What if there is a nonworking warranted item that the buyer does not discover during the inspection period?
Answer: If the buyer does not discover the item during the inspection period, the buyer cannot give the seller notice. Therefore, the seller continues to be obligated to repair the item and deliver it in working condition at COE.

Home Warranty Plan

The buyer and seller are advised to investigate the various home warranty plans and acknowledge that different home warranty plans have different coverage options, exclusions, limitations and service fees. Also, most plans exclude preexisting conditions. If a home warranty plan is to be purchased, the contract specifies who is responsible for ordering it, with what options, from what company, and at a cost not to exceed a specified amount.

Walkthrough(s)

The seller grants the buyer and buyer's inspector(s) reasonable access to conduct walkthrough(s) of the premises for the purpose of determining that any agreed upon corrections or repairs have been completed, warranted items are in working condition and that the premises are in substantially the same condition as of the date of contract acceptance. The walkthrough provision recognizes that more than one walkthrough may be required, i.e., the buyer may desire a walkthrough three days prior to COE to confirm agreed upon repairs have been completed.

Seller's Responsibility Regarding Inspections and Walkthrough(s)

The seller is obligated to make the premises available for all inspections and walkthrough(s) upon reasonable notice by the buyer. The seller is also obligated to have all utilities on, including any propane, until COE to enable the buyer to conduct these inspections and walkthrough(s).

REMEDIES SECTION

Cure Period

A party is given an opportunity to cure a noncompliance or potential breach of the contract. If a party fails to comply with any provision of the contract, the other party must deliver a notice to the non-complying party specifying the non-compliance before declaring a breach. If the non-compliance is not cured within three days after delivery of the notice (cure period), the failure to comply becomes a breach of contract.

The cure provision only applies when a party does or does not do something that would have otherwise been an immediate breach of contract. The cure notice provides a second chance to fix a problem before it becomes a breach — the cure notice does not address what happens when there is a breach.

The cure period applies to a noncompliance that would otherwise be a breach of contract. A breach of contract is the failure to perform a contractual duty, or in other words, a broken promise. The cure period does not apply to a contingency. A contingency is an event that must occur before a party is obligated to perform a contract. A contingency is a condition, not a promise. If a contingency does not occur, the party's obligation to perform the contract never arises, so the failure to perform a contingency is not a breach. In the event that a contingency does not occur, the contract is unenforceable.

The cure period was included in the contract for a variety of reasons, including:

- The cure period provides guidance on dealing with all failures to comply with the terms of the contract in a uniform manner and prompts compliance.
- The cure period should help eliminate the question of whether a breach has been waived — because an action or inaction is not a breach until the non-complying party is given notice and an opportunity to perform.
- The cure period can bolster the enforcement of the time is of the essence clause and the ability to cancel the contract for a breach. However, if a party wants to cancel due to a breach and there is a dispute, the parties should be referred to legal counsel for advice.
- There is some inherent fairness in giving a party the opportunity to rectify a noncompliance with the contract before the other party declares a breach and cancels the contract or takes legal action.

Question: *Can there be a breach without a cure period notice?*
Answer: No. There are no automatic breaches. The cure period notice is always a prerequisite to declaring a breach of contract.

Question: *Does the cure period apply to the loan contingency?*
Answer: No. The contract is contingent upon the buyer obtaining loan approval without conditions, in other words qualifying for a loan, by the COE Date (Section 2a). If the buyer in good faith fails to obtain loan approval, or qualify for a loan, by the COE Date, the buyer's obligation to perform the contract never arises. In such a case, the contract is unenforceable the next day, and the buyer is automatically entitled to the return of the earnest money without further action by either party.

Although the contract is unenforceable against the buyer if the buyer fails to obtain loan approval by the COE Date, the parties may, by mutual agreement, complete the transaction and close escrow thereafter if they choose to do so. However, any agreement to extend the COE Date should be reduced to writing and signed by both parties. *See,* A.R.S. §44-101(6) and NAR Code of Ethics Article 9 and Standard of Practice 9-1.

Question: *What action should a buyer take if, on the day of COE, the buyer discovers that the seller has failed to complete an agreed upon repair?*
Answer: The buyer should deliver a cure notice to the seller. The buyer may then delay closing for up to three days to allow the seller the opportunity to repair the item. In the alternative, the buyer may close escrow and if the seller fails to make the repair within three days, pursue the seller for the breach and recover the cost of the repair (in small-claims court, mediation, arbitration or litigation).

If the buyer delays COE for the three-day cure period and the seller still has not completed the repair, the seller is in breach of contract. Section 7b of the contract sets forth the remedies in the event of a breach: "the non-breaching party may cancel this contract and/or proceed against the breaching party in any claim or remedy that the non-breaching party may have in law or equity, subject to the Alternative Dispute Resolution obligations" set forth. However, if the buyer wants to cancel the contract due to the unrepaired item, the buyer's broker should refer the buyer to legal counsel. Although there is a remedy for every breach of contract, the remedy is not always cancellation.

Breach

As discussed above, if after receiving the notice of noncompliance the party does not perform the specified obligation, the non-complying party is in breach of contract. In that event, the non-breaching party may pursue all legal remedies, subject to the Alternative Dispute Resolution obligations set forth in the contract. The remedies for a breach of contract may include forfeiture of the earnest money, actual damages (money), forfeiture of the contract (cancellation), or specific performance (forcing the breaching party to perform). In the event of buyer's breach, the seller may accept the earnest money as the sole right to damages. In the event of buyer's breach arising from the failure to deliver the notice of the inability to obtain loan approval or the inability to obtain loan approval due to the waiver of the appraisal contingency, the seller agrees to accept the earnest money as the sole right to damages. This provision also states the obvious: an unfulfilled contingency is not a breach of contract.

Alternative Dispute Resolution (ADR) — Mediation and Arbitration

The buyer and seller agree to mediate any dispute or claim arising out of or relating to the contract, and all mediation costs will be paid equally. If mediation does not resolve the dispute, the unresolved dispute must be submitted to binding arbitration unless either party opts out within 30 days after the conclusion of the mediation conference by notice to the other. If a party opts out of arbitration, either party has the right to resort to court action.

Exclusions from ADR

The following matters are excluded from the requirement for mediation and arbitration:

- any action brought in the Small Claims Division of an Arizona Justice Court (up to $2,500)
- judicial or nonjudicial foreclosure or other action or proceeding to enforce a deed of trust, mortgage, or agreement for sale;
- an unlawful entry or detainer action
- the filing or enforcement of a mechanic's lien
- any matter that is within the jurisdiction of a probate court

The filing of a judicial action to record a *lis pendens* or order of attachment, receivership, injunction, or other provisional remedies is not a waiver of the obligation to submit the claim to alternative dispute resolution, or a breach of the duty to mediate or arbitrate.

Attorney Fees and Costs

The prevailing party in any dispute is entitled to an award of their reasonable attorney fees and costs.

ADDITIONAL TERMS AND CONDITIONS SECTION

Risk of Loss

If there is any loss or damage to the home prior to COE or possession, whichever is earlier, by reason of fire, vandalism, flood, earthquake, or act of God, the risk of loss is on the seller, unless the cost of repairing the loss or damage exceeds 10 percent of the purchase price. In that case, either seller or buyer may cancel the contract.

Permission

Buyer and seller grant broker(s) permission to advise the public of the contract.

Arizona Law

The contract is governed by Arizona law and any action relating to the contract is to take place in Arizona.

Time is of the Essence

The parties acknowledge that time is of the essence in the performance of the contractual obligations.

Compensation

The seller and buyer acknowledge that the broker(s) will be compensated for their services as previously agreed by separate written agreement(s), which shall be delivered by the brokers to the escrow company for payment at COE, if not previously paid. If the seller is obligated to pay the broker(s), the contract constitutes an irrevocable assignment of seller's proceeds at COE. If the buyer is obligated to pay broker(s), payment is to be collected from buyer as a condition of COE.

Copies and Counterparts

A fully executed facsimile or electronic copy of the entire contract is to be treated as an original contract. The contract and any other related documents may be executed by facsimile or other electronic means and in any number of counterparts, however copies may be signed. All counterparts are deemed to constitute one instrument, and each counterpart is deemed an original, except that the Lead-based Paint Disclosure Statement may not be signed in counterpart. (However, copies of the Lead-based Paint Disclosure may be signed, as discussed in chapter 14.)

Calculating Time Periods

This provision explains how time periods in the contract are to be calculated. The day of the act or event from which the time period begins to run is not included (i.e., the date of contract acceptance), and the last day of the time period is included. The provision explicitly states that contract acceptance occurs on the date that the signed contract (and any incorporated counteroffer) is delivered to and received by the appropriate broker. Acts that must be performed three days prior to the COE Date must be performed three full days prior; for example, if the COE Date is Friday, the act must be performed by 11:59 p.m. on Monday.

Days

All references to days are calendar days. A day begins at 12:00 a.m. and ends at 11:59 p.m.

Question: Contract acceptance occurred on Monday. When does five days after contract acceptance expire?
Answer: The day of the act or event from which the time period begins to run is not included, so day one is Tuesday. The last day to perform any acts required to be accomplished within five days after acceptance should be completed by Saturday at 11:59 p.m.

Question: If the cure period notice was sent at 5 p.m. on Monday when does the three-day cure period expire?
Answer: The three-day cure period expires at 11:59 Thursday night. This time period is calculated as follows:
- the day of the act or event from which the time period begins to run is not included, in this example, Monday. Therefore, Tuesday is day one, Wednesday is day two and Thursday is day three
- the last day of the time period is included, in this example, Thursday. Therefore, the non-complying party would be in breach at 12 a.m. on Friday

Entire Agreement

The contract, addenda and attachments constitute the entire agreement, supersede any other written or oral agreements and can be modified only by a signed writing. The failure to initial any page of the contract does not affect its validity or terms.

Subsequent Offers

The buyer acknowledges that the seller has the right to accept subsequent offers until COE. However, any subsequent offer accepted must be a backup offer contingent on the cancellation of the contract.

Cancellation

A party who wishes to exercise any right of cancellation allowed in the contract may cancel the contract by delivering a notice stating the reason for cancellation to the other party or to the escrow company. Cancellation becomes effective immediately upon delivery of the cancellation notice.

Question: Can a party cancel the contract for any breach?
Answer: No. Brokers are often faced with a transaction in which one party has breached the purchase contract and the non-breaching party is threatening cancellation. Although there is a remedy for every breach of contract, the remedy is not always cancellation. The remedy may be limited to compensation for financial losses. To justify cancellation, the breach generally must relate to a vital provision of the contract (a material term); the breach cannot relate simply to an incidental or minor contract provision. Therefore, a party threatening cancellation of a contract over the objections of the other party should be referred to legal counsel for advice.

Notice

Unless otherwise provided (i.e., for delivery of the title commitment, acceptance or cancellation), delivery of all notices and documentation required or permitted in the contract must be in writing, addressed as indicated in the referenced sections (Section 8r and Section 9a, which provide the identity and contact information for the brokers and salespersons involved in the transaction) and are deemed delivered and received when:
- hand-delivered
- sent via facsimile transmission

- sent via electronic mail, if e-mail addresses are provided
- sent by recognized overnight courier service

Therefore, the broker must check the office, fax and e-mail provided in the notice sections daily.

Question: Does the contract require the salesperson to receive notices via e-mail?

Answer: No. Notices may be sent by e-mail only if the salesperson provides an e-mail address in Section 8r or 9a. If no e-mail address is included, the other party may not deliver notice via e-mail. For clarity, the salesperson may wish to indicate "not authorized" on the e-mail line.

Question: When is a notice received pursuant to the contract?

Answer: Pursuant to Section 8m, notices are received when hand-delivered to the firm address, sent to the facsimile number or e-mail address provided in Section 8r or 9a. The notice is deemed received even if the notice is not picked up from the office, the fax machine is out of paper, or the e-mail is not opened.

Earnest Money

If applicable, the form of earnest money and where it will be deposited is addressed in this paragraph.

Release of Broker(s)

The parties expressly release, hold harmless and indemnify the broker(s) from liability and responsibility for the listed items relating to the premises. This provision emphasizes to the buyer the importance of conducting their due diligence investigation and inspection of the premises utilizing the appropriate professionals.

Question: Is a "hold harmless" clause enforceable?

Answer: Yes, a hold harmless clause is enforceable under certain circumstances. Such a clause will be given effect when it represents "an intentional relinquishment of a known right." Further, certain conditions must be met: there must be no public policy impediment to the limitation and the parties must "bargain" for the limitation.

In an Arizona case, *Aranki v. RKP Investments, Inc.*, 194 Ariz. 206, 979 P.2d 534 (App. 1999), the court considered whether the hold harmless clauses in the 1994 version of the AAR Residential Resale Contract (1994 AAR Contract) would protect a buyer broker from claims of negligence. The buyer's broker relied upon the clause in the contract that expressly released "all brokers . . . from any and all liability and responsibility regarding the condition" of the property and contained representations that the buyer would conduct all desired independent investigations of any and all matters concerning the purchase prior to closing. The *Aranki* court concluded that the hold harmless clauses in the 1994 AAR Contract did not immunize the buyer's brokers from liability because there was no evidence that the hold harmless terms were discussed or negotiated between the parties. Of importance to the court was that the parties did not initial the provision.

Other courts have enforced contractual hold harmless clauses. For example, in *Hamtil v. J.C. Nicols Real Estate*, 923 P.2d 513 (Kan. App 1996), the court dismissed a lawsuit brought by a buyer against the brokers involved in the transaction, based upon a separate hold harmless agreement signed by the buyers. The court held that real estate brokers may protect themselves from negligent misrepresentation actions by disclaiming knowledge of any property defects and having a buyer or seller acknowledge the disclaimer. The *Hamtil* court held that such real estate broker protection is not against public policy and, in fact, helps to clarify the law and the roles of those involved in real estate matters.

Similarly, in a 2004 case, a court upheld a hold harmless provision that stated in part:

> Buyer and seller agree that the real estate licensees involved in this transaction are not experts regarding whether any environmental or health hazards, defects in the mechanical equipment or systems, structural defects, or damage from wood-destroying insects exists in and on the property. Buyer and seller should seek expert advice and obtain inspections to determine if hazards,

defects or damage exist in and on the property. If inspections are not performed regarding all or part of the property, buyer is bound by whatever information an inspection would have revealed, and waives any claim, right or cause of action relating to or arising from any condition of the property that would have been apparent had inspections been performed. Unless otherwise provided in paragraphs relating to specific inspections, buyer accepts the property in its current condition.

Alires v. McGehee, 85 P.3d 1191 (Kan. 2004).

The AAR Resale Contract contains hold harmless provisions at Section 6h and Section 8o. These hold harmless provisions are conspicuously placed in the contract. The provisions should not be considered against public policy, the buyer's initials evidence that the provision was discussed, and the language clearly helps to clarify the broker's role in the transaction. Therefore, although these provisions will likely be strictly construed against the brokers in a transaction, they should be given effect according to their terms.

Terms of Acceptance

Contract acceptance occurs and the offer becomes a binding contract when acceptance is signed by the seller, and a signed copy delivered in person, by mail, facsimile or electronically and received by the specified broker by the specified time and date.

Broker on Behalf of Buyer

The broker and salesperson contact information is included in this paragraph for addressing the notice to the buyer, for agency confirmation and for earnest money receipt. All notices must be sent to the salesperson indicated unless otherwise provided.

Agency Confirmation

The agency relationship of the broker writing the offer is confirmed in this section. Both agency confirmations are contained on the same page so that any inconsistencies will be obvious.

SELLER ACCEPTANCE SECTION

Broker on Behalf of Seller

The listing broker's information is contained in this section. All notices to the seller must be sent to the salesperson indicated unless otherwise provided.

Agency Confirmation

The agency relationship of the listing broker is confirmed in this section.

Seller Receipt of Copy

The seller acknowledges receipt of a copy of the contract and grants permission to the broker to deliver a copy to the buyer.

Counter Offer

If a counteroffer is attached, the seller should sign both the offer set forth in the contract form and the counteroffer. If there is a conflict between the offer and the counteroffer, the provisions of the counteroffer are controlling.

Offer Rejected by Seller

If the offer is rejected, the seller should initial and date this provision.

Question: Why should the listing broker obtain the seller's initials on a rejected offer?
Answer: Many complaints against real estate licensees involve allegations that an offer was not submitted to the seller or not submitted to the seller in a timely manner. As a result, a box was added to the contract to prompt the seller to acknowledge that an offer was submitted and rejected on the date specified. The seller's initials evidence that both the listing broker and the buyer's broker complied with the Commissioner's Rule, R4-28-

802(B), which requires a broker to promptly submit all offers to the broker's client.

Conclusion

While no contract form is perfect, the AAR Resale Contract is designed to make transactions proceed more smoothly, set forth the obligations of the parties with specificity and reduce liability for the parties and the brokers. Further, the advantages of a standardized resale purchase contract for both the brokers and the parties involved can not be overstated.

KEY POINTS TO REMEMBER

- Provide the client with a copy of the contract before writing or submitting an offer and point out key provisions.

- Always attach an LSR to the offer.

- The buyer must conduct all desired inspection period due diligence before submitting a BINSR to the seller.

- Verbal negotiations do not extend the BINSR time frames.

- A cure period notice is always a prerequisite to declaring a breach.

CHAPTER 8

Residential Contract, Related Forms
And Other Addenda

There are numerous forms and addenda that are available for use in conjunction with the AAR Resale Contract. When executed by the parties, the addenda become a part of the contract and are enforceable pursuant to their terms. The disclosure forms are not a part of the contract, however, the information contained in the disclosure forms are representations on which the buyer may rely. Therefore, like the contract itself, all parties must be familiar with the addenda and disclosure forms that are used in a transaction.

The only AAR forms mandated by the AAR Resale Contract are the AAR Loan Status Report with the buyer's loan information completed (the lender portion of the form is not required) and the AAR Seller's Property Disclosure Statement (SPDS). The use of all other related AAR forms is simply encouraged for uniformity of practice.

LOAN STATUS REPORT (11/05)

The AAR Loan Status Report (LSR) is discussed in detail in the previous chapter on the AAR Resale Contract under the Financing section. The LSR must be attached to every offer, and its terms are incorporated into the contract. The purpose of the LSR is to describe the buyer's loan and allow the seller to evaluate the buyer's ability to obtain the necessary financing to complete the transaction.

THE RESIDENTIAL SELLER'S PROPERTY DISCLOSURE STATEMENT (8/05)

The AAR Resale Contract at Section 4a requires the seller to deliver a completed AAR Seller's Property Disclosure Statement (SPDS) form to the buyer within five days after contract acceptance. The SPDS is required by the AAR Resale Contract because the courts have held that where a seller of real property knows of facts materially affecting the value of the property that are not readily observable and are not known to the buyer, the seller is under a duty to disclose those facts to the buyer. This duty was first set forth in Arizona in the case of *Hill v. Jones,* 151 Ariz. 81, 725 P.2d 1115 (App. 1986) dealing with the disclosure of termites. Additionally, pursuant to the AAR Resale Contract at Section 5b, the seller warrants that the seller has disclosed to the buyer and broker(s) all known material latent defects and any information concerning the home known to the seller, excluding opinions of value, which materially and adversely affect the consideration to be paid by the buyer.[10]

The SPDS is designed to assist the seller in making the legally required disclosures and avoid inadvertent nondisclosures of material facts. The SPDS also assists the buyer in the inspection and investigation of the property. The proper use of the SPDS results in well informed buyers and reduces the likelihood of claims against the sellers and brokers involved in the transaction. The following is an overview of the Residential SPDS.

Seller Advisory

The Seller Advisory is the first page of the form and is designed to emphasize to the seller the legal obligation to disclose all known material

---

[10] *The AAR Vacant Land SPDS and Commercial SPDS forms are available for use in conjunction with the AAR vacant land and commercial contract forms.*

defects to the buyer. Additionally, the advisory provides the seller with guidance in completing the form.

Message and Instruction to the Seller

The message to the seller again explains that sellers are obligated by law to disclose all known material (important) facts about the property, and the SPDS is designed to assist in making these disclosures. Sellers are instructed to complete the form by answering all questions as truthfully and as fully as possible, to attach any available supporting documentation, and to use the explanation lines as necessary. If the seller does not have the personal knowledge to answer a question, the seller is instructed to use the explanation lines to explain.

Message and Instruction to the Buyer

The message to the buyer explains that although sellers are obligated to disclose all known (important) facts about the property, there are likely facts about the property of which the seller is unaware. Therefore, the buyer is told of the importance of taking an active role in obtaining information about the property. The buyer is instructed to review the SPDS and any attachments carefully and to verify all important information. The buyer is also instructed to ask about any incomplete or inadequate responses and inquire about any concerns not addressed on the SPDS. Finally, the buyer is instructed to review all other applicable documents, such as the CC&Rs and the title report, obtain professional inspections of the property, and investigate the area surrounding the property.

Ownership and Property

This section prompts for a variety of general information about the property, such as location, ownership and occupancy. Any seller, whether or not that seller has actually lived in the property, should be able to answer most, if not all, of the questions in this section.

This section informs the parties that an Affidavit of Disclosure is required by law if the property is in an unincorporated area and five or fewer parcels of land, other than subdivided land, are being transferred.

The parties are advised that if the owner is a foreign person or nonresident alien, a tax advisor should be consulted about possible mandatory FIRPTA withholding of funds. If the property was built prior the 1978, the parties are informed that a lead-based paint disclosure is required.

Additionally, the section informs buyers that a public report, which contains a variety of information about the subdivision at the time the subdivision was approved, may be available by contacting the ADRE or the homebuilder. Subdividers are required to give new home buyers in a subdivision public report. Subsequent buyers may also benefit from reviewing the public report, although some of the information may be outdated and no longer accurate. Public reports dating from January 1, 1997, are available on the ADRE Web site. Public reports issued before 1997 may be available by contacting the ADRE subdivision department, however, public reports over 20 years old are generally not available from the ADRE in any format.

A notice to buyers about homeowners insurance is also included to inform the buyer that the buyer's claims history and credit report, the property's claims history and other factors may affect the insurability of the property and at what cost. The buyer is also informed that an insurance company may cancel their homeowner's insurance within 60 days after the effective date; therefore, the buyer is urged to contact their insurance company.

Building and Safety Information

This section provides for information regarding the structural integrity of the property. The buyer is advised to contact a professional to verify the condition of the roof as a result of the frequency of claims from buyers alleging an undisclosed defective roof.

The seller is asked about any past or current presence of termites or other wood destroying organisms on the property. The treatment history of the property is requested, along with the name of any treatment provider and any warranty information. The buyer is also notified to contact the Structural Pest Control Commission for past reports or treatment history concerning the property.

Heating, cooling, plumbing, and electrical information is requested on the form. The seller is prompted to disclose any swimming pool, spa, hot tub, sauna or other water feature on the property and any problems with any of these items, as well as whether they are heated, and if so, the type of heat.

The seller is also asked specifically to disclose any knowledge of scorpions, rabid animals, bee swarms, rodents, or other creatures ever having been present on the property. This question was necessitated by claims involving the alleged nondisclosure of the presence of scorpions or other "pests" on the property. Although most sellers will answer affirmatively to the question, the buyer will be informed and unable to claim ignorance of these natural inhabitants of Arizona's desert environment after close of escrow.

Finally, this section prompts for information about any work or improvements to the property, whether permits were obtained, and other miscellaneous items.

Utilities

The seller is asked whether the property currently receives the listed utilities, and if so, to name the provider. The water source and any known information about drinking water problems are also requested. If the water source is a private or shared well, the seller is prompted to complete the Domestic Water Well/Water Use Addendum. The buyer is advised to contact the water provider for information about water supply.

Environmental Information

A variety of environmental information is requested. For example, the seller is prompted to disclose any issues relating to soil, drainage/grade, settlement/expansion, erosion, fissures or open mine shafts/tunnels or wells, noise from the surrounding area including airports and traffic noise and any odors or other nuisances. The seller is asked to disclose any past or present asbestos, radon, lead-based paint, pesticides, underground storage tanks or fuel/chemical storage on the property. If the property is located within a Superfund, WQARF, CERCLA or wetlands area, that information is solicited as well. The seller is asked specifically if the seller is aware of any past or present mold growth on the property. Additionally, the seller is prompted to disclose any conditions conducive to mold growth, such as dampness/moisture, flooding, water damage or water leaks of any kind.

Sewer/Waste Water Treatment

The topic of sewer or wastewater treatment is emphasized because of numerous claims involving alleged misrepresentations regarding sewer connections. For example, there have been situations in which the seller reasonably believed the property was connected to the sewer, and even paid sewer fees, when in fact the property was served by a septic tank. Therefore, the seller is asked if the entire property is connected to a sewer and if so, whether the sewer connection has been verified by a professional. Additionally, the buyer is advised to contact a professional to conduct a sewer verification test. If the property is served by an on-site wastewater treatment facility, i.e., a septic or alternative wastewater system, a variety of additional information is elicited. The parties are also notified that the ADEQ requires a pretransfer inspection of on-site wastewater treatment facilities on resale properties.

Other Conditions and Factors — Additional Explanations

These blank lines provide space for the seller to disclose any other important information concerning the property that might affect the buyer's decision-making process, the value of the property, or its use. The additional explanation lines can also be used for any other necessary explanations.

Seller Certification

The seller's signature certifies that the information in the SPDS is true, complete and that the seller will disclose any changes in the information in writing prior to close of escrow. A box is included to allow the seller to indicate by initialing that the SDPS has been reviewed and updated as of a specified date.

Buyer's Acknowledgment

The buyer acknowledges by signing that the information contained in the SPDS is based only on the seller's actual knowledge and is not a warranty. The buyer also acknowledges the obligation to investigate any material (important) facts in regard to the property. The buyer is encouraged to obtain professional inspections and to consider a home warranty. A notice has also been added to the SPDS form to advise the buyer that sellers and brokers are not obligated to disclose certain information, such as the fact that the property has been the site of a death or felony, owned or occupied by a person with HIV/AIDS or located in the vicinity of a sex offender. Finally, if the buyer disapproves of any items contained in the SPDS, the buyer must deliver written notice of the items disapproved as provided in the contract.

Question: Is the AAR SPDS form required by statute?
Answer: No. The seller is legally required to disclose known material facts, but the seller is not legally required to use the AAR form.

Question: Is the seller obligated to disclose material facts if the seller is not represented by a broker?
Answer: Yes. The seller has an obligation to make the required disclosures regardless of whether or not the seller is represented by a broker or uses the SPDS.

Question: Are all the questions on the SPDS material in every transaction?
Answer: No. Some of the questions on the SPDS are simply for informational purposes. What is material depends on the facts and circumstances of the transaction.

Question: If the seller answers the questions on the SPDS that are not material in that particular transaction, is the seller harmed?
Answer: No. If the disclosure is not material there should be no adverse consequences for providing the information.

Question: *Wouldn't it be better if sellers made their disclosures of material fact on a blank piece of paper, rather than utilizing the SPDS form?*
Answer: If a seller could remember all the material details of the property that need to be addressed, any writing would suffice. However, the SPDS serves to address statutory disclosures of which the seller may not be aware, to prompt the seller to disclose information the seller may not realize is material, and to assist the seller to make these disclosures fully and accurately.

Question: *Does the SPDS operate as a "warranty" of the condition of the property?*
Answer: No. The SPDS is not a warranty, but simply a disclosure of facts of which the seller is aware. The SPDS requires the buyer to acknowledge that the information in the SPDS is based only on the seller's actual knowledge and is not a warranty of any kind.

On occasion, a seller will express reluctance to complete a SPDS on the basis that the seller has never occupied the property or has never even seen the property. However, if the seller owns the property, the seller should be able to answer most of the questions in the Ownership and Property section of the AAR SPDS. For example, even an institutional seller who has never seen the property can usually:

- disclose the address of the property
- disclose whether the property is located in an unincorporated area
- identify the legal owner of the property
- disclose whether the legal owner is a foreign person or nonresident alien pursuant to the Foreign Investment in Real Property Tax Act
- indicate whether the property is in a community providing housing for older persons pursuant to the fair housing laws
- indicate whether the property is owner-occupied, lease, estate foreclosure, or vacant
- indicate if the property is vacant, and for how long

- indicate if the property is rented, and the expiration of the rental agreement, and disclose whether refundable deposits or prepaid rents are being held
- disclose whether the owner has entered into any agreement to transfer an interest in the property in any way

Additionally, most sellers know whether the property is in a home-owner's association (HOA) and whether there are HOA fees. Arizona law mandates seller disclosure of these and other HOA issues in HOAs with less than 50 units. The seller may also be aware of assessments, litigation, or liens affecting the property. Most of the questions on the SPDS ask only for information of which the seller is aware. However, if there are questions on the SPDS for which the seller does not know the answers, the seller can simply use the explanation lines to explain. The fact that certain information is unknown by the seller, and why, can be important to the buyer.

Despite the foregoing, some sellers still refuse to provide a SPDS. If a listing states that a SPDS is not available, or will not be provided, a buyer's broker should nonetheless advise the buyer to request the SPDS in the offer. The seller can respond to the offer requesting a SPDS with a counteroffer that a SPDS will not be provided. However, before the buyer accepts the counteroffer indicating that a SPDS will not be provided, a buyer's broker should provide the buyer with a blank copy of the SPDS form, which will enable the buyer to make an informed decision regarding whether to waive the SPDS. In these circumstances, a buyer's broker would be wise to obtain the buyer's written acknowledgment of receipt of the blank form.

A buyer should not waive a SPDS without seeing the SPDS form. Even a blank SPDS is valuable to the buyer. The buyer can and should utilize a blank SPDS as a checklist in conducting the desired inspections and investigations. The SPDS can prompt questions that will assist the buyer in evaluating the property. Clearly, the SPDS is a valuable tool for both buyers and sellers in a real property transaction. Therefore, every buyer should receive a SPDS.

BUYER'S INSPECTION NOTICE AND SELLER'S RESPONSE (BINSR) (8/05)

The BINSR form is designed to be used by the buyer to provide the seller with a signed notice of any inspection period items disapproved pursuant to Section 6i of the AAR Resale Contract. When executing the form, the buyer represents that the buyer has completed all desired:

- physical, environmental, and other inspections and investigations
- inquiries and consultations with government agencies, lenders, insurance agents, architects, and other persons and entities
- investigations of applicable building, zoning, fire, health, and safety codes
- inquiries regarding sex offenders and the occurrence of a disease, natural death, suicide, homicide or other crime on the premises or in the vicinity
- inspections and investigations pertaining to square footage, wood-destroying organisms or insects, sewer/on-site wastewater treatment system, flood hazard, swimming pool barriers, and insurance
- inspections and investigations of any other items important to the buyer

Further, the buyer acknowledges that the buyer has verified all information deemed important including:

- MLS or listing information
- all other information obtained regarding the premises

The BINSR provides a section for the buyer to accept the premises in its present condition and request no corrections or repairs or to reject the premises by disapproving of the listed items and electing to either immediately cancel the contract or provide the seller an opportunity to correct the disapproved items. The form also includes a section for the buyer to provide the seller notice of nonworking warranted items as required by Section 6k of the AAR Resale Contract.

The form contains a section for the seller's response, if the buyer provides the seller an opportunity to correct items disapproved. If the seller does not agree to correct all items disapproved, the buyer makes the election on the form to either cancel the contract or accept the seller's response and close escrow without correction of those items the seller has not agreed to correct.

The buyer disapproval, seller response process in the AAR Resale Contract is discussed in more detail in the previous chapter dealing with the Due Diligence section of the AAR Resale Contract.

DOMESTIC WATER WELL ADDENDUM AND DOMESTIC WATER WELL/WATER USE ADDENDUM TO SELLER'S PROPERTY DISCLOSURE STATEMENT (5/05)

Properties that are served by domestic water wells have unique concerns. These addenda are designed to be used when the premises is served by a domestic water well. The Domestic Water Well Addendum (DWWA) requires the seller to provide the Domestic Water Well/Use Addendum SPDS (DWW SPDS) and well records. The form also instructs the escrow company to send a change of well information/ownership form and transfer fee to the Arizona Department of Water Resources.

The DWW SPDS asks for a variety of information about the well, including ownership, registration and well-sharing agreements. The DWW SPDS prompts the seller to disclose any tests that indicate the well water may contain elements considered a health hazard or any problems with the well or well equipment. Information on the well's pumping capacity is also requested.

The DWW SPDS also advises the buyer to investigate current water use laws that may affect the property and to consult independent legal counsel regarding any water use/water rights issues. Also included is a notice on the General Stream Adjudications, which explains:

> General Stream Adjudications are court proceedings to determine the extent and priority of water rights in an entire river system. Arizona is undertaking a general stream adjudication

of both the Gila River and the Little Colorado River systems. A river system means all water appropriable by law and all water subject to claims based upon federal law. All affected property transfers should include assignment of statement of claimant forms from sellers to buyers.

For details regarding water uses and the watersheds affected by these adjudications or to obtain necessary statement of claimant forms or assignment of statement of claimant claim forms, contact the Arizona Department of Water Resources at 1-800-352-8488, 1-866-246-1414 or 602-417-2442.

The DWW SPDS asks whether a Statement of Claimant has been filed and, if so, asks for a copy and the claim number.

DISCLOSURE OF BUYER AGENCY AND SELLER WAIVER AND CONFIRMATION FORM (8/05)

The Disclosure of Buyer Agency and Seller Waiver and Confirmation (DBA) form is available for use in so-called limited or minimum service listing transactions in which the buyer's broker is instructed to present the offer directly to the seller. Brokers have been concerned about several issues presented by this type of listing agreement. AAR's DBA form was designed to address some of these issues, protect all parties in a limited service transaction and ensure compliance with the ADRE Commissioner's Rules.

The DBA form restates the ADRE Rule R4-28-1102 and states:

Arizona Department of Real Estate Rule R4-28-1102 requires that all negotiations be conducted exclusively through the seller's broker or the seller's broker's representative unless the seller waives this requirement in writing and no licensed representative of the seller's broker is available for 24 hours.

The DBA provides a means for the buyer's broker to ensure compliance with this rule evidencing the seller's waiver and confirmation that:

Seller has entered into an employment (listing) agreement with another broker pursuant to which the seller's broker will not be present to negotiate the offer, and agrees that all offers will be presented and negotiated by the buyer's broker directly with seller.

Seller waives the requirement that all negotiations be conducted exclusively through the seller's broker or the seller's broker's representative. Seller confirms that no licensed representative of seller's broker will be available for 24 hours based on the seller's agreement with the seller's broker.

Sellers who employ limited service brokers are essentially representing themselves. As a result, these sellers are prone to ask the buyer's broker questions about the transaction. Although the buyer's broker can respond to questions and discuss the offer with the seller, there are concerns that the seller may become confused about who the buyer's broker represents and the possibility of an unintentional dual agency situation. The DBA form makes it clear to the seller that the buyer's broker represents only the buyer, even though the buyer's broker is dealing directly with the seller. The DBA form clearly discloses that:

Seller acknowledges that buyer's broker is acting solely as buyer's agent and buyer's broker is NOT representing seller in regard to the property. As buyer's agent, buyer's broker has the fiduciary duties of loyalty, obedience, disclosure, confidentiality, and accounting to buyer. These duties require that all information given to buyer's broker by seller regarding the property and the transaction must be disclosed to buyer. Further, all acts of buyer's broker are exclusively for the buyer's benefit.

Thus, AAR's DBA form protects all parties in a limited service transaction by making a clear agency disclosure and provides a vehicle to ensure compliance with the ADRE Commissioner's Rules.

BUYER CONTINGENCY ADDENDUM (10/05)

This addendum is designed to be used when the AAR Resale Contract is to be contingent on the sale and closing of buyer's property. The addendum has two options: one for the transaction in which buyer's property is listed for sale, but the buyer has not yet entered into a contract for its sale, and another option for a transaction in which the buyer has entered into a contract for the sale of the property, but the transaction has not yet closed.

Option One: Contingent on the Sale and Closing of Buyer's Property

This option provides that the AAR Resale Contract is contingent on an accepted offer to purchase (sale) buyer's specified real property (buyer's property) by a specified date. If the buyer accepts an offer to purchase buyer's property, the buyer is obligated to deliver specified sale documents to the seller for review within five days after acceptance of the offer. Unless the seller cancels this contract within the time specified, the resale contract becomes contingent upon the closing of the pending sale of buyer's property by the specified date.

If the seller accepts a subsequent offer to purchase the premises before the sale of the buyer's property, the seller is obligated to deliver a notice to the buyer. Upon receipt of seller's notice, the buyer has the specified number of days to deliver to the seller a written agreement to remove the contingency and written documentation from the buyer's lender that the buyer can close escrow by the agreed-upon date without the sale and closing of buyer's property or the contract is deemed cancelled and the earnest money is released to the buyer.

Option Two: Contingent on the Closing of the Pending Sale of Buyer's Property

The AAR Resale Contract is contingent upon close of escrow on the buyer's specified real property by the specified date. The buyer is obligated to deliver the specified sale documents to the seller within five days after acceptance of the contract.

Provisions Applicable to Both Options

The seller may, within five days of receipt of buyer's sale documents, cancel the AAR Resale Contract if the seller reasonably believes that the closing of buyer's property will not occur by the specified date. Until the closing of the pending sale of buyer's property or cancellation of the contract, any subsequent offer accepted by the seller must be a backup offer contingent on the cancellation of the contract.

If the sale and closing of buyer's property is not completed by date specified, the contract is deemed cancelled and the buyer is entitled to a return of the earnest money. In such event, the buyer is obligated to deliver a notice that the sale and closing of buyer's property is not completed no later than the date specified. In the event of the buyer's breach arising from the buyer's failure to deliver the required notice, the seller agrees to accept the earnest money as the seller's sole right to damages.

ADDITIONAL CLAUSE ADDENDUM (10/05)

This Addendum contains clauses that may be applicable in a resale transaction.

Back-up Contract — Contingent upon Cancellation of Prior Contract

This clause is for use when writing a back-up contract contingent upon cancellation of a prior contract. The buyer acknowledges that the seller is obligated by a prior contract to sell the premises to another buyer. The seller retains the right to amend, extend, or modify the prior contract. Upon cancellation of the prior contract, the seller is obligated to promptly deliver notice to the buyer. Upon buyer's receipt of notice of cancellation of the prior contract, buyer's broker is instructed to open escrow and deposit the earnest money. The date of the seller's notice to the buyer is deemed the date of contract acceptance for purposes of all applicable contract time periods. The buyer can cancel the back-up contract any time prior to receipt of seller's notice of cancellation of prior contract.

Signature of Absent Buyer Spouse or Co-buyer

If one buyer is unavailable at the time the contract is written, this provision obligates the signing buyer to obtain the signature of the absent buyer spouse or co-buyer within a specified number of days after acceptance of the contract or deliver a disclaimer deed to the escrow company that eliminates the need for the absent signature.

Buyer's Costs

In addition to any costs the seller has agreed to pay in the contract, this provision obligates the seller to pay the specified amount toward buyer's costs.

Corporate Relocation Approval

If the seller is in the process of a corporate relocation, this provision makes the offer contingent upon corporate approval. The buyer agrees to cooperate with the seller in providing additional disclosures or executing additional addenda required by the corporation, provided that the buyer incurs no additional costs or liability.

All Cash Sale

In an-all cash sale, the buyer is obligated to provide the seller either a letter of credit or a source of funds letter from a financial institution documenting the availability of funds to close escrow as agreed within the specified number of days of contract acceptance.

Nonrefundable Earnest Money

The buyer's earnest money will be nonrefundable when this provision is utilized, unless the buyer elects to cancel pursuant to the Buyer Disapproval section of the contract (Section 6j), the contract is cancelled pursuant to the Risk of Loss section (Section 8b) or escrow fails to close due to seller's breach of contract. The buyer acknowledges that buyer's earnest money shall be nonrefundable even if the premises fails to appraise for the sale price or the loan contingency is unfulfilled.

Waiver of Appraisal

The buyer agrees to waive the appraisal contingency. In the event that the premises fails to appraise for at least the sales price, the buyer agrees that buyer's down payment will be increased in an amount equal to the difference between the appraised value and the purchase price.

Survey

If the parties agree to a survey, it will be performed by a licensed surveyor within a specified number of days after contract acceptance. The cost of the survey may be paid by either seller or buyer. The survey will be performed in accordance with the Arizona State Board of Technical Registration's Arizona Land Boundary Survey Minimum Standards. The survey instructions are also specified. The buyer has five days after receipt of results of survey or map to provide written notice of disapproval to the seller.

Tax-deferred Exchange

This provision is to be used when either seller or buyer intend to enter into a tax-deferred exchange pursuant to I.R.C. §1031, or otherwise. All additional costs in connection with any such tax-deferred exchange will be borne by the party requesting the exchange. The non-requesting party agrees to cooperate in a tax-deferred exchange provided that the non-requesting party incurs no additional costs and close of escrow is not delayed. The parties are advised to consult a professional tax advisor regarding the advisability of any such exchange. The non-requesting party and broker(s) are indemnified and held harmless from any liability that may arise from participation in the tax-deferred exchange.

Water

This provision is designed to be used in areas where water rights may be an issue. Arizona is undertaking General Stream Adjudications of both the Gila River and Little Colorado River systems, which are court proceedings to determine water rights. If the premises/property is affected by an adjudication, the parties are obligated to execute and file an Assignment of Statement of Claimant form. The Arizona Department of Water Resources and the ADRE *Buyer Advisory* provided by AAR provide sources of information on the court proceedings and other water availability or water quality issues. If water rights, availability or quality are a material matter, the buyer is instructed to investigate during the inspection period.

Other provisions may be added to this form as the need arises. Therefore, this form is not printed, but is available on Zipforms for AAR members and on the AAR Web site.

"AS IS" ADDENDUM (10/05)

A discussion of the AAR "AS IS" Addendum and "as is" transactions may be found in chapter 6.

OTHER AAR FORMS AND ADDENDA

Below is a list of other AAR forms and addenda that are not addressed in other chapters.

Addendum: This addendum is to be used when there is not sufficient room on a purchase contract to include all the terms being offered or to amend or add additional terms to an existing contract. This form is essentially blank lines. (Rev. 6/93)

Additional Compensation Consent: This is a consent form to be used to disclose that a broker has received compensation for providing services related to the transaction (other than brokerage services) as required by the Commissioner's Rules. (5/05)

Assumption/Carryback Addendum: This addendum provides additional terms for transactions in which the financing will include a seller carryback or an assumption of an existing first loan. (5/00)

Compensation Agreement for Unrepresented Seller: Compensation agreement between a buyer's broker and an unrepresented seller (for sale by owner). (Rev. 11/96)

Construction Contract for New Home (without Lot): This contract does not convey real property, but is a service contract between the owner and the builder for the construction of a new home. (Rev. 2/03)

Counter Offer: This form is designed to be used to make counteroffers to initial purchase offers. (Rev. 5/96)

Lead-based Paint Disclosure (Sales): This disclosure is to be used to meet requirements for lead-based paint disclosure for residential sales. (Rev. 2/02)

Lead-based Paint Disclosure (Rental): This form is to be used to meet requirements for lead-based paint disclosure for residential rental properties. (Rev. 4/97)

Multiple Counteroffer: This form is to be used when making counteroffers to multiple parties. (Rev. 11/03)

Purchase Contract for New Home (With Lot): This contract form is for the sale of newly constructed homes and the land. (Rev. 4/05)

Request for Loan Information: This request form is to be used by the seller to request loan information from their lender to determine equity, assumability and other pertinent information. (Rev. 4/91)

Spanish Translations

Additionally, AAR provides Spanish-translation companion pieces to the AAR Resale Contract and eight other AAR forms used in residential sales or leasing transactions. These translations are not actual forms, but are literal translations intended to assist Spanish-speaking buyers and sellers. However, Spanish-speaking buyers and sellers should nonetheless be advised to select their own translator to assist them in the transaction.

UNIFORM SPECIAL DURABLE POWER OF ATTORNEY FORM

A power of attorney is a written document by which one individual designates another person to act as the individual's agent. The requirements for the creation of a durable power of attorney (one that remains valid even if the individual is subsequently disabled or incapacitated) are set forth in Arizona statute at A.R.S. §14-5501. Further, either husband or wife may authorize the other by power of attorney to sign all documents relating to the transfer of real property pursuant to A.R.S. §33-454.

In the past, each of the many escrow/title companies required execution of a different Power of Attorney form, often resulting in delays in closings. As a result, the Land Title Association of Arizona (LTAA) and AAR designed a Uniform Special Durable Power of Attorney form that will be accepted by most title/escrow companies. The form, when properly executed, permits the agent appointed pursuant to the power of attorney "to sell, convcy, purchase, acquire, mortgage or otherwise encumber, transfer in trust, borrow money and execute and deliver notes therefore, loan money and receive notes and security therefore, and take or perform any other act necessary or appropriate regarding the real property" described in the power of attorney.

The form is available on the AAR Web site. Check with the title/escrow company you are working with to see if they will accept the Uniform Special Durable Power of Attorney form.

BUYER ADVISORY

Does a buyer in a real estate transaction know how to investigate the property being considered for purchase? Does a buyer know the questions to ask or where to go for reliable information? In an effort to address these issues, the ADRE Disclosure Law Instructor Development Workshop Committee developed the *Buyer Advisory* in 2002 as a tool to educate buyers. AAR updates the *Buyer Advisory* and maintains it on the AAR Web site. The *Buyer Advisory* is designed to be utilized online. It provides buyers with a wealth of information about issues that may be important in a real estate transaction, explains why certain issues may be important, and directs buyers, via hyperlink in the electronic version, to sources of additional information.

For organizational purposes, the *Buyer Advisory* is divided into three general sections: (1) common documents a buyer should review; (2) physical conditions in the property the buyer should investigate; and (3) conditions affecting the surrounding area that the buyer should investigate.

Some of the documents addressed in the *Buyer Advisory* include:

- *MLS Printout:* Buyers are advised that the MLS information may be incomplete or an approximation.

- *Disclosures:* The *Buyer Advisory* explains that the Public Report discloses a variety of material information about the property and provides a link to additional information from the ADRE. Buyers are cautioned to verify statements of concern and provided a link to a sample AAR SPDS form. The Affidavit of Disclosure and Lead-based Paint Form are also referenced.
- *CC&Rs:* The *Buyer Advisory* explains how a buyer agrees to be bound by the CC&Rs and provides a link to additional information.
- *HOA Governing Documents:* HOA articles of incorporation, bylaws, rules and regulations, and architectural control standards are discussed and links to information on HOAs in general are provided. Information on statutory HOA disclosures is also provided.
- *Title Report or Title Commitment:* The *Buyer Advisory* explains that the title report or commitment discloses documents that are exceptions to the title insurance (Schedule B Exceptions), which may affect the use of the property.
- *Loan Documents:* Buyers are provided sources of information on loans and the lending process.
- *County Assessor's Records:* The *Buyer Advisory* discusses the kinds of information included on the county assessor's records and provides a link to these records.
- *Inspection Reports:* The *Buyer Advisory* discusses home inspections and termite inspections.

Some of the physical property conditions addressed in the *Buyer Advisory* are:

- *Repairs and New Construction:* Buyers are advised to request documentation regarding work performed on the property and directed to the Registrar of Contractors for additional information. If the roof is 10 years old or older, a roof inspection by a licensed roofer is recommended.
- *Swimming Pools and Spas:* The *Buyer Advisory* explains that a pool or spa company inspection may be warranted and provided with

a link to a partial list of pool and spa contractors. A source for barrier information is provided along with a link to the required safety notice.

- *Square Footage:* Buyers are advised that the square footage noted in the MLS printout or the county assessor's records should not be relied upon, and a link is provided for a list of appraisers and architects who can measure the square footage of a property.

- *Sewer and On-site Wastewater Treatment Facilities:* The *Buyer Advisory* explains that even if the listing or SPDS indicates that the home is connected to the city sewer, a professional should verify it. The *Buyer Advisory* discusses pre-transfer inspection requirements for on-site wastewater treatment facilities and provides a link to additional information from the ADEQ.

- *Water and Well Issues:* The buyer is advised to investigate water availability and quality issues.

- *Soil Problems:* The *Buyer Advisory* discusses expansive soil, fissures, subsidence and other soil conditions.

- *Pests:* Buyers are advised to seek the advice of a pest control company about any concerns about pests.

- *Endangered and Threatened Species:* The buyer is advised to investigate issues relating to endangered and threatened species that may affect the use of the property.

- *Mold:* Mold concerns are addressed; buyers are directed to a pamphlet prepared by the Arizona Department of Health Services and Web site information provided by the EPA and the CDC for further information.

- *Flood Plain Status:* The *Buyer Advisory* explains that if the property is in a flood zone, an additional annual insurance premium may be required. The *Buyer Advisory* lists several sources of information to help determine if the property is in a flood hazard area or flood plain.

Some of the conditions that may affect the area surrounding the property addressed in the *Buyer Advisory* include:

- *Environmental Hazards:* Buyers are directed to several sources of information on environmental hazards, including a link to the Arizona Department of Environmental Quality Superfund maps.
- *Freeway Construction:* A link to the Arizona Department of Transportation maps to find the nearest future freeway routes and roads in the area slated for widening is included in the *Buyer Advisory*.
- *Crime Statistics:* Links to check the crime statistics for the cities of Phoenix, Tempe, Glendale, Mesa, Scottsdale, Chandler, Gilbert and Peoria are provided, along with a list of all Arizona city links where crime statistics for other cities may be obtained.
- *Sex Offenders:* The Arizona registry and community notification program is explained and a link to the sex offender Web site is provided.
- *Military and Public Airports:* The *Buyer Advisory* explains that the legislature has mandated the identification of areas in the immediate vicinity of military and public airports that are susceptible to a certain level of noise from aircraft. Links to the maps indicating these areas is provided.
- *Forested Areas:* Information on protecting property from wildfire is included.
- *Zoning/Planning/Neighborhood Services and Schools:* Sources of information on all of these issues is contained in the *Buyer Advisory*.

The *Buyer Advisory* also summarizes other methods to obtain information about a property. Because some brokers may wish to have the buyer acknowledge receipt of the *Buyer Advisory*, a Buyer's Acknowledgment section and prompt for initials are included.

The *Buyer Advisory* should result in more informed buyers by providing valuable information and resources and is updated as issues arise. A well-informed buyer will be less likely to encounter unpleasant surprises about the property after COE, which benefits not only the buyer, but the seller and real estate brokers involved in the transaction as well.

KEY POINTS TO REMEMBER

- A broker should read and understand the implications of any form or addenda prior to its use.

- The use of the AAR SPDS benefits buyers, sellers and brokers.

- A buyer should not waive an SPDS without seeing the SPDS form.

- The Disclosure of Buyer Agency and Seller Waiver and Confirmation form addresses agency and regulatory issues in limited or minimum service listing transactions.

- The *Buyer Advisory* assists the buyer in conducting due diligence and reduces broker liability.

CHAPTER 9

New Home Subdivisions

Purchasing a newly constructed home or a home to be constructed in a new home subdivision involves different considerations than buying a resale home in an established neighborhood. Generally, each new home seller has its own purchase contract, so there is no "standard" contract as there is in the resale market. AAR produces a Purchase Contract for New Home (With Lot) form; however, this form is used relatively infrequently. As a result, a new home purchase contract is generally much different than the AAR Resale Contract.

THE PUBLIC REPORT

Arizona law regulates the sale or lease of subdivided land, which is defined as land divided or proposed to be divided for sale or lease into six or more lots or parcels. A.R.S. §32-2181 *et seq.* A "subdivider" is anyone who offers for sale or lease six or more lots, parcels or fractional interests in a subdivision or subdivides land into a subdivision, or who undertakes to develop a subdivision. A.R.S. §32-2101(54). A subdivider may not sell or lease or offer for sale or lease any lots, parcels or fractional interests in a subdivision without first obtaining a public report from the ADRE. A.R.S. §32-2183(F). A subdivider must give a prospective new home buyer a copy of the public report and an opportunity to read and review it before the prospective buyer signs a contract to purchase a home in the subdivision. A.R.S. §32-2183(A).

Further, any agreement or contract for the sale or lease of a property interest in a development that requires a public report must contain substantially the following language in bold print or print larger than the other print used in the document above the signature portion of the document:

THE DEVELOPER SHALL GIVE A PROSPECTIVE PURCHASER A COPY OF THE PUBLIC REPORT AND AN OPPORTUNITY TO READ AND REVIEW IT BEFORE THE PROSPECTIVE PURCHASER SIGNS THIS DOCUMENT.

R4-28-803(A).

When a public report is required, the seller is obligated to complete a public report receipt and obtain the buyer's signature. R4-28-805. The rule requires the receipt to state in part:

PUBLIC REPORT RECEIPT

The developer shall furnish you, as a prospective customer, with a copy of the public report required by the Arizona Department of Real Estate. It is recommended that you read the report before you make any written offer to purchase or lease an interest in the development and before you pay any money or other consideration toward the purchase or lease of an interest in the development.

FOR YOUR PROTECTION, DO NOT SIGN THIS RECEIPT UNTIL YOU HAVE RECEIVED A COPY OF THE REPORT AND HAVE HAD THE OPPORTUNITY TO READ IT. BY SIGNING THIS RECEIPT, THE BUYER HAS ACCEPTED THE PUBLIC REPORT AND ACKNOWLEDGES THE INFORMATION IT CONTAINS.

The purpose of statutory provisions regulating subdivided lands "is to insure that consumers who purchase lots in residential developments are provided with adequate streets, utilities, drainage, and generally pleasant, healthy and livable surroundings." *Alaface v. National Investment Co.,* 181 Ariz. 586, 596, 892 P.2d 1375, 1385 (App. 1994). "Thus, the subdivision disclosure statutes have been enacted to protect members of the public from being misled into purchasing land that is unusable or unsafe for residential purposes." *Id.* In the *Alaface* case, the buyers purchased a vacant lot in Prescott, built a cabin on the lot and then discovered that water service was not available. The buyers had received no public report, in violation of the subdivision statutes.

The *Alaface* court stated that the public report requirements were enacted to protect buyers of subdivision lots and, in part, to protect them from buying residential lots not containing the utility services necessary to make the property safe and habitable. The court indicated that subdivision statutes are further intended to protect buyers of residential property from building improvements that are rendered unusable due to lack of facilities. Because the subdivision statutes were enacted for the protection and safety of the public, one who violates the subdivision statutes is guilty of negligence *per se. Id.,* citing *Brannigan v. Raybuck,* 136 Ariz. 513, 517, 667 P.2d 213, 217 (1983).

A buyer should carefully review the public report *before* signing a contract to purchase a new home because the report contains important information, such as:

- the identity of the subdivider/developer
- the physical characteristics of the subdivision
- disclosure of conditions or provisions that may limit the use or occupancy of the home
- homeowner's association information
- whether the subdivision is subject to any known flooding or drainage problems
- existing and proposed adjacent land use, including any unusual safety factors and uses that may cause a nuisance or adversely affect homeowners *(the ADRE recommends that the subdivider research within two miles of the subdivision for unusual safety factors and five miles for factors that may cause a nuisance or adversely affect lot owners)*

- gas pipelines within the boundaries of the subdivision or within 500 feet of the subdivision boundary
- environmental factors, including whether the subdivision is within a federal superfund or state WQARF site
- whether any portion of the subdivision is located in territory in the vicinity of a military or public airport
- the availability of utilities
- street and road maintenance
- flood protection or drainage facilities
- documents demonstrating acceptable arrangements have been made for completion of all facilities
- locations and availability of schools, shopping facilities, public transportation, medical facilities, ambulance service, and police service

A copy of any public report issued after 1997 is available to the public on the ADRE Web site.

UNSUBDIVIDED LAND

Unsubdivided land is more accurately described as a large lot subdivision. Arizona statute defines "unsubdivided lands" as "land or lands divided or proposed to be divided for the purpose of sale or lease, whether immediate or future, into six or more lots, parcels or fractional interests and the lots or parcels are 36 acres or more each but less than one hundred sixty acres each . . ." A.R.S. §32-2101(59). A public report is generally required if unsubdivided land (36 acres to 160 acres) is being sold by a subdivider, i.e., a person who owns six or more lots. A.R.S. §32-2195.

OTHER SUBDIVISION STATUTES AND RULES

All contracts for the purchase of subdivided land from a subdivider, owner or agent must clearly and conspicuously disclose:

- the nature of the document
- the buyer's right to receive a copy of the public report

- in the case of unimproved lots or parcels not exempted by regulation pursuant to §32-2185.01, the buyer's right to rescind the agreement as provided in §32-2185.01

Any contract, agreement or lease that fails to make these disclosures is not enforceable against the buyer.

Additionally, Arizona statutes and rules require that:

- The contract conspicuously discloses the nature of the document at or near the top of the document. R4-28-803(B).
- The contract indicates where the earnest money or down payment, if any, will be deposited and includes the name of the title company, the name of the broker's trust account, or other depository. R4-28-803(C).
- A contract where a down payment, earnest money deposit, or other advanced money is paid directly to the seller and not placed in escrow must conspicuously (in large or bold print) disclose this fact within the contract, and the buyer must sign or initial this provision. The disclosure must state: "Prospective purchasers are advised that earnest money deposits, down payments, and other advanced money will not be placed in a neutral escrow. This money will be paid directly to the seller and may be used by the seller. This means the purchaser assumes a risk of losing the money if the seller is unable or unwilling to perform under the terms of the purchase contract." R4-28-803(D).
- Subdivisions must have permanent access to the land over terrain that may be traversed by conventional motor vehicle. Any sale of subdivided land without permanent access is rescindable within three years. A.R.S. §32-2185.02.

LOT RESERVATIONS

A subdivider may take lot reservations before the ADRE issues a public report. A deposit may be accepted from a prospective buyer as a lot reservation if certain requirements are met. A.R.S. §32-2181.03. The reservation deposit for a single lot or parcel may not exceed $5,000 and must be maintained in an escrow account until cancellation or termination of the lot reservation or execution of a purchase contract. Within 15 calendar days after the public report is issued, the seller must provide the prospective buyer with a copy of the public report and a copy of the proposed purchase contract. The prospective buyer and prospective seller have seven business days after the prospective buyer's receipt of the public report and the proposed purchase contract within which to enter into a contract, or the lot reservation automatically terminates. A prospective buyer may cancel a lot reservation at any time before the execution of a purchase contract by delivering written notice of termination to the prospective seller.

BUYER CONSIDERATIONS WHEN ENTERING INTO A CONTRACT FOR A NEW HOME TO BE CONSTRUCTED

When a buyer decides to buy a new home that has yet to be constructed, there are many important decisions to make, such as design, flooring, countertops and colors. With all these decisions and all the excitement of buying a new home, the legal issues are often forgotten or ignored. However, there are a few issues that demand a buyer's attention. For example, before signing a new home contract, buyers should do the following:

Read the Subdivision Public Report

As discussed above, the purpose of the public report is to disclose important information about the subdivision. Therefore, a new home buyer should always read the public report before signing a purchase contract.

Read the CC&Rs and Other Homeowner's Association Rules

Most new homes are in a homeowner's association. Covenants, Conditions and Restrictions (CC&Rs) generally empower a homeowner's association to control certain aspects of the home's use. The CC&Rs may be very strict, especially those addressing landscaping, RV parking, and play equipment. It is essential that the buyer review and agree to these restrictions prior to entering into a contract; afterwards is generally too late. In addition to CC&Rs, a homeowner's association may be governed by articles of incorporation, bylaws, rules and regulations, and often architectural control standards, which should also be reviewed.

Read the Purchase Contract

Buyers must understand the importance of reading the purchase contract carefully and should be advised to keep the following questions in mind:

- *Who will hold the earnest money and other advance deposits?* If at all possible, all earnest money and other advance deposits should be held by the escrow company. If the deposits are held by the seller, the buyer may have a difficult time recovering those funds in the event the seller fails to perform.

- *Does the contract contain a financing contingency for the benefit of the buyer?* Unless the buyer plans to pay cash, the contract should contain a financing contingency stating that the contract is contingent upon the buyer qualifying for a loan. If the buyer is unable to qualify for a loan to buy the home, the buyer should be entitled to a return of the earnest money. Some new home contracts provide only that the seller has the right to cancel the contract if the buyer fails to qualify for a loan, which does not protect the buyer.

- *When will the home be completed?* The seller should be asked to give a realistic estimate as to when construction will be completed. A realistic completion date is important so that the quality of the construction will not be compromised by a contractor who is rushing to complete the home. A realistic completion date will help the buyer plan the move and avoid unanticipated housing costs. If the completion date is critical, the buyer may be able to negotiate a contract provision in which the seller agrees to pay a certain dollar amount to the buyer per day for late completion.

- *What are the buyer's remedies if there is a problem?* The remedies for problems may be specifically set forth in the contract. The contract should direct the buyer to the Arizona Registrar of Contractors (ROC), a governmental agency that regulates home builders. This agency can assist buyers with some construction defects. The contract may require that any disputes be resolved by binding arbitration, which may eliminate the right to a trial by judge or jury and the right to appeal.

NEW HOME DEFECTS AND DISPUTES

A new home seller/builder is held to impliedly warrant that the construction has been done in a workmanlike manner and that the home is habitable. *Columbia Western Corp., v. Vela,* 122 Ariz. 28, 592 P.2d 1294 (App. 1979). The implied warranty arises from the contractual relationship between the builder and the purchaser. However, the implied warranty extends to subsequent purchasers of the home. *Richards v. Powercraft Homes,* 139 Ariz. 242, 678 P.2d 427 (1984). As to subsequent purchasers, the warranty is generally limited to latent defects that manifest after the subsequent owner's purchase, which were not discoverable had a reasonable inspection of the structure been made prior to purchase. *Id.*

Unless a new home contract contains a commercially reasonable alternative dispute resolution procedure, a buyer is required give the seller a notice and opportunity to cure a defect before bringing an action related to the design, construction, condition or sale of the home. A.R.S. §12-1361 *et. seq.* Most new home contracts include an alternative dispute resolution clause. "If the contract contains an alternative dispute resolution procedure, the procedure shall conspicuously appear in the contract in bold and capital letters and a disclosure statement in at least twelve point font, bold and capital letters shall appear on the face of the contract and shall describe the location of the alternative dispute resolution procedure within the contract." A.R.S. §12-1366(A)(1).

The ROC may also be helpful in resolving any construction disputes. The purpose of the ROC is to assist consumers with any problems they

may have with a licensed contractor. A home buyer may file a complaint
at the ROC for:

- poor workmanship
- abandonment of the project
- failure to perform as agreed
- failure to pay subcontractors
- violation of building codes
- false or misleading advertising

KEY POINTS TO REMEMBER

- A new home buyer should always read the public report before
signing the purchase contract — afterwards is too late.

- A new home buyer should always read the CC&Rs before signing
the purchase contract — afterwards is too late.

- Lot reservations may be taken before the public report is issued,
but the buyer may cancel at any time.

- The buyer should be aware that if the earnest money is held by the
new home seller/developer, rather than in an escrow company, the
earnest money is at risk.

- Many disputes with new home seller/builders are subject to
statutory notice and opportunity to cure provisions.

CHAPTER 10

Vacant Land Transactions

Vacant land involves unique concerns both geologically and geographically and a variety of types of property. Vacant land transactions include "raw land" parcels that may be purchased for investment or agriculture, parcels for residential, commercial or industrial development with all, some or none of the infrastructure improvements incidental to the intended uses, or may simply involve a vacant lot in a residential subdivision. Accordingly, the level of sophistication of the parties and issues that should be addressed in the purchase contract for a vacant land transaction varies greatly. Some practitioners may find buyers and sellers prefer to engage legal counsel to draft the contract.

AAR VACANT LAND/LOT CONTRACT

Drafting a standard vacant land contract is a daunting task. AAR produces a Vacant Land/Lot Purchase Contract, which is under revision at the time of this writing. In addition to basic provisions similar to those found in the AAR Resale Contract, the revised AAR Vacant Land/Lot Contract will likely address the following issues:

- *Incidental Improvements:* Since the buyer is purchasing the property as vacant land, any fixtures and improvements on the property will be merely incidental and transferred in "as is" condition.

- *Land divisions:* Informing the buyer that lands proposed to be divided for purposes of sale or lease will be subject to state, county and municipal laws, ordinances and regulations. If state, county and municipal requirements relating to the division or splitting of the property are a material matter to the buyer, they should be verified by the buyer during the inspection period.

- *Site/Soil Evaluation:* A site/soil evaluation, which may include percolation or other tests, may be necessary to determine the suitability of the property for installation of a conventional septic tank or alternative on-site wastewater treatment facility. The parties should be aware that any site/soil evaluation is not binding on the state-delegated county agency in any future permitting decision as to the suitability of the design or type of system for the property.

- *Road Maintenance Agreements:* If there is such an agreement, the seller should provide the buyer with a copy. Additionally, if the road maintenance agreement is not recorded with the county recorder's office, the buyer should consult with the lender regarding any financing requirements in this regard.

- *Surveys:* A survey is often advisable in a vacant land transaction. If a survey is to be performed, it should be performed by or under the direction of a registered land surveyor and, at a minimum, be performed in accordance with the Arizona Board of Technical Registration's Arizona Land Boundary Survey Minimum Standards.

- *Water/Water Rights:* If water rights are a material matter to the buyer, these rights should be verified by the buyer during the inspection period. At close of escrow, if applicable, seller should assign to the buyer all of the water rights associated with the property.

- *Agricultural Foreign Investment Disclosure Act:* If applicable, the buyer and seller should comply with the Agricultural Foreign

Investment Disclosure Act and make the required disclosures to the U.S. Department of Agriculture.

- *Environmental Due Diligence:* The seller should disclose whether there has been any generation, storage, treatment, release or disposal of any hazardous waste or regulated substances on the property. The buyer should undertake the appropriate investigation into the previous ownership and uses of the property.

AAR ADDENDUM TO VACANT LAND PURCHASE CONTRACT REGARDING SUBDIVIDED OR UNSUBDIVIDED LAND (7/97)

The AAR Addendum to Vacant Land Purchase Contract Regarding Subdivided or Unsubdivided Land (Subdivision Addendum) was designed to comply with the contract disclosure requirements in the subdivision laws. The Subdivision Addendum should be used any time the seller has created or owns six or more fractional interest in a land, unless a statutory exemption from the subdivision laws applies to the transaction.

The Subdivision Addendum provides space to insert all pertinent information regarding the ADRE public report file number, buyer, seller and property involved. The addendum also provides the statutory definitions for subdivided land, unsubdivided land, and an unimproved lot or parcel.

The addendum contains the public report disclosure language mandated by the Commissioner's Rules, and the seven-day and six-month rescission language taken directly from the Commissioner's Rules, which require that this rescission language be included in any contract for the purchase or lease of an unimproved subdivided or unsubdivided lot or parcel.

Additionally, the Subdivision Addendum:

- contains the disclosure that the subdivision laws require unsubdivided land to have permanent access, unless waived by the ADRE
- contains the subdivision statutory requirements dealing with the manner in which the seller is obligated to transfer clear title to the buyer

- provides for disclosure regarding the adequacy of the water supply and puts the buyer on notice that additional disclosures from the seller may be required if the water supply is inadequate

KEY POINTS TO REMEMBER

- Land that is proposed to be divided will be subject to state, county and municipal laws, ordinances and regulations.

- The parties should be aware a site/soil evaluation is not binding on the state-delegated county agency in any future permitting decision as to the suitability of the design or type of on-site wastewater disposal system proposed for the property.

- Water rights and adequacy should be investigated during any inspection or due diligence period.

- Surveys should be performed in accordance with the Arizona Board of Technical Registration's Arizona Land Boundary Survey Minimum Standards.

- The AAR Addendum to Purchase Contract Regarding Subdivided or Unsubdivided Land (Subdivision Addendum) should be used with the AAR Vacant Land/Vacant Lot Purchase Contract to comply with the contract disclosure requirements in the subdivision laws.

Commercial Transactions

Commercial real estate covers a broad spectrum of property types, including industrial, office, multi-family, retail and hospitality real estate. Each property type has unique considerations of which the broker must be aware. Further, a commercial transaction is much more likely to involve one or more attorneys, who may draft the purchase contract and related transactional documents.

AAR COMMERCIAL REAL ESTATE PURCHASE CONTRACT

The AAR Commercial Real Estate Purchase Contract is designed for commercial transactions and reflects the realities of the commercial market. For example, all time periods run from the opening of escrow as opposed to contract acceptance. Additionally, in the AAR Commercial Contract, the buyer's financing contingency generally ends with the buyer's due diligence period. The following highlights some of the other significant terms in the AAR Commercial Contract.

Property, Price and Escrow

Earnest money, the property and the purchase price are all addressed on the first page of the form. The AAR Commercial Contract is used as escrow instructions, and the escrow company is instructed to immediately notify the buyer, seller and broker(s) in writing of the date of the opening of escrow. "Opening of escrow" is defined as the date when a fully executed contract and the earnest money have been delivered to the escrow company. The close of escrow is defined as recordation of the deed and any other documents required to complete the transaction.

Due Diligence and Inspections

The buyer's due diligence and inspection period is 30 days after opening of escrow, unless otherwise specified. During the due diligence period, buyer is obligated to satisfy itself with respect to the physical condition of the property, the condition of title to the property and as to the feasibility and suitability of the property for buyer's intended purpose. If prior to the expiration of the due diligence period, the buyer disapproves of the property, the buyer may either immediately cancel the contract or provide the seller an opportunity to correct the items disapproved. If the seller is unwilling or unable to agree to correct any of the items disapproved by buyer, including making any repairs in a workmanlike manner, the buyer may either cancel the contract or proceed with the transaction, in which case seller is not obligated to correct those items seller has not agreed to correct in writing.

The seller is obligated to make the property available to the buyer for all inspections during the due diligence period and a final walkthrough. The seller is responsible for providing all utilities for the buyer's inspections at the seller's expense.

Disclosures

The seller may provide the buyer with an AAR Commercial Seller Property Disclosure Statement (SPDS) or the buyer may waive review and approval of the SPDS. If the seller agrees to provide an SPDS, the completed form must be delivered to the buyer within five days after opening of escrow. The seller is also obligated to provide the buyer the following disclosures and information pertinent to the property in writing within five days or other specified days after opening of escrow:

- any information that may adversely affect the buyer's use of the property
- any known pending special assessments, association fees, claims or litigation
- copies of covenants, conditions and restrictions, articles of incorporation; by-laws; other governing documents; and any other documents required by law
- financial statements, copies of current rent rolls, lists of current deposits, personal property lists, copies of leases, rental agreements, service contracts
- a copy of the most recent survey, if available
- any and all other agreements, documents, studies, or reports relating to the property in seller's possession or control (unless the written contract that seller entered into with the consultant who prepared the report or study specifically forbids the dissemination of the report to others)

The buyer may provide written notice to seller prior to the expiration of the due diligence period of any items disapproved.

The seller is also obligated to immediately notify buyer in writing:

- of any changes in the previous disclosures made
- if the seller modifies any existing lease or other agreement affecting the property
- if the seller enters into any new leases, rental agreements, service contracts or other agreements affecting the property
- of any notice of violations of city, county, state or federal building, zoning, fire, or health laws, codes, statutes, ordinances, regulations, or rules filed or issued regarding the property that seller receives during the escrow period

Again, the buyer is allowed five days after receipt of notice of the foregoing to provide written notice to seller of any items disapproved.

Financing

If the sale is contingent upon buyer obtaining a satisfactory financing commitment, the buyer has 30 days or an otherwise specified number of days after the opening of escrow to obtain a financing commitment satisfactory to buyer in buyer's sole discretion, for a loan to purchase the property, or the buyer may cancel the contract and receive a refund of the earnest money. If the buyer does not deliver notice that the buyer has not received a satisfactory financing commitment, the buyer is deemed to have waived the financing commitment contingency and any right to cancel due to financing. The buyer is obligated to submit a formal loan application to a lender of buyer's choice within 10 days and both parties must promptly provide the lender with all materials and documents lender deems appropriate to facilitate processing of the loan.

Title and Escrow

The escrow company is instructed to obtain and distribute to the buyer and the brokers a commitment for title insurance in sufficient detail for the issuance of an Extended Owner's Title Insurance Policy together with complete and legible copies of all documents that will remain as exceptions to the buyer's policy of title insurance title commitment, within 15 days after opening of escrow. The buyer has until the expiration of the due diligence period to provide written notice to the seller of any items disapproved. The seller agrees to pay for and provide the buyer with a Standard Owner's Title Insurance Policy. The buyer may acquire extended coverage at the buyer's own expense.

In addition, the escrow company is instructed as follows:
- if the escrow company is also acting as the title agency but is not the title insurer issuing the title insurance policy, to deliver to the buyer and seller upon opening of escrow a closing protection letter from the title insurer indemnifying the buyer and seller for any losses due to fraudulent acts or breach of escrow instructions by the escrow company

- to allocate all closing and escrow costs equally, unless otherwise stated
- to provide the brokers copies of all notices and communications directed to or from seller or buyer and access to escrowed materials and information regarding the escrow
- to prorate real property taxes payable by the seller through close of escrow, based upon the latest tax bill available. The parties agree that any discrepancy between the latest tax bill available and the actual tax bill when received shall be handled as a post closing matter
- if the buyer takes an assignment of the existing casualty and/or liability insurance that is maintained by seller, to prorate the current premium through close of escrow
- to prorate rents; interest on existing notes, if transferred; utilities; and operating expenses through close of escrow. The parties agree to adjust any rents received after close of escrow as a post closing matter
- all deposits held by seller pursuant to rent/lease agreement(s) are to be either credited against the cash required of buyer at close of escrow or paid to buyer by seller at close of escrow as indicated
- the amount of any assessment that is a lien as of the close of escrow, is to be paid or prorated and assumed by buyer as indicated

The parties agree to promptly adjust any item to be prorated that is not determined or determinable at close of escrow as a post closing matter by appropriate cash payment to the other party outside of the escrow when the amount due is determined.

The parties are advised to consult a professional tax advisor regarding the advisability of a tax-deferred exchange pursuant to Internal Revenue Code §1031, or otherwise. The seller and buyer agree to cooperate in a tax-deferred exchange provided that close of escrow is not delayed. All additional costs in connection with any such tax-deferred exchange are to be borne by the party requesting the exchange. The non-requesting party and brokers are to be indemnified and held harmless from any liability that may arise from participation in the tax-deferred exchange.

Warranties

The seller warrants and agrees to maintain and/or repair the property so that, at the earlier of possession or close of escrow, all heating, cooling, mechanical, plumbing and electrical systems (including swimming pool and/or spa, motors, filter systems, cleaning systems and heaters, if any) and built-in appliances will be in working condition or as otherwise agreed in this contract. The seller also warrants that, at the earlier of possession of the property or close of escrow, the property shall be in substantially the same condition as on the date of the mutual execution of the contract.

The seller also warrants that payment in full will have been made for all rental and/or privilege taxes, labor, professional services, materials, machinery, fixtures, or tools furnished within the 150 days immediately preceding the close of escrow in connection with the construction, alteration or repair of any structure on or improvement made to the property. Finally, the seller warrants that seller has disclosed to the buyer and brokers all material latent defects and any information concerning the property known to seller, which materially and adversely affect the consideration to be paid by buyer.

The buyer warrants that the buyer has disclosed to seller any information that may materially and adversely affect the buyer's ability to close escrow. At the earlier of the removal of all contingencies, possession of the property or close of escrow, the buyer warrants that the buyer has conducted all desired independent investigations and accepts the property.

Remedies

The parties have a choice of remedies for breach of contract if the buyer is in breach. The parties may agree that in the event of a buyer's breach, the seller may cancel the contract and/or proceed upon any claim or remedy that the seller may have in law or equity, or in the alternative, the parties may agree that the seller will be entitled to the earnest money as seller's sole remedy. If the seller is in breach, the buyer may cancel the contract, collect the earnest money and/or proceed upon any claim or remedy that the buyer may have in law or equity.

The parties agree to mediate any dispute or claim arising out of or relating to the contract or services provided in relation to the contract, unless the matter is specifically excluded, such as a small-claims court case. All mediation costs are to be paid equally by the parties.

Additional Terms

Additional terms such as provisions addressing risk of loss, Arizona law, time is of the essence and counterparts are included. All references to days are construed as calendar days. The parties warrant to the other that they have had no dealings with any other broker in connection with the negotiation of the contract other than the named broker(s). The parties also acknowledge that brokers will be compensated for their services as agreed by separate written agreement.

ARIZONA COMMERCIAL INFORMATION EXCHANGE

The Arizona Commercial Information Exchange (AZCiE) is a state-wide Internet-based property listing service operated by AAR for commercial brokers. AZCiE is similar to a multiple listing service. It is a database of commercial properties (office, retail, industrial, land, etc.) for sale and lease. However, unlike a multiple listing service, the listings include no offer of compensation. Compensation agreements are negotiated between the brokers outside of AZCiE.

COMMERCIAL LEASE OR RENTAL LIEN LAW

An employing broker acquires lien rights when the broker has produced a tenant pursuant to a written agreement with the property owner for the lease of commercial property. A.R.S. §33-1071 *et.seq.* Thus, commercial real estate brokers have the right to file a lien for unpaid leasing commissions.

An employing broker acquires lien rights in a property owner's real property for the amount of compensation the owner agreed to pay for the broker's services in the lease or rental of the real property when:

- There is a written agreement between the broker and the property owner providing for the payment of a commission or other compensation, which discloses (above the portion of the agreement calling for the owner's signature) that the owner's failure to pay may give rise to lien rights.
- The broker produces a ready, willing and able tenant for the owner's property on the terms of the written agreement or terms otherwise acceptable to the owner, as evidenced by a written instrument signed by the owner.
- The broker complies with all of the notice and other requirements of the statute (discussed below).
- All the conditions for payment of the commission in the written agreement are satisfied.

The Preliminary Notice of Intent to Lien requirements pursuant to A.R.S. §33-1072(c) are:

- No later than 15 days before the tenant takes possession of the leased premises, the broker must record a "Broker's Preliminary Notice of Intent to Lien" at the county recorder's office.
- The broker must also deliver a copy of the preliminary notice, personally or by mail, to the owner and any escrow agent involved in the transaction.
- The preliminary notice must state that the broker is entitled to compensation under the terms of the written agreement with the owner and that the broker intends to claim a lien on the property.
- The preliminary notice must also contain all the information required to be included in the actual lien notice.

The broker's lien rights are extinguished if the broker fails to record the preliminary notice.

The lien attaches to the property when the broker produces a ready, willing and able tenant on the terms agreed upon with the owner and records a "Notice of Commercial Real Estate Broker Lien" at the county recorder's office. A.R.S. §33-1072 (A-B). The lien notice must be recorded within 90 days after the tenant takes possession of the property. The lien is perfected upon recording.

The lien notice should be titled "Notice of Commercial Real Estate Broker Lien" and must contain:

- the name and address of the broker's principal place of business
- the broker's real estate license number
- the name and mailing address of the property owner
- the real property interest of the property owner
- the amount of the lien
- the legal description of the property
- the street address of the property
- the broker's statement that compensation is due to the broker
- a notarized statement by the broker that the contents of the lien notice are true and accurate
- the use of the words "unknown" or "not available" or similar terms in the lien notice, in lieu of the above information, will invalidate the lien

A.R.S. §33-1073.

The following liens have express priority over the commercial broker's real estate lien:

- mechanic and materialmen's liens
- consensual liens, mortgages and deeds of trust recorded prior to the broker's preliminary notice

The lien may be foreclosed by a superior court action as if the lien were a mortgage. A.R.S. §33-1074. The foreclosure action must be brought within two years after recordation of the lien. A notice of *lis pendens*, pursuant to A.R.S. §12-1191, must be recorded within five days after filing the foreclosure action. The prevailing party in the foreclosure action shall be awarded costs and reasonable attorney fees.

The broker must record a satisfaction of lien within 30 days after being paid. A.R.S. §33-1075(A). The form of lien satisfaction required is detailed in A.R.S. §11-480. If the broker fails to record a satisfaction of lien within

30 days, the broker is liable for $1,000 and any actual damages pursuant to A.R.S. §33-712.

Lien waivers are required under certain circumstances. A.R.S. §33-1075(B-D). The broker must provide the owner with a "Waiver and Release of Claim of Lien" that extinguishes the broker's lien rights, in the form set forth in the statute:

- Within 30 days after satisfaction of a broker's claim of lien, if the broker is paid before recording a lien notice.
- Within 10 days after receipt of a written request of the owner and if the broker fails to record a lien notice within the 90 days after the tenant took possession of the premises.

If the broker fails to provide the waiver, the broker is liable for $1,000 and any actual damages pursuant to A.R.S. §33-712.

An owner or any other person with a legal or equitable interest in the property, a mortgagee, or other lien creditor, may record a surety bond in the form described in the statute, in the amount of one and one-half times the amount due to the broker, for the payment of the judgment that would be rendered against the property for enforcement of the lien. A.R.S. §33-1076. A power of attorney disclosing the authority of the person executing the bond on behalf of the surety must also be recorded. Upon recordation of the bond, the property is discharged of the lien.

Certain real property is not subject to the commercial real estate broker lien:

- property conveyed to a bona fide purchaser for value before the broker records the preliminary notice
- property encumbered by a bona fide lender for value before the broker records the preliminary notice
- residential property with fewer than five residential units
- property on which single-family mobile home lots, manufactured housing lots, residences or condominiums are sold by unit
  A.R.S. §33-1071(D)(E).

KEY POINTS TO REMEMBER

- All time periods in the AAR Commercial Contract run from the opening of escrow.

- The buyer's financing contingency, if any, ends with the due diligence period in the AAR Commercial Contract.

- The AAR Commercial Contract allows the parties to choose the remedy in the event of a buyer's breach.

- Arizona Commercial Information Exchange (AZCiE) is a database of commercial properties for sale or lease operated by AAR.

- An employing broker can acquire lien rights for the leasing commission after producing a tenant by following the statutory requirements.

CHAPTER 12

Sale of Manufactured and Mobile Homes

There are an increasing number of manufactured and mobile homes in Arizona. Some manufactured and mobile home sales involve the transfer of real property and others do not. Generally speaking, a real estate broker may sell an unaffixed manufactured/mobile home without a "manufactured/mobile home license" if the home is used, installed on the real property, and transferred with an interest in real property.

A DEPARTMENT OF BUILDING AND FIRE SAFETY LICENSE IS GENERALLY REQUIRED TO SELL MANUFACTURED/MOBILE HOMES

Generally, a license issued by the Office of Administration of the Arizona Department of Building and Fire Safety (DBFS) is required to act as a broker in the sale of manufactured homes, mobile homes and factory-built buildings (also known as modular) and subassemblies. The DBFS maintains and enforces standards of quality and safety for manufactured homes, mobile homes and factory-built buildings and reduces hazards to life and property through the maintenance and enforcement of the state fire code. Its purpose also includes consumer protection.

The DBFS consists of the Board of Manufactured Housing, the State Fire Safety Committee and the director of the department. The director's office consists of the Office of Manufactured Housing, the Office of the State Fire Marshal and the Office of Administration. Pursuant to A.R.S. §41-2194(3-4), it is unlawful to "engage in the business of a salesperson of manufactured homes, mobile homes or factory-built buildings . . ." or engage in the business of contracting to sell any new or used manufactured home, mobile home, factory-built building or subassembly (collectively referred to as "manufactured/mobile home") without a license issued by the DBFS.

THERE IS A LIMITED EXEMPTION FROM THE DBFS LICENSING REQUIREMENTS FOR REAL ESTATE LICENSEES

There is a limited exemption for real estate licensees in the DBFS licensing requirements. Pursuant to A.R.S. §41-2178(B)(1), the requirements of licensure from the DBFS do not apply to:

Real estate brokers and real estate salesmen licensed under section 32-2122 . . . with respect to used manufactured homes, mobile homes, factory-built buildings or subassemblies, if the manufactured home, mobile home, factory-built building or subassembly is listed in a contract for transfer of an interest in real property executed by its owner and is installed on the real property.

Question: What are the statutory requirements of the DBFS licensing exemption?
Answer: The requirements are the manufactured/mobile home must be:
- "used"
- "installed" on the property
- "listed" in a contract for transfer of an interest in real property executed by its owner

Question: *When is a manufactured/mobile home "used"?*
Answer: A used manufactured/mobile home is one "which has been sold, bargained, exchanged or given away from a purchaser who first acquired the unit which was titled in the name of such purchaser," "in good faith from a licensed dealer or broker for purposes other than resale." *See*, A.R.S. §41-2142(39) and A.R.S. §41-2142(27).

Question: *When is a manufactured/mobile home "installed" on the property?*
Answer: Pursuant to A.R.S §41-2142(18) a manufactured/mobile home is installed on the property when it is:
- connected to on-site utility terminals
- placed on a foundation system
- secured by ground anchoring

"Installation" does not require the filing of an affidavit of affixture for purposes of the exemption.

Question: *When is a manufactured/mobile home "listed" in a contract for transfer of an interest in real property executed by its owner?*
Answer: This occurs when both the manufactured/mobile home and the real property interest are transferred in the same purchase contract. In order to transfer both the manufactured/mobile home and an interest in the real property in the same purchase contract, the seller must either own the real property or have the right to directly assign the lease for the real property.

Question: *What is the significance of recording an affidavit of affixture?*
Answer: Except in limited circumstances set forth in A.R.S §33-1501, an affidavit of affixture may be recorded by a person who owns a mobile home that is installed on real property owned by the owner. A.R.S §42-15201 *et. seq.* A mobile home that has been permanently affixed to real property and for which an affidavit of affixture has been recorded:
- will be assessed as real property A.R.S. §42-15202
- any liens against the mobile home must be perfected in the same manner as real property or a fixture A.R.S. §28-2135

Pursuant to A.R.S. §33-1501, a person who owns a mobile home located in a mobile home park on real property that is not owned by that person may file an affidavit of affixture with the county recorder of the county in which the real property is located if: (1) the mobile home has been installed on the real property with all wheels and axles removed in compliance with applicable state and local mobile home installation standards; (2) the owner of the mobile home has entered into a lease for the real property on which the mobile home is located for a primary term of at least 20 years, and the lease specifically permits the recording of an affidavit of affixture; and (3) before filing the affidavit of affixture, a memorandum of lease is recorded that includes all of the requirements set forth in the statute. Once recorded, the mobile home and the leasehold interest to which it is affixed shall be treated as real property. Once an affidavit of affixture is recorded, most counties will classify the manufactured/mobile home as "single family" for taxation purposes.

KEY POINTS TO REMEMBER

- A license issued by the Office of Administration of the Department of Building and Fire Safety is generally required to act as a real estate broker in the sale of unaffixed manufactured/mobile homes.

- There is a limited exemption for real estate brokers in the Department of Building and Fire Safety licensing requirements.

- A real estate broker may list and sell an unaffixed manufactured/mobile home without a Department of Building and Fire Safety license if the manufactured/mobile home is:

  - used

  - installed on the real property

- listed in the purchase contract for the transfer of an interest in the real property executed by its owner (i.e., the seller owns the real property or has the right to directly assign the lease for the property)

- A mobile home that has been permanently affixed to real property and for which an affidavit of affixture has been recorded is generally considered real property.

- A real estate broker may list and sell a manufactured/mobile home if an affidavit of affixture has been recorded against a used manufactured/mobile home so that it is considered real property.

CHAPTER 13

. . . .

Financing

Financing is often the cornerstone of a real estate transaction and obtaining a loan can be a complicated process. A lender generally has no contractual agreement, agency relationship or fiduciary duty to the buyer. Therefore, it is essential for the brokers in the transaction to be active in the buyer's loan process and to follow up with both the buyer and the lender to insure that the loan approval process is completed by the close of escrow.

Lenders are typically paid for a successful closing, so the lender has the incentive to complete a loan. However, lenders need documentation from buyers and must often rely on outside sources with definitive requirements prior to approving a buyer for a loan. Lenders are also generally required to obtain a property valuation by an "approved" appraiser, as well as a title insurance policy that indicates the loan is in first position, subordinate only to property taxes. Thus, the lender should interact with all of the parties to the contract to assure that the proper documentation is submitted and all requirements are satisfied as the transaction develops toward a successful closing.

MONITORING THE LOAN PROCESS

AAR has developed the Loan Status Report (LSR), which is required to be included in any offer made on the AAR Resale Contract. The LSR provides the seller with valuable information about the buyer's ability to obtain financing. The AAR Loan Status Update (LSU), which is not required but is recommended, is designed to assist both brokers and buyers follow through on the loan process. These forms together essentially outline the steps necessary to obtain loan approval without conditions. The LSR sets forth the initial steps to loan approval:

- The buyer and lender discuss the loan amount and terms for which the buyer intends to qualify.
- The buyer and lender discuss the loan strategy.
- The lender reviews the buyer's Trimerged Residential Credit Report (TMRCR) and determines that the buyer is pre-qualified or credit-approved.
- The buyer completes and signs a 1003/application and delivers the loan application to the lender.
- The buyer provides to the lender all additional requested disclosures and supporting application documentation.
- The lender reviews the completed 1003/application and supporting documentation.
- The lender provides the buyer with a Good Faith Estimate indicating the cost of the mortgage, closing costs and interest rate.

The LSU continues the financing checklist outlining the documents, actions and conditions necessary to complete the loan process.

- The contract and all addenda are provided to the lender.
- The lender receives and reviews the title commitment.
- The lender receives and reviews the appraisal.

Assuming the property appraised for at least the sale price and there are no problems with the other submitted documentation, the underwriting process begins. Communication between the real estate brokers, the buyer and the lender continues to be vital during the underwriting phase.

- The lender submits the loan package to the underwriter. Mortgage bankers may submit the documentation to one underwriter, while mortgage brokers may submit the documentation to several underwriting companies.

- The underwriter gives loan approval with prior-to-loan-document conditions.
- All prior to loan document conditions are satisfied. At this point in the loan application, the buyer has loan approval without prior to loan document conditions.

Once the underwriting approval process is complete, the document and closing process begins. At this time, the lender generally submits instructions to the escrow company regarding documentation and closing costs.

- The lender orders the closing loan documents and instructions.
- The lender receives and approves the pre-audit from the escrow company.
- The lender receives the signed loan documents with prior-to-funding conditions.
- The lender orders the funds.

It is vitally important to remember that in most transactions the lender will update the condition of credit reports, employment status and buyer's funds immediately prior to funding, even though there may not be an official condition or indication that the lender intends to do so. In fact, the lender may update this information several times during the loan approval process. Thus, be aware that any changes the buyer may make in credit applications or employment or any major expenditure may place the loan approval and funding in jeopardy.

LENDER — MORTGAGE BROKER OR MORTGAGE BANKER

In discussing financing issues, the AAR forms use the term "lender"; however, the broker and buyer should be aware of the difference between a mortgage banker and a mortgage broker. A mortgage banker is an entity that originates, underwrites and funds a loan. A mortgage banker may also service the loan payments. *See,* A.R.S. §6-941 (5-6). A mortgage broker originates a loan and compiles the loan application, but does not underwrite or fund the loan. *See,* A.R.S. §6-901(6). The mortgage broker shops the buyer's loan package with mortgage bankers. Since mortgage brokers offer the products of many mortgage bankers, they may be able to find a loan product for a buyer with a low to moderate income or less than perfect credit history.

THE PRIVACY ACT

One of the most common questions about financing information is whether the lender is prohibited by the "privacy act" from disclosing the buyer's loan status to the seller or brokers involved in the transaction. The answer is "no." The Privacy Act of 1974 and the Privacy Act of 1980 generally pertain to governmental use of information. The privacy provisions contained in the Gramm-Leach-Bliley (GLB) Act do require financial institutions to protect the confidentiality of their customers' nonpublic information. *See,* 15 U.S.C. §6801. The GLB Act prohibits a financial institution from disclosing to a nonaffiliated third party any nonpublic personal information, except under certain circumstances. *See,* 15 U.S.C. §6802(a-d). However, the GLB Act does not prohibit the disclosure of nonpublic personal information:

- "as necessary to effect, administer or enforce a transaction requested or authorized by the consumer . . ."
- "with the consent or at the direction of the consumer . . ."

See, 15 U.S.C. §6802(e).

A real property purchase is certainly a transaction requested by the buyer. Further, the buyer explicitly authorizes the disclosure of this information in the AAR contracts. Therefore, the lender is not prohibited from disclosing loan status updates to the seller or brokers involved in the transaction.

AVOID LENDING SURPRISES AT CLOSE OF ESCROW

By staying active in the buyer's loan approval process and communicating with the lender, a broker should have a good idea prior to the close of escrow date whether or not the buyer will obtain loan approval and be able to close escrow as agreed. A good lender will communicate to the buyer and brokers, facilitate the loan approval process and, with the help of all parties, be able to fund the loan by the close of escrow date. No one wants an unpleasant surprise on the close of escrow date.

SELLER CARRYBACK FINANCING

Seller carryback financing occurs when a portion of the purchase price is financed by the seller. Generally, the buyer will execute a promissory note and deed of trust in favor of the seller, which will be recorded, generally in second position, at close of escrow. The AAR Assumption/ Carryback Addendum addresses the important provisions of this type of financing, such as:

- account servicing, typically the account servicing agency will require that payments on the carryback and prior encumbrances be made concurrently through a single payment to protect the seller's carryback position and lien on the property secured by the deed of trust.
- payment amount, impounds and loan term
- late payment penalties and default rate
- due-on-sale clause
- taxes and insurance

WRAPAROUND FINANCING

Wraparound financing is also referred to as a wrap, all-inclusive deed of trust or blanket mortgage. Wraparound financing occurs when a seller sells property that is already subject to an existing loan and takes back a loan for a purchase price that exceeds the existing first loan. The face amount of the carryback loan includes the remaining principal on the existing loan plus the amount being advanced on the second. The buyer does not pay off or assume the existing loan; the seller remains responsible to the lender for its payment. In other words, the seller "wraps" a larger loan around the existing loan.

A wrap is an alternative to paying off or qualifying to assume an existing loan. A wrap may be beneficial to the seller if the current interest rate is high, and the first loan is at a lower rate. A buyer may consider wraparound financing if the buyer cannot qualify to assume the existing loan encumbering the property or qualify for new financing.

Question: *Is wraparound financing legal?*
Answer: Although statutes in some states may prohibit wraparound loans, Arizona has no statute pertaining to this type of financing. However, if the loan documents forbid the loan from being wrapped, i.e., with a due-on-sale clause, an agreement to wraparound financing will result in a breach of the loan documents (which generally consist of a promissory note and deed of trust). If the seller breaches the terms of the loan documents, the lender will be entitled to all available legal remedies, including acceleration of the debt or foreclosure. Simply put, the seller may be responsible for paying the loan in full without the ability to collect the entire amount from the buyer because the seller is obligated to accept monthly payments under the conditions of the carryback.

Question: *Should wraparound financing be used if the loan encumbering the property contains a due-on-sale clause?*
Answer: No. Wraparound financing should only be considered when the seller's existing loan documents do not contain a due-on-sale clause. If the seller's loan contains a due-on-sale clause, the seller is contractually obligated to pay off the outstanding balance on the existing loan when the property is sold. In rare cases the lender may consent to a wraparound when it is in their best interest to do so.

Question: *May a nonassumable loan be wrapped?*
Answer: If the loan is not assumable, the loan documents generally contain a due-on-sale clause that the lender could use to call the loan due. Therefore, if the loan is not assumable, the loan should not be wrapped.

Question: *What are some lenders' concerns with wraparound financing?*
Answer: Many lenders do not want their loans wrapped, especially if the first loan has a below-market interest rate. From a business standpoint, lenders want to earn the highest rate of return possible. Additionally, lenders generally consider wraparound financing a high-risk transaction because the buyer oftentimes cannot qualify for a new loan.

Question: *How could a lender find out that the loan has been wrapped?*
Answer: Lenders often discover that a loan has been wrapped by the recording of the transfer of the property, the change of the tax liability, or the change of the insured's name on insurance policies. Lenders can also become aware of a wrap by receiving payments from the account servicing agent.

Question: *What are some buyer's concerns with wraparound financing?*
Answer: The buyer must ensure that the first loan is timely paid. With a wrap, the seller does not pay off the first loan, and the lender retains the right to foreclose on the property if payments are not made as required. Although the seller is responsible for making the payments on the first loan, the buyer generally has no guarantee that the seller will make these payments. Thus, the property could be foreclosed upon if the seller fails to make payments on the first loan. Therefore, a buyer should insist that all payments be made concurrently through a single servicing account maintained by a licensed escrow agent with adequate instructions regarding forwarding payments.

Question: *What are some seller's concerns with wraparound financing?*
Answer: The seller must ensure that the buyer is financially capable of making the required payments. Therefore, the seller should require the buyer to provide financial information to the seller, such as a credit report and income verification and seek professional assistance in interpreting the information, if necessary. The seller's credit status can also be in jeopardy if the buyer fails to make their payments timely, as the seller is still the primary borrower on the note and deed of trust that was wrapped.

Question: *Should a buyer considering a wrap request a copy of the seller's loan documents?*
Answer: Yes. The buyer should request and obtain a copy of the note and deed of trust to review the rights and obligations of the loan agreement, since the buyer will be subject to the same obligations. The buyer should confirm that a wrap would not trigger a due-on-sale clause, which requires the loan to be paid off if the property is transferred.

Question: *What kind of record-keeping is needed with a wraparound financing?*
Answer: The record-keeping for a wraparound mortgage can be complex. The seller must keep track of the payments made by the buyer and how much of each payment is attributable to principal and how much is attributable to interest. The amount of interest paid must be provided to the buyer for tax purposes. Therefore, the use of a servicing agent, such as an escrow company, is advisable for record-keeping purposes.

Question: *Do real estate brokers incur more liability in a transaction utilizing wraparound financing?*
Answer: Yes. Wraparound financing is risky for all parties involved. Additionally, because of the complexities involved in such a transaction, the purchase contract must adequately address numerous issues.

Question: *Should buyers and sellers be referred to legal and tax counsel before agreeing to wraparound financing?*
Answer: Yes. Because wraparound financing raises significant and complex issues, buyers and sellers should consult with independent legal counsel and tax professionals before entering into any transaction with a wrap.

TRUSTEE'S SALES

Most loans in Arizona are secured by a promissory note and a deed of trust, which is recorded against the property. If the property owner fails to make the payments on the loan or otherwise breaches the loan agreement, the lender may perform a nonjudicial foreclosure called a trustee's sale. The statutes governing trustee's sales are located at A.R.S. §33-801 *et. seq.* Pursuant to these statues, a property may not be sold at a trustee's sale until the ninety-first day after the date of the recording of the notice of the sale. A.R.S. 33-807(D).

ANTI-DEFICIENCY STATUTES

The so-called anti-deficiency statutes, A.R.S. §33-729(A) and §33-814(G), prohibit a lender from obtaining a deficiency judgment against a borrower after a trustee's sale or foreclosure of a purchase money loan encumbering property of two and one-half acres or less utilized for one-family or two-family residences. These statutes evidence the legislature's desire to protect homeowners from the financial disaster of losing their homes to foreclosure plus all their other nonexempt property on execution of a judgment for the balance of the purchase price. *See, Baker v. Gardner,* 160 Ariz. 98, 770 P.2d 766 (1988). Further, these statutes prohibit a lender from waiving the right to conduct a trustee's sale or foreclose and file a lawsuit against the borrower on the note for the entire unpaid balance. *Id.*

The anti-deficiency statutes also apply to a qualifying loan that has been refinanced. In *Bank One v. Beauvais,* 934 P.2d 809 (Ariz. 1197) the court addressed whether a refinanced loan is purchase money for the purposes of the anti-deficiency statutes. The *Bank One* court stated:

> . . . we believe the legislature did not intend that a loan would lose its character as a purchase-money obligation when . . . it is extended, renewed, or the remaining portion of the original loan is refinanced and the deed of trust on the property that was bought with the original loan continues or is renewed. Given the realities of the marketplace, to believe otherwise would put many homeowners, unable to make mortgage payments, at the peril of facing personal liability as well as the loss of their homes — a result the legislature intended to avoid through the

Anti-deficiency Statutes. In summary, we hold that regardless of whether [a promissory note is] an extension, renewal, or refinancing of [a purchase-money note], it retain[s] its character as a purchase-money note. *See, Lucky Invs., Inc. v. Adams,* 183 Cal. App. 2d 462, 7 Cal. Rptr. 57 (1960), cancellation and replacement with new notes, secured by the same property, transfers purchase-money status to new notes.

KEY POINTS TO REMEMBER

- Both brokers should actively follow up with the buyer and the lender to facilitate funding of the loan by COE.

- The AAR LSR should be included in every AAR Resale Contract.

- The AAR LSU should be utilized to keep the parties and brokers appraised of the progress of the buyers loan approval process.

- The AAR Assumption/Carryback Addendum addresses the issues involved in seller carryback transactions.

- A broker should understand the risks of wraparound financing and recommend that the client consult legal counsel.

CHAPTER 14

. . . .

Disclosure

All parties involved in a real estate transaction; sellers, buyers, brokers and lenders have some disclosure duty. Failure to disclose and associated misrepresentation claims generally make up the majority of real estate disputes. Many lawsuits against home sellers and brokers are brought by buyers alleging the failure to disclose a material defect in the property. These lawsuits are a drain not only on the individuals involved, but on the real estate industry as a whole.

GENERAL DISCLOSURE OBLIGATIONS

Discerning the disclosure obligations in a real estate transaction has become increasingly complex. Disclosure obligations originate from statutes, common law and administrative rule. Federal statutes, such as the lead-paint disclosure requirements, impose specific disclosure obligations upon sellers. Additionally, there are an increasing number of Arizona statutes that require certain disclosures, such as the planned unit development/condominium resale disclosure, pool barrier disclosure and airport disclosure requirements. The ADRE Commissioner's Rules impose specific disclosure obligations on real estate licensees. However, the general disclosure requirements in a real estate transaction originate from common (or court-made) law. The Arizona Courts have addressed a real estate broker's duty to disclose to both the client and the nonclient, as well as a seller's disclosure obligations to a buyer and a buyer's disclosure obligations to the seller.

A BROKER'S DUTY TO DISCLOSE TO THE CLIENT

A real estate broker's disclosure obligation to the client arises from the broker's fiduciary duty. Part of that fiduciary duty is the obligation to make a complete and full disclosure of all known material facts that might affect the client's decision to sell or buy a property. *See e.g., Jennings v. Lee*, 105 Ariz. 167, 461 P.2d 161 (1969). For example, in *Morley v. J. Pagel Realty & Insurance*, 27 Ariz. App. 62, 550 P.2d 1104 (1976), the listing broker presented an offer to the seller that provided for carryback financing, but no deed of trust. The sellers accepted the offer. After close of escrow, the buyers deeded the property to a third party for cash, defaulted on the note, and filed bankruptcy. The sellers then sued their broker for failing to inform them that they should have required the buyer to execute a deed of trust, which could have been recorded to secure the buyers' performance. The *Morley* court stated that the broker had a duty to effect a sale for the client on the best terms possible and to disclose to the client all the information the broker possessed pertaining to the prospective transaction. Thus, the broker was obligated to inform the sellers that they should require security for a carryback. The court also indicated that a broker should make all explanations commensurate with the education and understanding of the client, and if the broker is unable to give competent advice, the broker should allow the client the opportunity to obtain advice elsewhere.

Obviously, the specific disclosures and advice required of the broker depend on the transaction, the experience of the client, and the client's questions or concerns. The specific disclosures that a broker must make to a client also differ depending on whether the client is the seller or the buyer.

Some of the specific disclosure obligations of a listing broker to a seller imposed by common law, as reflected by the ADRE Commissioner's Rules, include the obligations to disclose:

- all offers (R4-28-802(B))
- any known information that the buyer is or may be unable to perform (*Lombardo v. Albu*, 199 Ariz. 97, 14 P.3d 288 (2000); *Mason v. Bulleri*, 25 Ariz. App. 357, 543 P.2d 478 (1975); R4-28-1101(B))
- if the broker, broker's family or a business entity in which the broker has an interest is the buyer (*Kimmell v. Clark*, 21 Ariz. App. 455, 520 P.2d 851 (1974); R4-28-1101(E))
- if the broker is receiving any compensation, rebate or profit for the transaction (and obtain written consent) (R4-28-1101(G))
- the name of each employing broker receiving compensation from the transaction (R4-28-701) (disclosure required to all parties).

Identifying the disclosure obligations to the seller client is relatively straightforward. Identifying the specifically required disclosure obligations a broker owes to the buyer client is more problematic. However, there are identifiable disclosure duties that a buyer's broker owes to a buyer, such as to disclose:

- all known material defects existing in the property. (R4-28-1101(B)(3))
- any known information that the seller is or may be unable to perform (R4-28-1101 (B)(1))
- the possible existence of a known lien or encumbrance on the property (R4-28-1101 (B)(4))
- if the broker, broker's family or a business entity in which the broker has an interest is the seller (R4-28-1101(E))
- if the broker is receiving any compensation, rebate or profit for the transaction (and obtain written consent) (R4-28-1101 (G))
- the name of each employing broker receiving compensation from the transaction (R4-28-701) (disclosure required to all parties)

A BROKER'S DUTY TO DISCLOSE TO THE NONCLIENT

A broker has no fiduciary duties in the absence of a broker-client relationship. *See, e.g., Norville v. Palant,* 25 Ariz. App. 606, 545 P.2d 454 (App. 1976). In the usual situation where one real estate broker secures a listing to sell real estate and another broker represents a buyer who makes an offer for the listed property, an agency relationship between the seller and the broker who represents a buyer is not established. *Buffington v. Haas,* 124 Ariz. 36, 601 P.2d 1320 (1979).

Even when there is no agency relationship, a broker does in fact have some disclosure obligations to the nonclient. However, the disclosure obligations a broker owes to the nonclient are narrower than the disclosure obligations owed to the client. For example, in the *Buffington* case the court found that a broker who did not represent the seller was not liable for failing to disclose that under the contract the seller did not retain a security interest in the property. The *Buffington* court stated: "there was not an agency relationship between the real estate salesman and seller. . . therefore the salesman had no obligation to inform the seller."

In a subsequent case, *Haldiman, v. Gosnell Development Corp.,* 155 Ariz. 585, 748 P.2d 1209 (App. 1987), the plaintiff argued that the court should impose a duty on real estate brokers to explain the implication of real estate documents even in the absence of an agency relationship. In this case, the real estate broker was employed by Gosnell to write purchase contracts for potential home buyers, which is what he did for the plaintiff. This brief relationship was the basis of the plaintiff's claim that the broker represented her and gave her real estate advice in the transaction. The court stated:

> [The plaintiff's] belief that [the broker] represented her, or was in essence her agent, does not, however, make him her agent. *See, e.g., Warren v. Mangels Realty,* 23 Ariz. App. 318, 321, 533 P.2d 78, 81 (1975) ("Warren's mental characterization of Mangels as his 'agent' could not by some magical process convert Mangels into one"). The facts are clear, despite [the

plaintiff's] belief and claim, that [the broker] was an employee of Gosnell and represented Gosnell only. An agent may not, in the absence of the principal's consent, act on behalf of an adverse party. *Valley Nat'l Bank v. Milmoe*, 74 Ariz. 290, 296, 248 P.2d 740, 744 (1952).

Id. 155 Ariz. at 589, 748 P.2d at 1213.

Therefore, the court held that the plaintiff had no cause of action for the seller's broker's failure to suggest that the purchase contract be conditioned upon financing and selling her home, or his failure to explain that she could not recover her deposits if she failed to close escrow for any reason.

Although a broker has no fiduciary duties to the nonclient, a broker still has a duty to deal fairly with a nonclient. Arizona courts have consistently held a broker accountable where the broker fails to deal fairly with a nonclient. Commissioner's Rule R4-28-1101(A), states:

A licensee owes a fiduciary duty to the client and shall protect and promote the client's interests. The licensee shall also deal fairly with all other parties to a transaction.

This rule acknowledges the broker's fiduciary duty to the principal while recognizing the broker's duty of fair dealing to other parties to the transaction.

In *Aranki v. RKP Investments, Inc.*, 194 Ariz. 206, 979 P.2d 534 (App. 1999), the Court of Appeals addressed the duty a broker owed to a nonclient and stated that "[a]s agents of the sellers, the [listing agent] owed a duty to the buyers different from the 'full and frank disclosure' they owed to their principals, the sellers . . . Their duty was to 'deal fairly with all other parties to a transaction'." In explaining the scope of the duty to deal fairly, the *Aranki* court stated:

The duty of fair dealing does not include investigations to discover defects in the sellers' property. The law does not, for example, require escrow agents, who act as fiduciaries for buyers and sellers alike, to investigate on behalf of their principals; such agents are merely bound to disclose circumstances that a reasonable agent would perceive as evidence of fraud. *See*

Burkons v. Ticor Title Ins. Co., 168 Ariz. 345, 353, 813 P.2d 710, 718 (1991); A.A.C. R4-28-1101 (B) (3).

The *Aranki* court found that the listing broker was not liable to the buyers for passing along information obtained from the seller without proof that the listing broker knew or should have known that the information might be false.

A broker's disclosure obligations to the nonclient were also discussed in *Lombardo v. Albu,* 199 Ariz. 97, 14 P.3d 288 (2000).[11] The trial and appellate court in this case both held that a buyer's financial information is confidential, and a buyer's broker has no legal duty to violate that confidence by disclosing such information to the seller. However, the Arizona Supreme Court held that such financial information is not confidential, and a buyer is obligated to disclose facts critical to the ability to perform. Because the buyer has the duty to disclose this information, the buyer's broker has the same obligation.

The *Lombardo* case resulted from a failed real estate transaction. The sellers, the Lombardo's, were in default on the second position deed of trust encumbering their home. The lender noticed a trustee's sale. As a result, the sellers and the lender entered into a loan workout agreement in which the sellers agreed to list and sell the home to pay the loan. Three months later, the sellers listed the home for sale. The buyers interested in purchasing the home were represented by a buyer's broker. At some point, the buyers conveyed to the buyer's broker that the husband had financial problems. However, the buyers believed the wife could obtain financing and submitted an offer in the wife's name only. The buyer's broker did not disclose the buyer's (husband's) financial situation to the sellers. The sellers entered into a purchase contract with the buyer wife that was contingent upon financing and obtained an extension on the loan workout agreement. However, the buyer was unable to obtain the necessary funds to close escrow on the agreed-upon date. Therefore, the close of escrow date and trustee's sale were extended, in exchange for the payment of the

---

[11] *AAR filed an amicus curie brief in this case both at the Court of Appeals and the Supreme Court.*

buyer's earnest money to the foreclosing lender. Ultimately, the buyers failed to close escrow, and the second lien holder foreclosed on the home.

The sellers sued all parties involved in the transaction, including the buyer's broker. The sellers alleged that had they been told about the buyer's financial history that they would have sought other conditions in the contract, such as the right to keep the home on the market. The trial court granted the buyer's broker summary judgment. On appeal, the sellers argued that the Commissioner's Rules were rules that the public could use as the basis for lawsuits against real estate licensees and R4-28-1101(B) stated that a broker "shall disclose to all other parties to the transaction . . . [a]ny information that the buyer . . . is, or may be, unable to perform . . ."

The Court of Appeals agreed with the trial court that the buyer had no duty to disclose financial information to the sellers because such information was confidential. Further, the court commented that the seller could obtain such information by requesting a credit check or loan pre-approval and thus the information was not "latent" information that could require affirmative disclosure. Based on that analysis, the appeals court concluded that the Commissioner's Rule requiring a buyer's broker to disclose confidential information about the buyer to the seller resulted in a breach of fiduciary duty to the buyer. Therefore, the Court of Appeals held that a buyer's broker, like the buyer, had no duty to disclose adverse financial information to the seller.

The Arizona Supreme Court reversed the Court of Appeals decision. The Supreme Court began its opinion by stating the buyer and seller have legal duties to each other "arising out of their contractual relationship." The court stated:

> This [duty] includes the covenant of good faith and fair dealing. Buyers and sellers must deal fairly with each other. And, the buyer and seller have duties to each other to disclose facts that are material to the transaction.
>
> The major consideration flowing from the buyer to the seller is the price. The buyer cannot present himself as a ready, willing, and able buyer if he knows that there is a significant risk that the deal will never close because of his inability to

perform. This would violate the buyer's duty to deal fairly under the contract and the legal duties imposed by [the common law in the] *Restatement (Second) of Contracts §161 and Restatement (Second) of Torts §551.*

199 Ariz. at 97, 14 P.3d at 290. *(Emphasis added.)*

Regarding the duties of the buyer's broker to the sellers, the Supreme Court quoted with approval a section of the *Restatement (Second) of Agency,* which states:

Although the making of a contract by the agent does not constitute a representation by him that his principal is known by him to be solvent or honorable, *if the agent knows that the principal does not intend to perform the contract because of hopeless insolvency or other reason, the making of the contract for him under such conditions subjects the agent to liability.* [Citations omitted.] Likewise, if the agent fails to reveal circumstances that make it impossible for the principal to perform, the other party has the remedies given for misrepresentation.

199 Ariz. at 100, 14 P.3d at 291. *(Emphasis added).*

The Supreme Court held that information regarding the buyer's ability to perform is not confidential information, "[b]ut even if it were. '[a]n agent is privileged to reveal information confidentially acquired by him in the course of his agency in the protection of a superior interest of himself or of a third person'." *Id.* The Supreme Court was also asked to determine whether a violation of the ADRE Commissioner's Rules should impose civil tort liability upon real estate brokers, but the court declined to decide that issue.

After the Supreme Court issued its decision, the case was remanded (sent) back to the trial court to determine if the buyer's broker breached the duty to disclose the buyer's financial information to the sellers. After hearing the facts, the trial court found that the buyer's broker did not breach the duty to disclose, the Court of Appeals agreed and the case finally ended after 8 years of litigation.

THE SELLER'S OBLIGATION TO DISCLOSE TO THE BUYER

A seller has a duty to disclose known facts materially affecting the value of the property that are not readily observable and are not known to the buyer. This duty was delineated by the court in *Hill v. Jones*, 151 Ariz. 81, 725 P.2d 1115 (App. 1986). In *Hill v. Jones*, the buyer and sellers entered into a contract for a home with a wood floor. The sellers disclosed no past termite damage, and the termite report indicated no visible evidence of infestation or previous treatment. The termite inspector did not see the treatment holes in the patio because of stacked boxes and did not find the termite damage inside the house because a large plant covered the area.

After close of escrow in the *Hill* case, the buyers learned from a neighbor that the house had past termite infestation, and the buyers discovered that part of the wood flooring was crumbling. When the lawsuit was filed, the buyers learned that the sellers had received two termite guarantees from the previous owner, had treated the house twice for termites and that existing termite damage had not been repaired. In examining the case, the court announced the seller's duty to disclose known material facts to the buyer in Arizona and stated that under certain circumstances nondisclosure of a known fact may be equivalent to the assertion that the fact does not exist. Therefore, nondisclosure may be equated with and given the same legal effect as fraud and misrepresentation.

An Arizona court has also held that an "as is" clause provision in a contract does not shield the seller from liability for failure to disclose known material defects in the property. *S. Development Corp. v. Pima Capital Management Co.*, 201 Ariz. 10, 31 P.3rd 123 (App. 2002). The seller is obligated to make the required disclosures regardless of the "as is" clause. See chapter 6, "As Is" Contracts for a more detailed discussion of the *S. Development Corp.* case.

Further, if the buyer asks the seller about an aspect of the property, the seller has a duty to disclose the information, regardless of whether or not the seller considers the information material. *Universal Inv. Co. v. Sahara*

Motor Inn, Inc., 127 Ariz. 213, 215, 619 P.2d 485, 487 (1980). Sellers also have a legal duty to disclose facts when disclosure is necessary to prevent a previous statement from being misleading or a misrepresentation: for example, if something changes. However, a seller does not generally have a legal obligation to correct defects in the property, as long as the defects are disclosed.

The Seller's Statutory Duty to Disclose

In addition to the common law duty to disclose, there are an ever-increasing number of specific disclosures that sellers are required by statute to make, such as:

- lead-based paint disclosure in pre-1978 properties (Title X)
- swimming pool barrier disclosure (A.R.S. §36-1681(E))
- planned Community/Condominium disclosure information (A.R.S. §33-1806 & 33-1260)
- notice of soil remediation (A.R.S. §33-434.01 and 49-701.02)
- disclosure affidavit for property in unincorporated areas, unless the property is located in a subdivision (A.R.S. §33-422)
- military airport (A.R.S. §28-8484)
- public airport information (A.R.S. §28-8486)
- subdivision disclosures/public reports (A.R.S. §32-2183)
- dangerous drug lab disclosure (A.R.S. §12-1000)

A BUYER'S OBLIGATION TO DISCLOSE TO THE SELLER

Like all the other parties in a real estate transaction, a buyer of real property has certain disclosure obligations. As discussed previously, a buyer has a duty to disclose to the seller all known facts materially affecting the transaction. *Lombardo v. Albu,* 199 Ariz. 97, 14 P.3d 288 (2000). Because the major consideration flowing from the buyer to the seller is the price, the buyer must disclose to the seller all facts materially affecting the buyer's ability to pay the purchase price. A buyer cannot present himself or herself as a "ready, willing, and able" buyer if the buyer knows that there is a significant risk that he or she will be unable to perform by purchasing the home. This would violate the buyer's duty to deal fairly. Therefore, buyers have a legal duty to disclose facts that are critical to their ability to perform. Buyers entering into AAR contracts also assume a contractual duty to disclose as well. In AAR contracts, the buyer "warrants that the buyer has disclosed to seller all information which may materially and adversely affect the buyer's ability to close escrow or complete the obligations of" the contract.

Modern lending practices involve a highly complicated structure of credit scoring and other variables. A buyer's ability to qualify for a real estate loan is affected by numerous factors. Therefore, when financing is involved, a buyer should consult a lender and instruct the lender to complete an AAR LSR in a residential resale transaction, listing all conditions to financing before submitting an offer to purchase a home. A lender generally will not commit to providing the buyer with financing until close of escrow because the ability to obtain loan approval may be affected by other aspects of the buyer's financial situation, any material change in the buyer's financial status, or by adverse property conditions.

Additionally, if there are other factors that may prevent the buyer from performing, the buyer must disclose these as well. For example, the buyer must disclose factors such as the buyer:

- must sell their existing home or other property to qualify for financing
- must lease a property to qualify for financing
- must complete a sale before the funds for the down payment will be available
- has filed bankruptcy

The buyer of real property has legally mandated disclosure duties. However, by providing an LSR or otherwise, specifying all conditions to loan approval, with the offer, the buyer can generally fully comply with these obligations.

SPECIFIC DISCLOSURE REQUIREMENTS

Affidavit of Disclosure

By statute, a seller of five or fewer parcels of land, other than subdivided land, in an unincorporated area of a county and any subsequent seller of such a parcel is required to furnish a written Affidavit of Disclosure to the buyer at least seven days before the transfer of the property, and the buyer is obligated to acknowledge receipt of the affidavit. A.R.S. §33-422. The buyer has the right to rescind the sales transaction for a period of five days after receipt of the Affidavit of Disclosure. The seller must record the executed Affidavit of Disclosure at the same time that the deed is recorded.

Question: What land is subject to the statute?
Answer: The statutory requirements apply to all land sold in five or fewer parcels in unincorporated areas that are not located in a subdivision.

Question: Does the statute apply only to vacant land?
Answer: Although, much of the property in unincorporated areas is vacant land, the statute states that the requirements apply to "land, other than subdivided land." The term "land" is undefined. Additionally, the statute refers to the land as "property" and "parcel." Therefore, the statute should be interpreted to apply to all land (sold in five or fewer parcels, other than subdivided land) in an unincorporated area, whether the land is improved, unimproved, vacant, residential or commercial.

Question: What is an unincorporated area?
Answer: An unincorporated area is land located outside the corporate limits of a city or town. *See,* A.R.S. §9-101 *et.seq.*

Question: What is subdivided land?
Answer: Pursuant to A.R.S. §32-2101(55) subdivided land means "improved or unimproved land or lands divided or proposed to be divided for the purpose of sale or lease, whether immediate or future, into six or more lots, parcels or fractional interests."

Question: *What kind of information must be disclosed in the affidavit?*
Answer: The affidavit must contain information addressing issues such as legal access, physical access, road maintenance, floods and floodplains, utilities and services, water, wells, septic systems, percolation tests, and zoning deficiencies.

Question: *Is the form of affidavit required?*
Answer: Yes. The required form of affidavit is prescribed by the statute.

Question: *Should the listing agent complete the affidavit on the seller's behalf?*
Answer: No. The seller should complete the disclosure affidavit.

Question: *What if the seller does not know some of the required disclosure information?*
Answer: The form of affidavit does not allow for an "unknown" response to some of the disclosure items. If the seller does not know and does not have access to information required to be disclosed, the seller should indicate that the information is unknown and provide any necessary explanation on the explanation lines of the form. If additional space is required, the seller should indicate that fact on the explanation line, write the information on a separate sheet of paper (leaving a one-half inch margin on all sides of the paper for recording purposes), mark the paper as exhibit "B" (the legal description should be exhibit "A") and attach the exhibit to the affidavit.

Question: *Is a trustee in a foreclosure exempt from the statute's requirements?*
Answer: Yes. For the purposes of the statute, "seller" and "subsequent seller" do not include a trustee of a deed of trust who is selling property by a trustee's sale or any officer who is selling property by execution sale to enforce a judgment or to foreclose a mortgage.

Question: *Is a seller who is subject to the statute required to make any other disclosures?*

Answer: Yes. The statute only requires the disclosure of limited issues regarding the land. A seller is still required to disclose all known material defects. Thus, the affidavit should be used in conjunction with the appropriate SPDS.

Question: What action must a buyer take to rescind a transaction after receiving the affidavit?
Answer: The statute simply provides that "the buyer has the right to rescind the sales transaction for a period of five days after the Affidavit of Disclosure is furnished to the buyer." Thus, no specific procedure is required to rescind the transaction. Written notice of rescission from the buyer to the seller during the five day time period should be sufficient.

Question: What if the information disclosed in the affidavit changes?
Answer: A new affidavit may be recorded. The statute specifically provides that a subsequently recorded affidavit supersedes any previous affidavit.

Question: How is the statute enforced?
Answer: The statute contains no enforcement mechanism or penalty. However, a seller could have civil liability to the buyer for the failure to furnish the Affidavit of Disclosure. Further, a buyer's remedies against the seller for the failure to deliver the Affidavit of Disclosure could include not only damages, but rescission of the sale as well. Additionally, if the seller failed to otherwise disclose material facts that would have been disclosed in the affidavit, the seller would have civil liability for the nondisclosure pursuant to common law.

Meth Lab (and other Dangerous Drug Lab) Disclosure

A.R.S §12-1000 requires property owners to clean up properties used as dangerous drug laboratories and to disclose that the property has been used as a drug lab until the clean-up is complete. The statute applies to residential property, mobile homes and recreational vehicles. The following addresses the general statutory requirements as they apply to residential real property.

Discovery by the Police Triggers the Statutory Requirements

If a police officer discovers a clandestine drug laboratory or arrests a person for having chemicals or equipment used in the manufacture thereof, on a property, the officer will:

- deliver a notice of removal to the owner or manager, if on the site at the time of the discovery or arrest
- send the notice of removal by certified mail within two business days after the discovery or arrest to the owner's address on file with the county assessor, to the owner's on-site manager, the county health department, and the appropriate local fire department
- remove the gross contamination and order the removal of all persons from the residually contaminated portion of the property
- affix the notice of removal in a conspicuous place on the property A.R.S. §12-1000(A)

The notice of removal is required to have "WARNING" in large bold type at the top and bottom of the notice and state:

- that a clandestine drug laboratory was seized or a person was arrested on the property for having chemicals or equipment used in the manufacturing of methamphetamine, ecstasy or LSD on the real property
- the date of the seizure or arrest
- the address or location of the real property, including the identification of any dwelling unit, room number, apartment number or vehicle number
- the name of the law enforcement agency or other agency that seized the clandestine drug laboratory or made the arrest and the agency's contact telephone number
- that hazardous substances, toxic chemicals or other waste products may still be present on the property
- that it is unlawful for any unauthorized person to enter the residually contaminated portion of the property until the owner, landlord or manager establishes that the portion of the real property noticed as residually contaminated has been remediated by a drug laboratory site remediation firm

- that it is a class 6 felony to violate this law
- that it is a class 2 misdemeanor to disturb the posted notice of removal
- that the owner of the property shall remediate the residually contaminated portion of the property in compliance with the law
- that if an owner fails to provide any notice required by the law, the owner is subject to a civil penalty and a buyer, tenant or customer may void a purchase contract, rental agreement or other agreement

A.R.S. §12-1000(B).

Disclosure to Buyers and Tenants is Required until Remediation is Complete

Until the property is remediated, the following is required:

To Buyers

Within five days after a buyer signs a contract to purchase the property, the owner must notify the buyer in writing that methamphetamine, ecstasy or LSD was manufactured on the property or that an arrest was made pursuant to this law. The buyer must acknowledge receipt of the notice. A buyer may cancel the real estate purchase contract within five days after receiving the notice. If the owner does not comply with this requirement, the buyer may cancel the purchase contract.

To Tenants

The landlord must notify a prospective tenant for a dwelling unit that was the subject of the notice in writing that methamphetamine, ecstasy or LSD was manufactured on the real property or that an arrest was made pursuant to this law. The tenant must acknowledge receipt of the notice before taking possession of the property or before signing a rental agreement for the property. The notice must be attached to the rental agreement. If the landlord does not comply with this requirement, the tenant may void the rental agreement.

Similar notice and opportunity to cancel provisions apply to room rentals, mobile homes, and recreational vehicles. A.R.S. §12-1000(F)(5).

The Owner is Required to Remediate the Property and Restitution is Required

The owner is required to remediate the residually contaminated portion of the property by retaining a registered and licensed drug laboratory site remediation firm. A.R.S. §12-1000(C). A person who operates a clandestine drug laboratory and who is not the owner of the real property is required to pay restitution to the owner of the property for all costs that the owner incurred to remediate the property. A.R.S. §12-1000(I).

A drug laboratory site remediation firm is required to comply with the requirements established and the best practices and standards for remediation of residual contamination adopted by the State Board of Technical Registration. A.R.S. §12-1000(D). When remediation is complete, the remediation firm will remove the posted notice and issue a document stating that the residually contaminated portion of the real property has been remediated. Within 24 hours after the remediation is complete, the remediation firm is required to deliver the document to each person and entity that received the notice of removal and the law enforcement agency that issued the notice.

After the remediation document has been issued by the remediation firm, the owner, landlord or manager of the property is no longer required to give any buyer or tenant notice and an opportunity to cancel the contract or lease, and any person may use, enter, occupy, rent or sell the real property.

Noncompliance May Result in Civil and Criminal Penalties

There are civil and criminal penalties for noncompliance. If an owner fails to provide any notice required by the law, the owner is subject to a civil penalty of $1,000 and is liable for any harm resulting from the failure to comply with these notice requirements. A.R.S. §12-1000(G). A person who knowingly violates an order or notice of removal is guilty of a class

6 felony. A person who knowingly disturbs a notice of removal posted on the real property is guilty of a class 2 misdemeanor. A.R.S. §12-1000(J).

Lead-based Paint Disclosure

A seller must make certain lead-based paint disclosures before a buyer is obligated under contract to buy a home constructed before 1978 (target housing).

In 1992, Congress passed the Residential Lead-based Paint Hazard Reduction Act (also referred to as Title X or the Act). The law required the EPA and HUD to promulgate joint rules and regulations for lead-based paint disclosure. As a result, the Code of Federal Regulations (24 CFR Part 35, Subpart H and 40 CFR Part 745, Subpart F) and the final joint EPA and HUD Rule (61 FR 9064) were promulgated to implement the Act. There are literally hundreds of pages of statutes, regulations and rules addressing the Act.

Disclosures Required before Buyer is Obligated

The federal law (42 USCS §4852d) and subsequent rules and regulations require that before a buyer (or tenant) is obligated under any contract to purchase a home constructed prior to 1978, the seller must:

- Provide the EPA-approved lead hazard pamphlet, *Protect Your Family From Lead in Your Home.*
- Disclose any known information regarding lead-based paint hazards to buyers and brokers.
- Disclose and provide any available lead based paint records or reports to buyers.
- Permit a 10-day opportunity (or other agreed upon time period) to conduct a lead-based paint risk assessment or inspection, unless waived by the buyer.

Contract Requirements

Every contract to sell target housing must contain (or provide as an attachment):

- a lead warning statement consisting of the required language
- a statement by the seller disclosing any known information regarding lead-based paint hazards
- a disclosure of the lead-based paint records or reports available to the seller
- a statement signed by the seller that the seller has complied with all notification requirements
- a statement signed by the buyer that the buyer:
  - affirms the receipt of the above disclosures
  - received the pamphlet *Protect Your Family From Lead in Your Home*
  - has read and understands the lead warning statement
  - received or waived an opportunity to conduct a lead risk assessment or inspection before becoming obligated under the contract
- a statement that:
  - the broker has informed the seller of the seller's obligations under 42 USC 4852d
  - the broker is aware of his/her duty to ensure compliance with these requirements (*See,* 24 CFR §35.92)

The AAR Disclosure of Information on Lead-based Paint and Lead-based Paint Hazards (Sales) form may be used to satisfy these requirements. Sellers and brokers must retain a copy of the executed disclosure form for at least three years.

Lead-based Paint Disclosure after Contract Acceptance

The rules state: "[i]f any of the disclosure activities . . . occurs after the purchaser or lessee has provided an offer to purchase or lease the housing, the seller or lessor shall complete the required disclosure activities prior to accepting the purchaser's or lessee's offer and allow the purchaser or lessee an opportunity to review the information and possibly amend the offer." (24 CFR Part 35, Subpart H, §35.88(b); 40 CFR Part 745, Subpart F §745.107; *see also,* 61 FR 9064). However, there are times when the necessary lead-based paint disclosures are not even available until after contract acceptance. Therefore, the required timing of the disclosures was an industry problem for some time.

AAR worked closely with NAR's legal counsel to draft contract language that would accommodate the concerns of the EPA in such an event. This issue is addressed by HUD and the EPA in Part III of the *Interpretive Guidance for the Real Estate Community on the Requirements for Disclosure of Information Concerning Lead-based Paint in Housing* (August 2, 2000). The *Interpretive Guidance* contains questions and answers concerning the lead-based paint disclosure requirements and confirms that the lead-based paint disclosure information can be provided to the buyer after contract acceptance if the buyer has the unilateral right to cancel the contract after receipt of the disclosures. Therefore, either lead-based paint disclosure option in the AAR Resale Contract should be acceptable to the EPA and HUD. However, it is always best to provide the buyer with the disclosure before a contract is executed, if at all possible.

Use of MLS Lead-based Paint Disclosure Forms

Upon listing target housing for sale, some Multiple Listing Services require the listing agent to have the seller prepare and sign all of the appropriate lead-based paint disclosure forms. All of the required disclosure information is input into the MLS with the notation that the seller's and listing agent's original signatures are on file. The electronic lead-based paint disclosure is therefore available to any MLS participant who searches that particular listing. Thus, before any buyer submits an offer on the target housing, the buyer can receive and sign this MLS lead-based paint disclosure form.

The EPA has indicated that such MLS electronic lead-based paint disclosures are acceptable as long as: (1) the buyer receives and signs the completed lead-based paint disclosure form "before the point of obligation"; and (2) the buyer's agent obtains a copy of the original disclosure form signed by the seller from the listing broker and attaches it to the form signed by the buyer. The two lead-based paint disclosures must "add up" to a single completed form for the file. In other words, although it is permissible to get the disclosure signed in this manner, brokers must still have a complete disclosure in the file signed by both the seller and the buyer.

For example, when dealing with target housing the following steps should be followed:

- The listing agent should have the seller complete and sign the lead-based paint disclosure form when the listing agreement is executed.
- The listing agent should sign the lead-based paint disclosure form and input the disclosures in the MLS.
- The buyer's agent should print the MLS lead-based paint disclosure form with the listing information.
- Before the buyer submits an offer: (a) the buyer and the buyer's agent should sign the MLS lead-based paint disclosure form, (b) check line 146 in the AAR Resale Contract, initial line 152, check that the lead-based paint disclosure is included as an addendum on line 26, and (c) attach the disclosure to the offer.
- Upon acceptance of the offer, the listing agent should attach a copy of the lead-based paint disclosure form containing the signatures of the seller and listing agent and deliver the signed contract with both disclosures attached to the buyer's agent.
- Both the listing broker and the buyer's broker should retain copies of the executed lead-based paint disclosure forms in their respective files.

The MLS lead-based paint disclosure form available when an MLS listing is printed allows the lead-based paint disclosure to be made to the buyer before contract acceptance, but does not satisfy the requirement for having signatures of all parties on the lead-based paint disclosure form in the files of both brokers. The EPA has indicated that it is permissible to have these electronic disclosures signed in counterpart (signatures on separate completed lead-based paint disclosure forms) provided that both the listing broker and the buyer's broker retain copies of the lead-based paint disclosure forms containing signatures of all parties.

Penalties for Violations

The EPA and HUD issued *Guidelines for Assessments of Civil Penalties for Violations of the Disclosure Rule,* which addresses violations of the disclosure requirements and provides procedures to determine the appropriate enforcement response to violations. No warnings will be given. Immediate civil penalties will be issued. Responsible parties include listing brokers, selling brokers, buyer's brokers, real estate brokerage firms, and property management firms. This guideline also contains a matrix of different types of violations and the suggested penalties. In addition to civil sanctions, a person who knowingly or willfully violates this law is subject to criminal sanctions. (15 USC §2615(b)). These sanctions include imprisonment for not more than one year and criminal fines of $25,000 for each day of violation.

Exempted Properties

The following properties are excluded from the lead-based paint disclosure requirements:
- property constructed after 1977
- housing for elderly (retirement communities composed of persons over the age of 62) or disabled housing unless a child under the age of six years will reside therein
- foreclosure transactions
- short-term leases (100 days or less where no renewal or extension can occur)
- lease renewals where the disclosures were previously made and no new information since the initial disclosure was provided
- purchase, sale or servicing of mortgages
- sale or lease of zero-bedroom dwellings

61 FR 9064 at Section IV(A).

Landlords are also obligated to make these lead-based paint disclosures before the tenant is obligated under a lease agreement. The AAR *Disclosure of Information on Lead-based Paint and Lead-based Paint Hazards (Rentals)* may be used for this purpose. However, the act does not

require that tenants be given an opportunity to conduct a lead-risk assessment or inspection. Further, landlords may have their properties certified
lead-free by an approved lead paint inspector.

Polybutylene Plumbing

Sellers with homes containing polybutylene plumbing pipes should
disclose that fact in writing to potential buyers. Any buyer considering purchasing a home containing polybutylene plumbing pipes should
obtain a professional inspection of the pipes. Sellers and buyers should
also be made aware that funds may be available in certain circumstances
to offset the cost of replacing these pipes.

Polybutylene plumbing is flexible plastic plumbing pipe with plastic or
metal fittings. Several million homes built or replumbed between January
1, 1978 and July 31, 1995, are plumbed with either polybutylene plumbing
and/or yard service lines. Although not all polybutylene plumbing has
been a problem, two class action settlements, *Cox v. Shell* and *Spencer v.
Dupont*, have been entered into to compensate owners who have experienced polybutylene plumbing leaks.

Under the terms of the *Cox* settlement, class members who have
qualifying plumbing leaks may be entitled to unreimbursed leak expenses
and plumbing replacement. The *Cox* settlement applies to homes where
the polybutylene pipes were installed between January 1, 1978 and July
31, 1995. The *Cox* settlement requires the occurrence of a qualifying leak
to be eligible for relief. For mobile homes and yard lines, the leaks must
occur within 10 years, and the claim must be filed within 11 years after
the date of installation. For site-built homes with plastic insert fittings,
the leak must occur within 13 years, and the claim must be filed within
14 years after the date of installation. For site-built homes with metal fittings, the leaks must occur within 16 years, and the claim must be filed
within 17 years after the date of installation.

Under the terms of the *Spencer* settlement, class members may be reim-
bursed 10 percent of leak expenses and 10 percent of plumbing replacement
costs for leaks, if the pipes were replaced. The *Spencer* class action includes

homes that were plumbed inside using polybutylene plumbing connected with acetyl plastic insert fittings. The homeowner must own or have owned a home with the polybutylene system and must have had it replumbed in order to be considered for reimbursement under the *Spencer* settlement. Generally, the *Spencer* settlement will reimburse qualified class members if the plumbing system is replaced within 15 years of its installation.

Stigmatized Property

Pursuant to A.R.S. §32-2156, sellers, lessors and brokers are not obligated to make certain disclosures. The statute states:

A. No criminal, civil or administrative action may be brought against a transferor or lessor of real property or a licensee for failing to disclose that the property being transferred or leased is or has been:

   1. The site of a natural death, suicide or homicide or any other crime classified as a felony.

   2. Owned or occupied by a person exposed to the human immunodeficiency virus or diagnosed as having the acquired immune deficiency syndrome or any other disease that is not known to be transmitted through common occupancy of real estate.

   3. Located in the vicinity of a sex offender.

B. Failing to disclose any fact or suspicion as set forth in subsection A shall not be grounds for termination or rescission of any transaction in which real property has been or will be transferred or leased.

Nonetheless, if a buyer asks a seller about one of these issues, the seller cannot lie. The seller must respond with the truth or refuse to respond based on the statute.

Compensation Sharing Disclosure

R4-28-701 requires that: "[a] real estate broker shall disclose to all the parties in a transaction, in writing before closing, the name of each employing broker who represents a party to the transaction and who will receive compensation from the transaction."

KEY POINTS TO REMEMBER

- If a broker has knowledge of a material defect, the broker must disclose it in writing.

- Buyers and sellers should be educated about their specific disclosure duties.

- An Affidavit of Disclosure must be provided to the buyer on all transactions of one to five parcels in an unincorporated area of the county, if the property is not in a subdivision.

- Federal law requires specific lead-based paint disclosures on homes constructed prior to 1978.

- Although the Stigmatized Property Act does not obligate the seller or brokers to disclose certain issues such as a death or felony on the property, a seller or broker must answer truthfully or state that the information will not be disclosed if the buyer inquires.

CHAPTER 15

Escrow and Title Issues

ESCROW INSTRUCTIONS

An escrow is primarily a conveyancing device designed to carry out the terms of a binding contract of sale previously entered into by the parties. *Higgins v. Kittleson,* 1 Ariz. App. 244, 249, 401 P.2d 412, 417 (1965). The purchase contract is often used as escrow instructions. For example, the AAR contracts specify that they are to be used as escrow instructions. Nonetheless, an escrow company often requests the parties to execute supplemental instructions. If the contract is not used as escrow instructions, the escrow company will generally provide a preprinted escrow instruction form. If escrow instructions are provided by the escrow company, either in whole or in part, the parties should read the instructions carefully and strike any undesirable provisions.

Escrow instructions are "designed to carry out the terms of a binding contract of sale previously entered into by the parties." *Young v. Bishop,* 88 Ariz. 140, 353 P.2d 1017 (1960). Consequently, escrow instructions cannot alter the terms of the underlying purchase contract "unless the parties specifically and clearly state such alteration or modification in writing with specific reference to the fact it changes the original contract." *Allan v. Martin,* 117 Ariz. 591, 574 P.2d 457 (1978).

An escrow agent must comply with the terms of the escrow instructions. *Tucson Title Insurance Co. v. D'Ascoli,* 94 Ariz. 234, 236, 383 P.2d 119, 121 (1963). An escrow agent that fails to follow the escrow instructions breaches its contract, and the parties to the escrow may recover any resulting damages. *Burkons v. Ticor Title Ins. Co.,* 168 Ariz. 345, 813 P.2d 710 (1991). If there is a question as to the intention of the parties, the escrow agent has a duty to contact the buyer and seller for clarification. *Id.* Further, if the escrow agent is aware of facts and circumstances that a reasonable escrow agent would perceive as evidence of fraud, then the escrow agent has a duty to disclose. *Id.* The title/escrow industry is regulated by the Arizona Department of Financial Institutions for escrow services and the Arizona Department of Insurance for title operations.

CLOSING PROTECTION LETTER

The escrow company may be only the agent for the actual title insurer, who is liable for the financial backing for the title insurance. This is often the case when the escrow company name includes the term "agency." The AAR contracts require that if the escrow company is not the title insurer, that the title insurer provide a closing protection letter indemnifying the parties for any losses due to fraudulent acts or breach of escrow instructions by the escrow company.

Additionally, A.R.S. §6-841.02 requires an escrow agent that is a title insurance agent to disclose to a residential buyer and seller that the title insurer may offer a closing protection letter that provides protection for the loss of escrow monies due to fraud or dishonesty of the escrow agent. If an escrow agent does not make the disclosure, the title insurer must reimburse the buyer or seller, as applicable, for any escrow monies that are lost and that are not recovered from the Arizona escrow recovery fund established by A.R.S. §6-847.01.

TITLE COMMITMENT

The AAR contracts require the escrow company to obtain and distribute to the buyer a Commitment for Title Insurance form together with complete and legible copies of all documents that will remain as exceptions to the buyer's policy of title insurance (title commitment). Pursuant to the AAR contract, the buyer has an opportunity after receipt of the title commitment to provide notice to the seller of any of the exceptions disapproved. Buyer's brokers can reduce their liability and experience fewer problems during escrow by promptly reviewing the title commitment with the buyer.

Important Information in the Title Commitment

Before issuing the title commitment, the title company issuing the title insurance policy will perform a title search on the property. The results of the title search that may be an issue in the transaction will be included in the title commitment. Thus, the title commitment may contain important disclosure issues, such as:

- easements
- CC&Rs and other deed restrictions
- access problems
- whether the property is in the vicinity of a military airport
- prior leases

The title commitment may also reveal problems that could delay the close of escrow, such as:

- court orders/divorce decrees
- probate issues
- foreclosures
- bankruptcies
- judgment liens
- state and federal tax liens
- environmental liens
- other matters of record affecting title

Understanding the Title Commitment

The title commitment is divided into several sections: Schedule A, Schedule B exceptions, Requirements, and Exclusions, and should be accompanied by the "underlying documents." The underlying documents are copies of the actual documents referred to in Schedule B.

Schedule A: Schedule A sets forth the search date, the amount of insurance coverage, the name of the insured, and the legal description of the property being insured. Check the policy to be issued in Schedule A of the title commitment to insure that the best policy type available will be issued. The American Land Title Association (ALTA) Homeowner's Title Insurance Policy is generally considered the best available for residential transactions.

Schedule B: Schedule B may be the most important part of the title commitment, but buyers are often unaware that they need to read the exceptions to coverage. Schedule B lists the specific exceptions from coverage that the title company discovered during its title search. It also generally includes certain standard exceptions such as mineral and water rights. The title insurance policy will not insure against loss, nor will the title insurer pay costs, attorney fees, or expenses, resulting from title problems listed in Schedule B. Additional boilerplate exceptions coverage may be contained in an addendum to the commitment. Buyers should carefully review Schedule B of the title commitment for disclosure items and for restrictions on the use of the property.

The broker should refer the buyer to the escrow officer or an attorney if there are questions or concerns about the exceptions in Schedule B. If an exception is unacceptable to the buyer, the broker may be able to convince the title company to eliminate the exception by obtaining a release, affidavit, waiver, quit claim deed or other document. The title insurance company may also be willing to delete some Schedule B exceptions if the problem is further explained or cured before closing. Or, the buyer may be able to obtain an endorsement so that the title policy will cover any damages arising from the defect.

Requirements: The requirements section lists what things must be done before escrow can close and title insurance will be issued. If a requirement cannot be met, close of escrow may be prevented or delayed. The common requirements include the payment of taxes, recording a release and reconveyance of the deed of trust currently encumbering the property, recording the deed, and recording the deed of trust securing the new loan. Other requirements may include approval by the trustee in bankruptcy, recording a disclaimer deed from a spouse, redemption of a certificate of purchase for past-due taxes, recording a court order evidencing the authority for one person to act on another's behalf, and releases of various other types of liens. Talk to the escrow officer about fulfilling any unusual requirements as soon as possible to avoid a delay in close of escrow.

Exclusions: There are also standard exclusions from the title insurance policy, including generally:

- any law, ordinance or governmental regulation relating to the use of the property
- any governmental police power, unless recorded
- rights of eminent domain, unless recorded
- defects, liens, encumbrances, adverse claims or other matters agreed to by the buyer
- claims arising from bankruptcy or other creditors' rights laws

Specific Title Commitment Issues

Easements: An easement gives persons other than the owner access to or a right-of-way over the homeowner's property. Common easements include utility easements and roadway or access easements. Easements may be an issue if the buyer is planning on building a pool or adding improvements to the home. An easement may have a wide sweeping affect on a property, for example, if the property is subject to railroad or similar easement. Many times railroad and similar easements affect the entire parcel and are not confined to any particular section or area.

CC&Rs and Other Deed Restrictions: A declaration of covenants, conditions and restrictions (CC&Rs) for a homeowner's association may be recorded against the property. The CC&Rs empower the homeowner's association, if there is one, to control certain aspects of the home. If there is no homeowner's association, the CC&Rs can be enforced by the other homeowners. A homebuyer should always carefully read the CC&Rs (and any other association documents) because the buyer will be obligated to comply with all the rules and restrictions. Use the CC&Rs table of contents to point out the section on use restrictions to the buyer. Explain to the buyer in a new home transaction that the CC&Rs must be reviewed before signing the contract. In a resale transaction, the AAR Resale Contract allows the buyer five days to review and disapprove of the CC&Rs.

Access: Failure of the public record to disclose a right of access to the land will be noted in the title commitment. Although landlocked property can be sold (except in the case of subdivided land, A.R.S. §32-2185.02), the lack of access must be disclosed to the buyer.

Military Airports: To ensure disclosure to buyers in areas in the vicinity of a military airport, the ADRE is required to record a disclosure notice on all affected property. This disclosure notice should be reflected in the title commitment.

Judgments: A recorded judgment is a lien on all real property of the judgment debtor. A judgment lien against the seller usually must be paid prior to close of escrow.

Bankruptcy: If the seller has filed bankruptcy, the bankruptcy trustee will have to approve of the sale prior to close of escrow or a court order may be necessary. The seller's bankruptcy attorney should be able to assist in obtaining the approval, but be sure to allow enough time for the process.

Liens: There are numerous types of liens that may need to be paid and released before escrow can close. These liens may include state and federal tax liens. State tax liens are extinguished if the state takes no action for six years. By filing a Notice of Federal Tax Lien, the government establishes its interest in the property and any property acquired after the lien is filed. Mechanics liens and liens arising from environmental laws may also become an issue.

ENDORSEMENTS

In addition to the coverage available under the title insurance policy, a buyer can obtain additional coverage through endorsements. These endorsements may be available for little or no cost. For a list of available endorsements, visit the ALTA Web site or talk to the escrow officer.

THE TITLE INSURANCE POLICY

The title insurance policy will be issued as of close of escrow. Title insurance does not insure that a title defect will not occur; it insures that if a defect that occurred prior to the policy date becomes apparent, the buyer will be indemnified if the defect cannot be cured. A standard policy generally insures against the title to the property being vested other than stated in the policy; any defect in or lien or encumbrance on the title; unmarketability of title; and lack of a right of legal (not necessarily physical) access. The ALTA Homeowner's Title Insurance policy provides coverage for additional defects. The policy generally contains the same sections as the title commitment and includes:

- insuring provisions, which are the items the policy covers
- exclusions from coverage
- conditions and stipulations, which provide definitions, information on how to make a claim, and the title company's responsibility and options for handling a claim
- schedule A
- schedule B items excepted from coverage
- endorsements that provide additional coverage

FORMS OF HOLDING TITLE

As the AAR contracts all state, the manner in which a buyer takes title may have significant legal, estate planning and tax consequences. Therefore, a buyer should obtain legal and tax advice before determining how to take title. The buyer has until close of escrow to make this decision. The common ways to hold title are summarized as follows.

Tenancy in Common: Co-ownership where the parties have no survivorship rights. All grants of real property made to two or more persons create estates in common and not in joint tenancy, except grants or devises in trust, or to executors, or to husband and wife. A.R.S. §33-431(A).

Joint Tenancy with Right of Survivorship: Co-ownership in which upon the death of one co-owner the title automatically conveys to the surviving co-owner. A grant to two or more persons may, by express words, vest the estate in the survivor upon the death of a grantee or devisee when expressly declared in the grant, transfer or devise to be a joint tenancy with right of survivorship. An estate in joint tenancy with right of survivorship may also be created by grant or transfer from a sole owner to the owner and others, or from two or more owners to themselves or to one or more of them and others. A.R.S. §33-431(B).

Community Property: Co-ownership by married persons. Upon the death of one spouse, the deceased spouse's interest may be conveyed by will or intestate succession.

Community Property with Right of Survivorship: Co-ownership by spouses in which upon the death of one spouse, title to the property is vested in the surviving spouse. "A grant or devise to a husband and wife may by express words vest the estate in the surviving spouse on the death of one of the spouses when expressly declared in the grant, transfer or devise to be an estate in community property with right of survivorship. An estate in community property with right of survivorship may also be created by grant or transfer from a husband and wife, when holding title as community property or otherwise, to themselves or from either husband or wife to both husband and wife." A.R.S. §33-431(C).

Sole and Separate: Sole ownership of a property. A spouse may hold title as his or her sole and separate property, however, the spouse not on title must generally execute a disclaimer deed.

Entities: A properly formed partnership, corporation, or limited liability company may also hold title to real property.

DEEDS

The deed is the written document by which the seller, as grantor, transfers the property to the buyer, as grantee. The formal requirements for executing a deed may be found at A.R.S. §33-401, which requires written instrument signed and notarized by the grantor. However, a deed or conveyance containing any defect, omission or informality in the certificate of acknowledgment and which has been recorded for longer than 10 years in the office of the county recorder of the county in which the property is located is deemed to have been duly acknowledged on and after the date of its recording. A.R.S. §33-401(C). The language necessary for deed conveyances is set forth at A.R.S. §33-402.

Deeds should be recorded in the office of the county recorder in which the property is located. If a deed is not recorded, it is binding between the grantor and grantee, but void as to creditors and subsequent purchasers for valuable consideration without notice. A.R.S. §33-412.

There are several kinds of deeds, differing primarily in the covenant (promise) by the grantor. The most common forms of deeds are:

- *Warranty Deed or General Warranty Deed:* A grantor in a warranty deed warrants on behalf of the grantor, heirs and assigns, to convey clear title to the property. Pursuant to A.R.S. §33-435, "[i]f the word "grant" or the word "convey" is used in a conveyance by which an estate of inheritance or fee simple is to be passed, the following covenants and none other, on the part of the grantor for himself and his heirs, to the grantee and his heirs and assigns, are implied unless restrained by express terms contained in the conveyance: (1) [t]hat previous to the time of execution of the conveyance the grantor has not conveyed the same estate or any right, title or interest therein, to any person other than the grantee, and (2) [t]hat the estate is at the time of execution of the conveyance free from encumbrances," including taxes, assessments and all liens.

- **Special Warranty Deed:** A deed in which the grantor warrants the title only against defects arising during the period of the grantor's ownership of the property.
- **Quit Claim Deed:** A deed in which the grantor conveys whatever interest the grantor may have in the property, but the grantor does not warrant that the grantor has any interest.
- **Beneficiary Deed:** A deed that conveys an interest in real property to a grantee beneficiary that is only effective on the death of the owner. A.R.S. §33-405. A beneficiary deed may designate multiple grantees who take title as joint tenants with right of survivorship, tenants in common, a husband and wife as community property or as community property with right of survivorship, or any other tenancy that is valid under the laws of this state. A beneficiary deed may be revoked at any time by the owner by an executed and recorded revocation before the death of the owner. Pursuant to A.R.S. §33-405(K) a beneficiary deed is sufficient if it complies with other applicable laws, and if it is in substantially the following form:

  Beneficiary Deed

  I (we) _____ (owner) hereby convey to

  _____ (grantee beneficiary) effective on

  my (our) death the following described real property:

  (Legal description)_____

  (Signature of grantor(s))

  (Acknowledgment)

KEY POINTS TO REMEMBER

- The AAR contracts serve as escrow instructions.

- The title commitment and Schedule B documents contain important disclosures and should be reviewed carefully.

- The title commitment requirements may reveal problems that could delay close of escrow.

- The buyer should obtain legal and tax advice before determining how to take title.

- There are several kinds of deeds, differing primarily in the promise made by the seller/grantor.

CHAPTER 16

Due Diligence

The more informed a buyer is about the property being purchased, the less likely the buyer will make an objectionable discovery or assert a claim after close of escrow. The type of due diligence that a buyer undertakes will vary depending on the type of property. However, regardless of the type of property, a buyer should conduct all desired inspections and investigations of the property before being bound to purchase the property. In most residential resale, commercial and vacant land transactions, the contract will provide for a "due diligence" contingency period in which to perform all desired inspections and investigations. In new home sales, the buyer will generally have no contingency period after entering into the contract; therefore, all possible due diligence items should be undertaken before signing a contract. Some of the more common due diligence items include document review, governmental inquiries and physical inspections.

DOCUMENT REVIEW

Title Commitment

The title commitment reflects the condition of title as of the time and date the commitment is issued. Upon receiving the commitment, the buyer should read Schedule B, which lists the specific items of record that the title examiner has determined to be encumbering the property and are therefore exceptions and exclusions from coverage. The buyer should also review all of the documents listed in Schedule B of the commitment, which may include easements, patents, deeds, and liens. If these items are not cleared from the title, they will not be covered by the title insurance policy, and the buyer will take title subject to these items. The chapter on title insurance contains a more detailed discussion of the title commitment. The title commitment is discussed in greater detail in chapter 15.

Conditions, Covenants & Restrictions (CC&Rs)

If the property is subject to deed restrictions or located in a homeowner's association (HOA), condominium complex or planned community, the buyer, must read the CC&Rs and other governing documents. Many CC&Rs contain a table of contents, which is a good place to start a review of the document. The CC&Rs are likely divided into various sections, such as: definitions, developer's rights, use restrictions, easements, membership, voting rights, assessments, fees, penalties, maintenance responsibility, and insurance. At a minimum, a buyer must thoroughly understand the use restrictions, since these will affect the buyer's day-to-day use of the property. At times there are questions about the scope of a restriction or whether a restriction has been waived. The buyer should be encouraged to clarify these issues with the HOA, management company, or legal counsel. Additionally, the buyer should determine what fees must be paid upon transfer.

Seller's Property Disclosure Statement (SPDS)

Most resale sellers will provide an AAR SPDS. This document poses a variety of questions for the seller to answer about the property and its condition. Many specific disclosure issues are listed on the form, and additional information is provided to assist the buyer in obtaining all desired information. The residential resale SPDS is discussed in greater detail in chapter 8.

Public Report (Subdivisions)

The purpose of this document is to point out material information about the development. The public report is required to be given to buyers by the subdivider of a new home subdivision, and a new home buyer should thoroughly review the public report before signing any contract. A public report is also required when selling unsubdivided lands, which are land or lands divided or proposed to be divided into six or more lots or parcels, 36 acres or more each, but less than 160 acres each. A resale buyer may also benefit from reviewing the public report, even though some of the information may be outdated. The public report and other subdivision issues are discussed in chapter 9.

Affidavit of Disclosure

If the buyer is purchasing five or fewer parcels of land other than subdivided land in an unincorporated area of a county, the seller is required by law to provide the buyer with an Affidavit of Disclosure. Although, much of the property in unincorporated areas is vacant land, the statute states that the requirement applies to "land, other than subdivided land" and the term "land" is undefined. Additionally, the statute refers to the land as "property" and "parcel." Therefore, the statute should be interpreted to apply to all land (sold in five or fewer parcels, other than subdivided land) in an unincorporated area, whether the land is vacant, residential or commercial. For additional information about the affidavit see chapter 14.

Economic Investigation

The commercial buyer will generally want to perform an economic investigation of the property. The buyer will want to review all financial statements, copies of any rent rolls, lists of deposits, personal property lists, leases, rental agreements, and service contracts relating to the property. The buyer will also want to insure that no tenant on the property is the subject of a bankruptcy, probate or insolvency proceeding and obtain estoppel agreements from all tenants at close of escrow.

PHYSICAL INSPECTION

Home or Property Inspections

When dealing with residential property, regardless of whether the home is new or a resale, a qualified home inspector should be retained. At a minimum, a home inspector will perform an inspection and submit a written report that specifies any systems and components that need repair, monitoring or evaluation by other professionals. The buyer should carefully review this report with the inspector and ask the inspector about any item of concern. When dealing with commercial property, a qualified engineer is probably the best choice of inspectors. The buyer may also want to conduct other specialized property inspections.

Home inspectors must be certified by the Board of Technical Registration. A.R.S. §32-122.02. A home inspector will perform a visual physical examination of readily accessible installed systems and components listed in *The Standards of Professional Practice for Arizona Home Inspectors.* R4-30-301.01. The Arizona Standards of Practice are adopted from the American Society of Home Inspectors (ASHI) 1992 Standards of Practice, through the Arizona Chapter of the American Society of Home Inspectors and are available on the Board of Technical Registration Web site.

The inspector will submit a written report that describes the systems and components and specify any systems and components that are in need of immediate major repair and any recommendations to correct, monitor or evaluate by appropriate professionals.

Pursuant to the standards, inspectors are not required to report on:
- the life expectancy of any component or system
- the causes of the need for a major repair
- the methods, materials and costs of corrections
- the suitability of the property for any specialized use
- compliance or noncompliance with applicable regulatory requirements
- the market value of the property or its marketability
- the advisability or inadvisability of purchase of the property

- any component or system that was not observed
- the presence or absence of pests such as wood-damaging organisms, rodents, or insects
- cosmetic items, underground items, or items not permanently installed

The buyer should carefully review this report with the inspector and ask the inspector about any item of concern. Pay attention to the scope of the inspection and any portions of the property excluded from the inspection.

Wood-destroying Insects and Other Wood-destroying Organisms

Termites are commonly found in some parts of Arizona, and a termite inspection is a common lender requirement. Investigating evidence of termites or other wood infestation is the job of the pest control inspector. The Structural Pest Control Commission regulates these inspectors pursuant to A.R.S. §32-2301; A.A.C. R4-29-101 *et. seq.* The Structural Pest Control Commission can also provide the buyer with information regarding past termite treatments to the property. A Wood-destroying Insect Inspection Report (WDIIR) is a document prepared by a licensed pest control business that details any termite damage or presence. The WDIIR's first page provides basic information about the inspection such as whether there were any obstructions or areas inaccessible to inspection and whether there is visible evidence of infestation or previous treatment. The second page of the WDIIR identifies areas of concern and contains a space for the inspector to draw the property with these details. Additional information may be obtained at the Structural Pest Control Commission Web site.

A structural fungi inspection report is also available. A fungi inspection report reflects evidence of the existence or absence of fungi (mold) that was visible and accessible on the inspection date.

Pool Barriers

Arizona state law requires an enclosure surrounding a swimming pool (defined as a body of water that is 18 inches or more in depth at any point, is wider than eight feet and is intended for swimming) on residential property. A.R.S. §36-1681. However, the statute allows cities and counties to adopt their own ordinances, provided that the ordinance is equal to or more stringent than the provisions of the statute. Ordinances vary widely between cities and counties. The buyer must investigate swimming pool barrier regulations so that the home can be in compliance when the buyer takes occupancy.

Sewer, Septic and Other On-site Wastewater Treatment Facilities

Even if the listing or SPDS indicates that the property is connected to a sewer, it should be verified by a plumber, home inspector, or other professional. Some counties and cities can perform this test as well. If the property has a septic tank or other on-site wastewater treatment facility, it must be inspected by a qualified inspector within six months prior to COE, pursuant to Arizona Department of Environmental Quality (ADEQ) Rule R18-9-A316. (For details of the rule's requirements, see chapter 7.)

Soil Conditions

Some areas of Arizona are subject to expansive soil, fissures, subsidence and other soil conditions. Properties built on such soils may experience significant movement causing a major problem. If it has been disclosed that the property is subject to any such soil conditions or if the buyer has any concerns about the soil condition or observes evidence of cracking, the buyer should secure an independent assessment of the property and its structural integrity by a professional engineer.

Environmental Concerns

The broad scope of environmental liability requires an environmental investigation if there is any indication of hazardous waste having been on the property. Generally, the first step in an environmental investigation is a Phase I Report. A Phase I investigation generally includes document review, investigation with governmental agencies, a site inspection of the property, interviews with individuals who have information on the history of the property and other sources of information. A Phase II report will depend upon the results of the Phase I Report and generally consist of soil and water sampling, tests and analysis. A Phase III Report is generally the remediation indicated by the Phase I and Phase II Reports.

In addition, a buyer may also wish to investigate indoor air quality. For example, mold growth in property has been an issue of concern in recent years. A mold inspection may be performed by a qualified environmental inspector. Radon and other air quality concerns may also be of concern to a buyer.

GOVERNMENTAL INQUIRIES

Building Code

If the home has been remodeled, the buyer should be encouraged to verify that the proper permits were obtained. Residential construction permits are needed when existing homes are remodeled or additions are made. For instance, in Phoenix, a permit is needed for improvements such as:

- room additions
- garage or carport conversions
- porch enclosures
- patio covers
- detached garages, sheds, gazebos or structures that are larger than 120 square feet in roof area
- fences or walls that are higher than six feet/retaining walls over four feet high
- installation or alteration of a driveway
- remodeling, repairs or additions that require electrical, mechanical, plumbing or structural changes

To determine whether the required permits were obtained for a home remodel or addition, the buyer should contact the city development services department. If the buyer determines that the proper permit was not obtained, the parties can work with the city to obtain the permit, assuming that the remodel or addition was performed in compliance with the then-existing code.

County Assessor/Tax Records

The county assessor's records contain a variety of valuable information including the assessed value of the property for tax purposes and some of the physical aspects of the property, such as the reported square footage (which should always be verified for accuracy).

Flood Plain Status

If the property is in a flood zone, an additional annual insurance premium of several hundred dollars may be required. If the property is in an area deemed high risk, the buyer may be required by the lender to obtain flood hazard insurance through the National Flood Insurance Program. The location of a property in a flood plain will also have an effect on the availability of a building permit.

Water/Well Issues

If the buyer intends to use water from a well, springs, lakes, ponds, reservoirs, canyons or ravines, the buyer should investigate current water use laws. Arizona is undertaking general stream adjudication of both the Gila River and the Little Colorado River systems to determine the extent and priority of the associated water rights. All affected property transfers should include an Assignment of Claimant form from the seller to the buyer.

If the property is served by a well, the buyer should also investigate the adequacy of the water and any potability problems. The buyer should investigate any problems with the water pressure and all well equipment. Finally, the buyer should insure that the well is registered and review copies of all Department of Water Resources records related to the well.

If the property is served by a private water company or a municipal water provider the Arizona Department of Water Resources may not have made a water supply determination and the buyer should contact the water provider for information.

Freeway Construction

A buyer may be concerned about future road construction. The Arizona Department of Transportation maps indicate the nearest future freeway routes and roads in the area slated for widening.

Crime Statistics

A buyer may want to investigate the crime statistics in the area. Some statistics are available online. In other instances that buyer may need to visit or call the local law enforcement agencies to obtain the crime statistics in the area.

Military and Public Airports

There are many statutes with the purpose of preserving military bases and granting authority to the appropriate governing body dealing with encroachment. To ensure disclosure to prospective buyers in these areas, public report disclosures are specified, and the ADRE is required to record a disclosure notice on all affected property. Cities and counties are also required to identify the boundaries of these areas in their general or comprehensive plan. Maps for military and public airports may be accessed through the ADRE Web site.

Surveys

The buyer should consider verifying the boundaries and acreage of the property. This information may be obtained by a survey conducted by a licensed surveyor in accordance with the State Board of Technical Registration's *Arizona Land Boundary Survey Minimum Standards.*

Development Investigation

Lands proposed to be divided for purposes of sale or lease are subject to state, county and municipal regulation. If the buyer intends to split the land, the buyer should investigate the laws and regulations relating to the division or splitting of property. The buyer should also determine water availability, the suitability of the property for installation of an on-site wastewater disposal system, the cost of providing other utilities, soil condition, and a host of other issues.

KEY POINTS TO REMEMBER

- The more due diligence performed by the buyer, the less likely the buyer will make an objectionable discovery after close of escrow.

- Buyers should be educated about what documents to review, when they should be reviewed and why.

- Buyers should always obtain a general property inspection and any other specific inspections warranted.

- If the home has been remodeled, the buyer should determine whether the proper permits were obtained.

- Buyers should perform all due diligence during any due diligence inspection or contingencies period — and before executing a new home contract.

CHAPTER 17

Homeowner's Associations

Arizona, like many areas of the country, has experienced a dramatic increase in the number of homeowners associations (HOAs). A transaction involving a property in an HOA will involve additional buyer considerations, such as restrictions, rules, and transfer fees, for which the broker must be prepared. Additionally, the transaction will likely involve other challenges for the broker. Therefore, it is critical that brokers understand the basics of HOA law and anticipate these challenges to properly represent their clients.

Condominium and planned community HOAs are regulated by statute. A.R.S §33-1201 *et.seq.* (Condominiums); A.R.S. §33-1501 *et.seq.* (Planned Communities). The distinction between condominiums and planned communities involves the ownership of common areas. In a condominium community, each unit owner owns an undivided percentage ownership of the common area. In a planned community the common area is owned by the HOA.

These condominium and planned community statutes govern matters such as the penalties an HOA may impose, meeting and record requirements, liens, and required disclosures on the resale of a home. Additionally, there are statutes regulating HOA lawsuits related to dwelling design, construction, condition and sale. A.R.S §12-1361 *et.seq.* Developments that have mandatory HOA membership but do not contain any common areas do not fall within the statutory definition of either condominiums or planned communities.

In most of these developments, restrictive covenants are recorded against the property, commonly referred to as Covenants, Conditions and Restrictions (CC&Rs), which empower the HOA to control certain aspects of property use within the development, often including oversight and approval authority over the construction of new homes and alterations of existing ones. When a person buys a home in such a development, the person receives a copy of the CC&Rs and agrees to be bound by their terms. The CC&Rs form an enforceable contract between the homeowners as a whole and the individual homeowners. Buyers should be mindful that the CC&Rs may be lengthy. HOAs may from time to time amend the CC&Rs and oftentimes those amendments are attached at the end of what can be a bulky document. Buyers should be advised to use any table of contents to focus on use restrictions and other issues of particular concern, but to carefully review every page.

In exercising control over an individual's property, the courts have traditionally held HOAs to a standard of reasonableness and good faith. If the HOA acts reasonably based on the CC&Rs, the courts will uphold the HOA decision. As in all situations, reasonableness may depend on the circumstances. For example, in *Makeever v. Lyle,* 125 Ariz. 384, 389, 609 P.2d 1084, 1089 (App. 1980), the HOA allowed an owner to expand his condo into the common area. The *Makeever* court ruled against the HOA and held that although the HOA had broad powers, allowing the unauthorized taking of the common property was unreasonable. However, in *Heritage Heights Home Owners Ass'n. v. Esser,* 115 Ariz. 330, 334, 565 P.2d 207, 211 (App. 1977), the court held that the HOA's decision to allow those who had no prior knowledge of CC&Rs violation time to comply, while strictly enforcing CC&Rs against those who knowingly violated CC&Rs, was reasonable.

Further, in *Powell v. Washburn,* 211 Ariz. 553, 125 P.3d 373 (2006), the court indicated that CC&Rs will be interpreted to give effect to the intention of the parties as determined from the language of the document in its entirety and the purpose for which the covenants were created. In *Arizona Biltmore Estates Ass'n v. Tezak,* 177 Ariz. 447, 449, 868 P.2d 1030, 1032 (App. 1993), the court addressed the intention of the parties in creating the CC&Rs. In this case, an HOA successfully brought an action against a property owner to prevent the property owner from parking a large bus on their property. Although the CC&Rs at issue did not specifically prohibit buses, the court found that the bus fell within the type of vehicles the CC&Rs were intended to restrict.

HOA DISPUTES

The condominium and planned community hearing office has been established to address disputes between an owner and a condominium association or planned community association. A.R.S. 41-2198 *et. seq.* An owner or the HOA may petition for a hearing concerning violations of condominium documents or planned community documents or violations of the statutes that regulate condominiums or planned communities.

PLANNED COMMUNITIES — RESALE DISCLOSURES

A "planned community" is defined as a development that "includes real estate owned and operated by a nonprofit corporation or unincorporated association of owners that is created for the purpose of managing, maintaining or improving the property and in which the owners of separately owned lots, parcels or units are mandatory members and are required to pay assessments to the association for these purposes." A.R.S. §33-1802(4).

By statute, within 10 days after receipt of a written notice of a pending sale, the homeowners' association (if the association has 50 or more units) or the seller (if the association has less than 50 units) must provide in writing to the buyer certain information.

Information required by law to be provided upon resale include:
- a copy of the bylaws and the rules of the association

- a copy of the declaration of CC&Rs
- a dated statement containing:
    - the telephone number and address of a principal contact for the association, which may be an association manager, an association management company, an officer of the association or any other person designated by the board of directors.
    - the amount of the common regular assessment and the unpaid common regular assessment, special assessment or other assessment, fee or charge currently due and payable from the seller
    - a statement as to whether a portion of the unit is covered by insurance maintained by the association
    - the total amount of money held by the association as reserves
    - if the statement is being furnished by the association, a statement as to whether the records of the association reflect any alterations or improvements to the unit that violate the declaration. The association is not obligated to provide information regarding alterations or improvements that occurred more than six years before the proposed sale. Seller remains obligated to disclose alterations or improvements to the premises that violate the declaration. The association may take action against the buyer for violations apparent at the time of purchase that are not reflected in the association's records.
    - if the statement is being furnished by the seller, a statement as to whether the seller has any knowledge of any alterations or improvements to the unit that violate the declaration
    - a statement of case names and case numbers for pending litigation with respect to the premises or the association
- a copy of the current operating budget of the association
- a copy of the most recent annual financial report of the association. If the report is more than 10 pages, the association may provide a summary of the report in lieu of the entire report
- a copy of the most recent reserve study of the association, if any

- any other information required by law
- a statement that provides "I hereby acknowledge that the declaration, bylaws and rules of the association constitute a contract between the association and me (the purchaser). By signing this statement, I acknowledge that I have read and understand the association's contract with me (the purchaser). I also understand that as a matter of Arizona law, if I fail to pay my association assessments, the association may foreclose on my property." The statement shall also include a signature line for the purchaser and shall be returned to the association within 14 calendar days. A.R.S. §33-1806

CONDOMINIUMS — RESALE DISCLOSURES

A "condominium" is a complex "portions of which are designated for separate ownership and the remainder of which is designated for common ownership solely by the owners of the separate portions." A complex is not a condominium unless the undivided interests in the common elements are vested in the unit owners. A.R.S. §33-1202(10). The creation and management of condominiums is governed by A.R.S. §33-1201 *et. seq.*

A public report is required for the sale of a new condominium. A.R.S. §32-2101(55).

Specific statutory disclosures are required on the resale of a condominium. *Id.* By statute, within 10 days after receipt of a written notice of a pending sale, the HOA (if the association has 50 or more units) or the seller (if the association has less than 50 units) must provide in writing to the buyer certain information.

Information required by law to be provided upon resale include:

- a copy of the bylaws and the rules of the association
- a copy of the declaration CC&Rs
- a dated statement containing:
  - the telephone number and address of a principal contact for the association, which may be an association manager, an association management company, an officer of the association or any other person designated by the board of directors

- the amount of the common expense assessment for the unit and any unpaid common expense assessment, special assessment or other assessment, fee or charge currently due and payable from the selling unit owner
- a statement as to whether a portion of the unit is covered by insurance maintained by the association
- the total amount of money held by the association as reserves.
- if the statement is being furnished by the association, a statement as to whether the records of the association reflect any alterations or improvements to the unit that violate the declaration. The association is not obligated to provide information regarding alterations or improvements that occurred more than six years before the proposed sale
- if the statement is being furnished by the unit owner, a statement as to whether the unit owner has any knowledge of any alterations or improvements to the unit that violate the declaration
- a statement of case names and case numbers for pending litigation with respect to the unit filed by the association against the unit owner or filed by the unit owner against the association. The unit owner or the association is not required to disclose information concerning the pending litigation that would violate any applicable rule of attorney-client privilege under Arizona law
- a copy of the current operating budget of the association
- a copy of the most recent annual financial report of the association. If the report is more than 10 pages, the association may provide a summary of the report in lieu of the entire report
- a copy of the most recent reserve study of the association, if any
- a written statement: "I hereby acknowledge that the declaration, bylaws and rules of the association constitute a contract between the association and me (the purchaser). By signing this statement, I acknowledge that I have read and understand the

association's contract with me (the purchaser). I also understand that as a matter of Arizona law, if I fail to pay my association assessments, the association may foreclose on my property." The statement shall also include a signature line for the purchaser and shall be returned to the association within 14 calendar days. A.R.S. §33-1260(3)(H)

Restricting Condo Rentals

Some condo HOAs have amended their CC&Rs to eliminate rentals in the community. Such an amendment arguably requires unanimous consent. A.R.S. 33-1227(D) states:

Except to the extent expressly permitted . . . an amendment shall not create or increase special declarant rights, increase the number of units or change the boundaries of any unit, the allocated interests of a unit or the uses to which any unit is restricted, in the absence of unanimous consent of the unit owners."

This requirement for unanimous consent applies only to condos; the Planned Community Statutes have no similar provision.

BUYER CONSIDERATIONS WHEN PURCHASING A HOME LOCATED IN AN HOA

In addition to dues, fees and assessments, some of the other issues that a buyer should consider when purchasing a home in an HOA are:

- *The restrictions contained in the CC&Rs:* these restrictions may affect parking, pets, children, the ability to rent the property and a variety of other issues of importance to any homeowner.
- *Architectural restrictions:* these restrictions may prohibit certain alterations and improvements and/or require approval of others.
- *HOA rules and regulations:* rules and regulations generally govern the use of common areas as well as individually owned homes.

- *Financial health of the HOA:* there must be enough reserves to pay for the repair and maintenance of the common area.
- *CC&Rs violations:* any violations must be addressed prior to close of escrow.
- *Rental restrictions:* some HOAs restrict rentals or require approval of all tenants.
- *Management companies:* some HOAs are managed by management companies and some are not. HOA management companies are unregulated and their level of service and related fees vary.
- *New home/developer control:* issues regarding when control will be relinquished to the homeowner should be addressed, if applicable.
- *Restricting resale for a certain time after close of escrow:* antispeculation clauses are of particular importance to an investor or a buyer who intends to own the home for a short period of time.
- *Lawsuits between the HOA and developer/builder:* these lawsuits may be lengthy and expensive.

OTHER HOA TRANSACTIONAL CHALLENGES

For the brokers, handling a transaction for a home located in an HOA may raise unique transactional challenges, such as:

- *Locating the contact person:* in an attempt to address this issue, A.R.S. §33-1807(J) requires the HOA to record a notice with the contact information for the association, designated agent or management company for the association.
- *Obtaining the CC&Rs and other information in a timely manner:* HOAs often do not provide the necessary documents and disclosure within 10 days and a buyer may not receive these documents until just prior to COE. The listing broker should consider obtaining as much of the information as possible as soon as practical after listing the home for sale.
- *For Sale signs:* the type/size/color of for sale signs in the HOA may be restricted. Therefore, additional marketing may be needed.

FEES RELATED TO THE TRANSFER OF A PROPERTY IN AN HOA

There are often fees that must be paid upon the transfer of a property in an HOA. Most HOAs charge fees to produce the statutorily required disclosures. The statute allows the HOA to charge "reasonable" fees, but the amounts vary greatly depending on the association.

There are often other fees related to the transfer of the home as well. These fees can amount to thousands of dollars and are referred to by a variety of names, such as asset preservation fees, capitol reserve fees, etc. An informal survey reflects the following examples of fees charged by different HOAs across the state:

- *Phoenix:* percentage of the sales price, such as one-half of one percent of the sales price ($5,000 on a million dollar home)
- *Tucson:* "buyer's transfer fees" in the $1,200–1,300 range, working capital contribution" and "transfer process fees," which may be in the $400–$650 range, "capital preservation fees" and "community enhancement fees" as high as three-quarters of one percent of the sales price
- *Flagstaff:* Transfer fee $750
- *Sun City:* Capital preservation fee $2,100; Resale transfer fee $300
- *Sun City West:* Asset preservation fee $1700; Resale transfer fee $180; Resale disclosure packet fee $75
- *Surprise:* CARE fee $525; Resale transfer fee $100; Resale disclosure statement fee $100
- *Prescott:* Transfer fee $100–$300; Reserve fund $300–$500; Working capital $300–$500; ARC Review fees $300–$2500
- *Peoria:* Transfer fee $638–$800; resale statement fee $300; City property management fee $100; Capital preservation fee $638.31; Front yard grass assessment $120/year; Reserve fund $690

Therefore, whether acting as a listing broker or buyer's broker, it is imperative to find out what fees are due and payable at close of escrow and discuss these fees with the client before submitting or accepting an offer to ensure that the client is not surprised by substantial unanticipated fees at close of escrow.

AAR HOA CONDOMINIUM/PLANNED COMMUNITY ADDENDUM

The AAR HOA Condominium/Planned Community Addendum is designed to be used in residential resale transactions involving property in an HOA. The form provides a notice to both the seller and the buyer that an HOA may require varying fees, deposits or other payments at close of escrow and that these fees may be labeled as community reserve, asset preservation, capitol reserve, working capital, community enhancement or future improvement fees, payments, deposits, or otherwise. The addendum addresses which party will be responsible for paying any HOA dues, fees, and assessments related to the sale. The form language provides that any inspection or certification fee charged by the HOA will be paid by the seller.

The addendum also obligates the seller to notify the HOA of the pending sale or to make the required disclosures, depending on the size of the association. For reference purposes, the form includes a list of the information required by statute to be provided to the buyer. The buyer is allowed five days after receipt of the HOA information to provide the seller notice of any items disapproved.

KEY POINTS TO REMEMBER

- The restrictions contained in the CC&Rs are generally enforceable.

- A buyer should always read the CC&Rs, especially the use restrictions, before signing a new home contract and within five days of receipt on a resale (using the AAR Resale Contract).

- The HOA (or seller) is required by law to provide the buyer with certain information upon resale of a home in a planned community or condominium complex.

- There may be substantial fees due upon the sale of a home in an HOA of which the parties should be aware before entering a purchase contract.

- If the resale home is in an HOA, always include the AAR HOA Addendum in the AAR Resale Contract.

CHAPTER 18

Claims and Remedies

BREACH OF CONTRACT

Most real estate transactions are completed without dispute. However, there are times when one party or the other refuses to perform due to anxiety, stress, financial issues or other factors that are outside the parties' contractual agreement. In such a case, the nonperforming party is in breach of contract. A breach of contract is a nonperformance of a contractual duty, or in other words, a broken promise. A breach may be a violation of any of the terms or conditions of a contract without legal excuse.

There are other times, when a party indicates that the party will not perform a contractual obligation before the time for performance is due. For example, when a seller states two weeks before the close of escrow date, that he or she will not close escrow on the agreed upon date. This is known as an anticipatory breach of contract. An anticipatory breach of contract occurs when the party expresses a positive and unequivocal manifestation not to render the required performance when it is due. *See, Oldenburger v. Del Webb,* 159 Ariz. 129, 765 P.2d 531 (1988); *Kammert Bros. Enterprises, Inc. v. Tanque Verde Plaza Co.,* 102 Ariz. 301, 428 P.2d 678 (1967). A mere implication that a party will not perform is not sufficient to constitute an anticipatory breach of contract. *Rancho Pescado, Inc. v. Northwestern Mutual Life Ins. Co.*, 140 Ariz. 174, 680 P.2d 1235 (App. 1984).

REMEDIES FOR BREACH OF CONTRACT

The specific remedies for a breach of contract may be set forth in the contract. All AAR contracts contain a remedies section, which sets forth the parties rights and obligations. These contracts also contain alternative dispute provisions for dispute resolution.

Upon a breach, the party seeking relief generally has one or all of the following remedies:

- cancel the contract
- pursue specific performance
- request damages resulting from the breach
- accept the earnest money as liquidated damages.

See, Higgins v. Kittleson, 1 Ariz. App. 244, 247, 401 P.2d 412, 415 (1965).

Cancellation

A contract may be cancelled for a material breach, misrepresentation or fraud. All of the AAR contracts include cancellation as an available remedy for a breach of contract. However, contract cancellation is not the remedy for every breach. To justify cancellation, the breach generally must relate to a vital contract provision. Cancellation is generally not warranted for a breach of a minor contract provision that can be rectified by monetary damages. Thus, a party threatening cancellation of a contract over the objections of the other party should be referred to legal counsel for advice.

Specific Performance

Specific performance is an available remedy for the refusal to complete the purchase or sale of real estate. *Kimbel v. Statler*, 20 Ariz. 81, 176 P. 843 (1918); *Sabin v. Rauch*, 75 Ariz. 275, 255 P.2d 206 (1953). Specific performance is ordinarily available to enforce real estate contracts because land is viewed as unique and an award of damages is usually considered an inadequate remedy. *Woliansky v. Miller*, 135 Ariz. 444, 661 P.2d 1145 (1983); *See Glad Tidings Church v. Hinkley*, 71 Ariz. 306, 226 P.2d 1016 (1951). However, the court has wide discretion in determining whether damages are an adequate remedy and specific performance is never a matter of absolute right. *Id.* In cases where the purchaser does not desire the real property for personal use but instead wants to acquire the land merely for investment profit, damages would theoretically be an adequate remedy. Before a buyer is awarded specific performance, the buyer generally must satisfy the court that the buyer is ready and able to perform. However, in a case where the seller repudiates the contract, the buyer is not required to tender performance before commencing a specific performance action.

Damages

Damages are the monetary compensation that may be recovered in court for the loss suffered by a party due to the other's breach of contract. For example, in *Woodward v. Chirco Construction Co.*, 141 Ariz. 514, 516, 687 P.2d 1269, 1271 (1984), the court explained that a plaintiff "can seek to recover in contract for defects in the structure itself as such defects render the home less than purchaser bargained for." The court wrote "if a fireplace collapses, the purchaser can sue in contract for the cost of remedying the structural defects." *Id. (Distinguishing between contract claims and tort or personal injury claims).*

Liquidated Damages

Liquidated damages is the term used when a specific sum of money has been agreed upon by the parties as the amount of damages to be recovered for breach of contract. All of the AAR contracts contain a liquidated damages clause. A liquidated damages clause serves as an economical alternative to the costly and lengthy litigation involved in a breach of contract action. When liquidated damages are specified in a contract, the terms of the contract generally control. *Davis v. Tucson Arizona Boys Choir Soc.*, 137 Ariz. 228, 233, 669 P.2d 1005, 1010 (App. 1983); *Roy H. Long Realty Co. v. Vanderkolk*, 26 Ariz. App. 226, 228, 547 P.2d 497, 499 (1976).

The earnest money is designated as the liquidated damage amount in the AAR contracts. However, be aware that if there is an unreasonably large amount of the earnest money at issue, that the court may refuse to enforce the liquidated damages clause. A liquidated damages clause that fixes an unreasonably large sum of liquidated damages may be unenforceable because it is deemed to be a penalty. Restatement (Second) of Contracts §356 (1981). A liquidated damages clause will be considered a penalty unless two conditions are met. First, the amount fixed in the contract must be a reasonable forecast of just compensation for the harm that is caused by any breach. Second, the harm that is caused by any breach must be one that is incapable or very difficult of accurate estimation. *Larson-Hegstrom & Associates, Inc. v. Jeffries*, 145 Ariz. 329, 701 P.2d 587 (App. 1985).

However, not all large liquidated damage sums are unreasonable. For example, in *Pima Sav. and Loan Ass'n v. Rampello*, 168 Ariz. 297, 812 P.2d 1115 (App. 1991), the buyer contracted to purchase a condominium complex from Pima Savings for $4.7 million. The contract's liquidated damage clause stated: "*If the closing does not occur due to default of buyer, the parties agree that Pima shall be paid the sum of two hundred ninety thousand dollars ($290,000.00) as liquidated damages, which sum the parties agree is a reasonable sum considering all of the circumstances existing on the date of this agreement . . .* "When the buyer failed to close, the buyer argued that the liquidated damage clause was unenforceable as a penalty. The court noted that the "liquidated damage amount was little more than six percent of the total contract price and was reasonable on its face and, when all the facts were considered, reasonable at the time of the contract." Therefore, the clause was enforceable.

ALTERNATIVE DISPUTE RESOLUTION

Many purchase contracts contain alternative dispute resolution clauses, generally mediation and/or arbitration. All AAR contracts require the parties to mediate any dispute before taking further action. The AAR Resale Purchase Contract requires mediation and defaults to binding arbitration, unless one of the parties opts out.

Mediation

Mediation is a process in which the parties meet with an impartial person who helps to resolve the dispute informally and confidentially. Mediators cannot impose binding decisions. The parties must agree and sign an agreement before any settlement reached at the mediation is binding.

Under Arizona law, an agreement in a written contract, to submit a dispute or claim to mediation is valid and enforceable. If one party files a lawsuit without offering to mediate, the court will either dismiss the claim as premature or "stay" the litigation pending mediation. If a party refuses to mediate when a dispute arises, the refusal to mediate may be construed as bad faith or breach of contract.

At times the buyer and seller are reluctant to mediate. The parties may think that mediation is just a waste of time or will be used only for gathering evidence in support of the complaining party's claim. Some of these concerns are the result of a lack of understanding of the mediation process. In a mediation, a neutral party called the mediator attempts to assist the parties to negotiate a mutually acceptable solution to the dispute. The mediation process allows the parties to vent their anger and tell their story to a neutral party. It may also allow the parties to realistically evaluate the merits of their claim or defense and consider the risks of litigation. Finally, mediation can produce a creative solution to a dispute, which may not be possible in court.

Most mediations follow a similar pattern. First, the mediator will have all parties meet in the same room. The lawyer, or a party, for each side makes an opening statement. During this opening statement, each side explains the party's claim or defense, evidence and desired outcome. Thereafter, the mediator will generally separate the parties into different rooms to discuss the party's position in detail. The mediator will privately point out the strengths and weaknesses of each party's position. The mediator then engages in shuttle diplomacy conveying positions, concerns, offers and counteroffers between the still separated parties. The mediator's goal is to achieve a binding written agreement between the parties.

Any concern that one party may use the mediation for the purpose of informal discovery to gather evidence to use against the opposing party is largely unwarranted. Anything told to the mediator in confidence should be kept confidential. The Arizona Rules of Evidence preclude the introduction of evidence of settlement negotiations in a trial for the purpose of proving liability, the validity of a claim, or its amount. Offers made during mediation should not be allowed as evidence in any trial or hearing regarding the matter.

Mediation is less expensive and time consuming than litigation. Mediation fees are typically split between the parties so individual costs are further reduced. Most disputes are resolved within two and one-half to three hours. Agreeing to mediate does not mean that the parties are agreeing to settle, but simply means the parties are trying to resolve a dispute without going to court. The parties do not give up any right to pursue other legal remedies if mediation is not successful.

Arbitration

Arbitration is a process that is similar to litigation in the courts. An arbitrator or panel of arbitrators hears evidence and testimony and makes a decision of who wins and who loses. An arbitration can be binding, which means the parties agree that the arbitrator's decision cannot be appealed to superior court, or nonbinding, which means that the decision can be appealed.

Pursuant to the AAR Residential Resale Contract, if mediation does not resolve the dispute, the unresolved dispute must be submitted to binding arbitration, unless either party opts out within 30 days after the conclusion of the mediation conference by written notice to the other. If neither party opts out of arbitration, the parties must agree upon an arbitrator and cooperate in the scheduling of an arbitration hearing. If the parties are unable to agree on an arbitrator, the dispute must be submitted to the American Arbitration Association (AAA) in accordance with the AAA Arbitration Rules for the Real Estate Industry. The decision of the arbitrator is final and nonappealable.

In the case of *Harrington v. Pulte Home Corp.*, 211 Ariz. 241, 119 P.3d 1044 (Ariz. 2005), the court addressed the issue of whether an arbitration clause in the Pulte Homes standardized purchase contract violated the doctrine of reasonable expectations because the plaintiff buyers claimed that the waiver of a jury trial was not explicitly referenced or knowingly made, and the clause lacked notice regarding the substantial arbitration fees the buyers must pay. The court rejected the buyers' arguments that an arbitration clause could only be effective through knowing and voluntary consent. The court held the arbitration clause was presumptively valid and enforceable, whether or not any buyer read it or appreciated its full effect, unless the sellers had reason to believe that the buyers would not have accepted the clause if they knew it was in the contract.

LITIGATION

If the parties do not resolve their dispute via alternative dispute resolution, litigation may be the only option. A case generally must be litigated in the county where the property is located.

Small-claims Court

Many disputes in which the amount at issue is $2,500 or less can be quickly and easily resolved in small-claims court. The AAR contracts do not require mediation if the parties file an action in the Small Claims Division of an Arizona Justice Court, so long as the matter is not transferred from the Small Claims Division. The procedures in small-claims cases are intended to be simple enough for a person to represent him or herself. Therefore, lawyers are generally not allowed in small-claims court. The case will be heard by either a judge or hearing officer, who then makes a decision. This decision is final and there is no right to an appeal.

Justice Court

A lawsuit may be filed in the Justice Court if the amount involved, exclusive of interest, costs and attorney fees is less than $10,000. Lawyers may represent a client in Justice Court.

Superior Court

If the claim exceeds $10,000, the claim must be filed in the Superior Court to resolve the dispute. To file such a lawsuit, the buyer or seller will probably want to hire an attorney. Certified Real Estate Specialists may be located through the Arizona State Bar.

CLAIMS AGAINST BROKERS

Claims against brokers may be filed in a variety of forums, such as:

- Superior Court/Justice Court/Small-claims Court
- ADRE
- State and local REALTOR® Associations
- Attorney General's Office

The majority of claims against brokers come from buyers, and the vast majority of those claims are related to property condition. Some of the most common property condition claims involve:

- water issues (availability, waterlines, well issues)
- permit/code/zoning issues
- termites or termite damage
- sewer/septic issues
- presence of mold
- boundary/encroachments
- acreage/square footage
- structural (cracks, settlement) conditions
- electrical problems
- roof leaks

Of course not all claims involve property condition. Some claims involve issues related to the transaction or transaction documents. Transaction-related complaints include:

- earnest money disputes
- problems with offer/acceptance
- financing problems
- discrimination
- pre-possession & post-possession agreement disputes

A lawsuit will include not only the factual basis of the claim, i.e., the property condition or problem with the transaction documents, but will also assert that the facts give rise to a specific legal cause of action. The legal causes of action that may be alleged in a lawsuit include:

- professional negligence
- breach of fiduciary duty
- failure to disclose
- violation of real estate statutes
- innocent misrepresentation
- negligent misrepresentation
- intentional misrepresentation
- fraud
- consumer fraud
- breach of contract

If a broker is found liable, the consequences will depend upon the type of claim and the forum in which the claim was pursued. Some of the possible consequences are:

- forfeiture of commission (for breach of fiduciary duty, regardless of damages)
- actual damages (the amount of money required to compensate the plaintiff)
- punitive damages (money awarded to punish)
- ADRE sanction (civil penalties to loss of license)
- association sanction (education requirements and monetary penalties to loss of membership)
- criminal penalties
- attorney's fees & costs

Errors and Omissions Insurance

Because of the potential liability, every broker should consider errors and omissions (E&O) insurance. E&O Insurance generally covers the amounts a protected person is legally required to pay as damages for loss that result from performing real estate duties, such as:

- listing or selling

- property management
- estimating market value
- counseling clients
- referrals

Most E&O policies have deductibles and limits of coverage for each wrongful act and for each policy year. E&O policies also have exclusions and commonly do not cover:

- criminal acts
- punitive damages
- securities
- physical injury to person or property
- advertising injury
- commission disputes
- family/personal transactions
- fair housing/discrimination
- activities other than real estate duties

Most E&O policies define a "claim" as a written demand for money or services alleging an error, omission or negligent act. If a buyer or seller makes such a demand, the broker should:

- notify the designated broker or manager, who will:
  - notify the E&O carrier in writing
  - obtain a claim number
- cooperate with carrier and attorney
  - although the attorney is paid by the insurance company, the attorney represents the broker

ADRE Investigation of Cases Involving Civil Litigation

ADRE Substantive Policy Statement No. 2005.07 states that:

A Complainant's filing of a civil suit has no bearing on whether the Department will pursue an alleged violation of a statute or rule within the Department's jurisdiction. The Department shall commit the appropriate resources to investigate possible violations.

The Department monitors and regulates real estate licensees, but does not determine a licensee's civil liability to third parties. A finding by the Department that a violation warranting administrative action did or did not occur, is not dispositive of liability and does not create any presumption regarding whether or not civil liability exists.

The Department's investigations shall not be utilized for the purpose of circumventing the Arizona Rules of Civil Procedure or as a means of discovery of evidence for use in civil litigation. The Department will not intentionally place itself in the position of providing discovery and building a prima facie case for a complainant, only to have the complainant use the Department's investigative file as evidence in a civil suit. It is not the Department's role to assist a complainant to develop a case that will assist them in pursuing damages.

The Department shall not delay an investigation to await the outcome of a civil court proceeding. Such a delay may discourage or financially inhibit a complainant's pursuit of a civil cause of action. Such a delay might also encourage a licensee to assert the Department's inaction as an argument in the licensee's favor.

Real Estate Recovery Fund

The ADRE maintains a real estate recovery fund for the benefit of any person "aggrieved by any act, representation, transaction or conduct of a licensed real estate" broker. The recovery fund pays for actual and direct out-of-pocket losses, including reasonable attorney fees and court costs up to thirty thousand dollars for each transaction, regardless of the number of persons, brokers or parcels of real estate involved.

A.R.S. §32-2186 *et. seq.*

KEY POINTS TO REMEMBER

- The failure to perform any promise in a contract (after expiration of any applicable cure period) generally constitutes a breach of contract.

- Upon breach of contract, the non-breaching party always has a remedy, but the available remedy is not always cancellation.

- The AAR contracts all contain alternative dispute resolution provisions.

- The majority of claims against brokers are related to property defects.

- A broker who receives a written demand for money or services should immediately notify their designated broker or manager.

CHAPTER 19

Fair Housing

Any allegation that a broker has committed a fair housing violation is serious business. Even if vindicated, the defense of a fair housing claim is costly both emotionally and financially. What may be surprising to some is that the majority of fair housing claims in recent years involve reasonable accommodations for the handicapped.

To avoid a potential career-ending claim, a broker must first be aware of what constitutes a fair housing violation. Second, if faced with a situation implicating a violation, the broker must be confident enough to stop the conversation, announce that the broker does not engage in discrimination, and immediately contact the manager or designated broker so that the situation can be properly handled and documented.

"It is the policy of the United States to provide, within constitutional limitations, for fair housing throughout the United States." 45 U.S.C. §3601. The first civil rights legislation enacted by Congress was the Civil Rights Act of 1866, which states: "All citizens of the United States shall have the same right in every territory and state, as is employed by the white citizens thereof, to inherit, purchase, lease, sell, hold and convey real and personal property." Thus, the Civil Rights Act of 1866 prohibits all racial discrimination in the sale or rental of property. Numerous other statutes now address the area of civil rights. The following information focuses on the Fair Housing Act and related statutes.

FEDERAL FAIR HOUSING ACT (45 U.S.C. §3601 ET. SEQ.) (24 CFR100.1 ET. SEQ.)

The Fair Housing Act (Title VIII of the Civil Rights Act of 1968) was designed to eliminate discrimination in housing based upon an individual's race, color, religion and national origin. The act was amended in 1974 to prohibit discrimination based on sex. The act was amended again in 1988 to include the prohibition of discrimination based on handicap or familial status.

The Fair Housing Act prohibits the following if based upon race, religion, color, national origin, sex, familial status, or handicap, i.e. protected classes:

- refusal to sell a dwelling
- refusal to rent a dwelling
- refusal to negotiate for the sale or rental of a dwelling
- to otherwise make unavailable or deny a dwelling
- to discriminate in the terms, conditions or privileges of the sale or rental of a dwelling
- to discriminate in the provision of services or facilities in connection with a dwelling
- to make, print or publish or cause to be made, printed or published any statement, or advertisement regarding the sale or rental of a dwelling that indicates any preference, limitation or discrimination
- to represent to any person that a dwelling is not available, if untrue
- to induce or attempt to induce any person to sell or rent by representations regarding entry or prospective entry into the neighborhood of a person (blockbusting)

45 U.S.C. §3604(a-e).

Dwelling Defined

A dwelling is defined as:

- any building, structure or part of a building or structure that is occupied as, or designed or intended for occupancy as, a residence by one or more families
- any vacant land that is offered for sale or lease for the construction or location of a building, or structure or part of a building or structure as described above.

42 U.S.C. §3602.

Handicap Defined

A mental or physical impairment that substantially limits at least one major life activity, a record of such impairment, or being regarded as having such an impairment. 42 U.S.C. §3602(h). "Handicap" does not include the current illegal use of or addiction to a controlled substance. In regard to handicapped individuals, it is also unlawful to:

- refuse to permit, at the handicapped person's expense, reasonable modifications necessary for the full enjoyment of the premises (except that such permission may be conditioned upon the agreement to restore the premises, if reasonable)
- refuse to make accommodations in rules, policies, practices, or services necessary to afford the handicapped person the equal opportunity to use and enjoy the dwelling
- to design and construct multifamily dwellings (generally four or more units) after September 13, 1988, without specified handicapped access

However, a dwelling is not required to be made available to an individual if the tenancy would result in a direct threat to the health and safety of others or would result in substantial physical damage to the property of others.

45 U.S.C. §3604(f).

Familial Status Defined (A.R.S. §41-1491.01)
- domiciled with a child under age 18
- pregnant women
- persons in the process of obtaining legal custody of a child under 18

Prohibition against Discrimination in Residential Real Estate Transactions

A person whose business includes residential real estate-related transactions may not discriminate in making a transaction available or in the terms of the transaction. A "real estate-related transaction" is defined as:
- making or purchasing loans or providing other financial assistance either:
  - to purchase, construct, improve, repair or maintain a dwelling
  - to secure residential real estate
- selling, brokering or appraising residential real property
42 U.S.C. §3605.

Exemptions

The following are exempted from the Act:
- single-family house sold or rented without the use of a real estate broker (with other restrictions) (42 U.S.C. §3603(b)(1))
- owner-occupied with no more than four units (42 U.S.C. §3603(b)(2))
- housing operated by religious organizations and clubs that limit occupancy to members, unless the membership in the religion is restricted on account of race (42 U.S.C. §3607)
- housing for older persons

Requirements to Qualify as "Housing for Older Persons"

The requirements are:
- intended for, and solely occupied by, persons 62 years of age or older
- intended and operated for occupancy by persons 55 and over

- at least 80% of the units are occupied by at least one person 55 years of age or older
- the community publishes and adheres to policies and procedures that demonstrate intent
- the community complies with rules for verification of occupancy

Good Faith Attempt at Compliance (42 U.S.C. §3607)

"A person shall not be held personally liable for monetary damages for a violation of [the Fair Housing Act] if such person reasonably relied, in good faith, on the application of the [housing for older persons exemption.]" "[A] person may only show good faith reliance on the application of exemption by showing that:

- such person has no actual knowledge that the facility or community is not, or will not be, eligible for such exemption
- the facility or community has stated formally, in writing, that the facility or community complies with the requirements for such exemption"

Related Federal Laws

- *Equal Credit Opportunity Act (ECOA) (15 U.S.C. 1691-1691f):* Forbids discrimination in all lending, including housing loans. Makes discrimination unlawful with respect to any aspect of a credit application on the basis of race, color, religion, national origin, sex, marital status, age or because the applicant's income derives in whole or in part from any public assistance program.
- *Americans with Disabilities Act of 1990:* Title III of the Americans with Disabilities Act prohibits discrimination against persons with disabilities in places of public accommodations and commercial facilities.
- *The Rehabilitation Act of 1973:* Prohibits employment discrimination against individuals with disabilities in the federal sector and mandates nondiscrimination under federal grants and programs.

ARIZONA FAIR HOUSING ACT (A.R.S. §41-1491 ET. SEQ.)

The Arizona Fair Housing Act provides the same substantive protections as the Federal Fair Housing Act. However, the Arizona Fair Housing Act provides different procedures for the administrative complaint processing than the Federal Act.

Related State Laws

- A.R.S. §33-1317: Prohibits discrimination by a landlord against a tenant with children. *See also,* A.R.S. §33-303.
- A.R.S. §20-1548: Prohibits discrimination in the issuance or extension of mortgage guaranty insurance.
- A.R.S. §41-1442: Prohibits discrimination in places of public accommodation
- A.R.S. §41-1492.02: Prohibits discrimination by public accommodations and commercial facilities.
- A.R.S. §32-2153(A)(19): Allows the ADRE to suspend or revoke a license, deny the issuance of a license or deny the renewal or right of renewal of a license for violating the federal fair housing law, the Arizona civil rights law or any local ordinance of a similar nature.

HANDICAP DISCRIMINATION CLAIMS

The National Fair Housing Alliance and the Department of Housing and Urban Development (HUD) have reported that nationally the number one complaint in 2005 was discrimination on the basis of handicap, followed closely by discrimination on the basis of race.

Two Arizona cases that deal with reasonable accommodation in relation to a claim of discrimination on the basis of handicap are:

Cimarron Foothills Community Association v. Kippen, 206 Ariz. 455, 79 P.3d 1214 (App. 2003). In this case the homeowners operated an elder-care facility out of their home, using a large recreational vehicle (RV) to transport the residents. Contrary to applicable conditions, reservations and restrictions (CC&Rs), they did not keep the RV in a garage. The association sought an injunction to force the homeowners to comply with the CC&Rs. The homeowners counterclaimed, alleging that under the Federal Fair Housing Act that parking the RV on their lot was reasonable and necessary to afford the residents equal opportunity to use and enjoy their home. The court found that the homeowners failed to demonstrate that but for the accommodation, their residents would be denied the opportunity to enjoy the housing of their choice and therefore the proposed accommodation was not a required reasonable accommodation under the Fair Housing Act.

Canady v. Prescott Canyon Estates Homeowners Association, 204 Ariz. 91, 60 P.3d 231 (App. 2002). In this case the community had a minimum age restriction of 55 years of age for at least one resident and a further rule that no one under 35 years of age could reside in the community. The prospective buyers entered into a contract to buy a home there, but were informed that their 26-year old severely disabled son, who lived with them due to his disabilities, could not live there. The sale was cancelled and a discrimination complaint was filed with the Arizona Attorney General's Office, which found reasonable cause to believe that the defendants had unlawfully discriminated. In the resulting lawsuit, the Court of Appeals held that the homeowners association's refusal to waive the age restriction was discrimination under both the federal and state acts, and the association had a duty to reasonably accommodate disabled persons by waiving the age restrictions.

KEY POINTS TO REMEMBER

- A broker may not discriminate based upon race, religion, color, national origin, sex, familial status, or handicap, i.e., protected classes.

- Advertisements may not indicate any preference or limitation based on the protected classes.

- A handicap is a mental or physical impairment that substantially limits at least one major life activity and has been the most common fair housing violation claim in recent years.

- It is unlawful to refuse to reasonably accommodate handicapped persons.

- If faced with a situation implicating a violation, a broker should stop, announce that the broker does not discriminate, and immediately contact the broker's manager, designated broker or legal counsel.

CHAPTER 20

RESPA

Real estate brokers, title/escrow companies, lenders, and inspectors all rely on each other in a real estate transaction. Because brokers generally have the initial relationship with the client, title/escrow companies, lenders, and inspectors often compete for the business that the broker's client brings. Competition based on service to the client is legitimate and results in a higher level of professionalism in the industry. Competition based on kickbacks and prohibited referral fees result in higher costs to the client and expose the broker and affiliated industries to civil and regulatory penalties. Therefore, a broker must recognize the difference between legal marketing techniques and illegal kickbacks and referral fees.

The Real Estate Settlement Procedures Act of 1974 (RESPA)[12] is a federal law enacted to insure that buyers are provided with sufficient information about the nature and costs of financing and closing escrow on a home (defined in the law as the settlement process). RESPA is also intended to protect buyers from unnecessarily high close of escrow charges. RESPA

---

[12] *RESPA was amended in 1976 and 1983 (minor revisions); in 1992 (addressing affiliated business relationships and computer loan origination); and in 1996 (further revisions, including addressing certain employer payments to bona fide employees). Various other amendments to the law have been proposed.*

requires that buyers receive disclosures at various times that spell out the costs associated with the close of escrow, lender and escrow practices and fees, such as the Good Faith Estimate. Section 8 and Section 9 of RESPA have the greatest impact on real estate brokers.

KICKBACKS AND REFERRAL FEES
SECTION 8 (12 U.S.C. §2607; 24 C.F.R. §3500)

Section 8 (a) Prohibits Kickbacks and Referral Fees
Section 8(a) states:
> No person shall give and no person shall accept any fee, kickback, or thing of value pursuant to any agreement or understanding, oral or otherwise, that business incident to or a part of a real estate settlement service involving a federally related mortgage loan shall be referred to any person.

Thus, Section 8 prohibits a person from giving or accepting any "thing of value" for referrals of settlement service business.

Section 8(b) Prohibits Unearned Fees
Section 8(b) prohibits a person from giving or accepting any part of a charge for services that are not performed. Section 8(b) states:
> No person shall give and no person shall accept any portion, split, or percentage of any charge made or received for the rendering of a real estate settlement service in connection with a transaction involving a federally related mortgage loan other than for services actually performed.

Section 8 Definitions (12 U.S.C. §2602)
A "settlement service" includes any service provided in connection with a real estate transaction, including title insurance, attorney services, surveys, credit reports, appraisals, pest and fungus inspections, and loan origination (the taking of loan applications, processing, underwriting and

funding). If the service is provided at or before close of escrow, it is probably a settlement service.

A "thing of value" is very broadly defined. A thing of value includes any payment, advance, funds, loan, service or other consideration.

A "federally related mortgage" includes any loan (other than temporary financing such as a construction loan) that is secured by a first or subordinate lien on residential real property designed principally for the occupancy of one to four families. In other words, a federally related mortgage covers virtually all financing secured by a lien on residential property.

Examples of Reported Section 8 Enforcement Actions

HUD has increased its enforcement staff and stepped up its pursuit of RESPA violators. For example, HUD settled a case against four Detroit real estate brokers for $80,000. HUD alleged that the title company paid these brokers for the use of conference rooms at rates substantially higher than their fair market value. Additionally, a broker agreed to pay $250,000 to settle HUD charges that it violated RESPA by offering gifts and other incentives to agents who referred business to its affiliated title company.

Section 8(c) Exceptions

Not all fees, salaries, compensation or payments for settlement services violate Section 8. RESPA does not prohibit:
- payments to attorneys for services actually rendered
- compensation by a title company to its duly appointed agent for services actually performed in the issuance of a policy of title insurance or by a lender to its duly appointed agent for services actually performed in the making of a loan
- payment of a bona fide salary, compensation or payment for goods or facilities actually furnished or for services actually performed
- payments pursuant to cooperative brokerage and referral arrangements or agreements between real estate agents and brokers
- affiliated business arrangements so long as certain requirements are met

An affiliated business arrangement is an arrangement in which a person (or associate) who is in a position to refer business incident to or a part of a real estate settlement service involving a federally related mortgage loan has either an affiliate relationship with or an ownership interest of more than one percent in a settlement service provider and either directly or indirectly refers business to that provider or affirmatively influences the selection of that provider. *See, 12 U.S.C. §2602.* To qualify for the affiliated business arrangement exemption, a disclosure must be made of the existence of the arrangement, and a written estimate of the charge or range of charges for the service is made at or before the time of the referral. Further, the buyer cannot be required to use the service. Additionally, the only thing of value that is received from the arrangement is a return on the ownership interest.

HUD has and will investigate sham affiliated business arrangements. For example, a title company in Florida reportedly paid $3.2 million to settle allegations that it was entering into sham affiliated business arrangements in an attempt to funnel improper payments to builders, real estate agents and mortgage brokers.

Question: *Can a real estate brokerage lease office space to a lender or other settlement service provider without violating RESPA?*
Answer: Yes. HUD interprets Section 8 to allow the rental of office space in this situation if the rental payments are reasonably related to the market value of the office space. If the rental payments exceed the market value of the office space, a RESPA violation may have occurred.

Question: *Can a real estate broker and title company advertise their services on the same brochure?*
Answer: Joint advertising is not prohibited by RESPA. However, if one party is paying less than a pro-rata share for the brochure, there could be a RESPA violation.

Question: Can a lender give a real estate broker note pads with the lender's name on it?

Answer: Note pads with the lender's name are allowable as normal promotional items. However, if the lender gives the real estate broker note pads with the real estate broker's name, the note pads could be a thing of value given for referral of loan business, because it defrays the broker's marketing expense.

Question: Does the offering of a package of settlement services or the offering of discounts to consumers for the purchase of multiple settlement services violate RESPA?

Answer: A package of services or a discount will not be considered a prohibited required use if it is optional to the purchaser. The discount must be a true discount below the prices that are otherwise generally available and must not be made up by higher costs.

Question: Do lender fee programs comply with RESPA?

Answer: Some may and some may not. RESPA does not prohibit a lender from paying the lender's agent or contractor for services actually performed in the origination or processing of a loan. Thus, the program may comply with RESPA if a real estate agent is actually providing loan services, the appropriate RESPA-required disclosures are made, and the buyer is notified that the buyer is not obligated to use the real estate agent as their loan originator.

Do not enter into a compensation agreement with a lender without checking with the designated broker or legal counsel. Also, make sure that you are being paid for actually performing substantial services (see, HUD Statement of Policy 1999-1), the appropriate required disclosures are made, and the buyer is notified that the buyer is not obligated to use the offered services.

TITLE INSURANCE — SECTION 9 (12 U.S.C. §2608; 24 C.F.R. SEC. 3500.16)

Section 9 of RESPA prohibits a seller from requiring the buyer to buy title insurance from a specific title insurance company. Section 9 of RESPA states:

(a) No seller of property that will be purchased with the assistance of a federally related mortgage loan shall require directly or indirectly, as a condition to selling the property, that title insurance covering the property be purchased by the buyer from any particular title company.

(b) Any seller who violates the provisions of subsection (a) of this section shall be liable to the buyer in an amount equal to three times all charges made for such title insurance.

"Required use" means:

A situation in which a person must use a particular provider of a settlement service in order to have access to some distinct service or property, and the person will pay for the settlement service of the particular provider or will pay a charge attributable, in whole or in part, to the settlement service.

Question: *Is it a RESPA violation if the seller requires the buyer to use a specific title company when the seller is paying for the buyer's title insurance?*
Answer: HUD has indicated that it "will not enforce Section 9 of RESPA against a seller who selects the title insurance company if the seller is paying for the owner's title insurance policy, and does not require the buyer to use the title insurance company for the simultaneously issued lender's policy."[13]

---

[13] *See correspondence from Rebecca J. Holtz, acting Director, Office of Consumer and Regulating Affairs, HUD RESPA/ILS Division dated August 2000 and related enclosures and correspondence available on the AAR Web site.*

Question: *Is it a RESPA violation if the seller requires the buyer to use a specific title company and pays for the buyer's title insurance with funds from the buyer's closing costs?*

Answer: Yes. HUD has indicated that it would take action "in situations where a seller required a buyer to pay the seller an amount toward closing costs, and the seller used a portion of the buyer's paid closing costs for the owner's title insurance without providing the buyer with a choice of that title company."

Question: *What is the safest course for a seller who wants to require the use of a certain title insurance policy?*

Answer: Based on HUD's position, the safest course for a seller who insists on using a particular title company is to pay for both the buyer's title insurance policy and the lender's title insurance policy. Additionally, the seller should not require the buyer to pay any closing cost that could be attributable to the cost of the title policies.

Question: *What are the penalties for a violation of Section 9 of RESPA?*

Answer: Pursuant to 12 USC §2608(b), any seller who violates Section 9 is liable to the buyer in an amount equal to three times all charges made for such title insurance. Additionally, the seller may face sanctions from HUD (Section 3500.19(c)) and the Arizona Department of Real Estate (A.R.S. §32-2153(B) (10)).

In addition to RESPA's restrictions on the practice of the seller requiring the use of a particular title insurance company, there are other legal and practical considerations.

Question: *What is the effect of a seller's counteroffer changing the title company to be used in a transaction?*

Answer: If the buyer submits an offer, and the seller responds with a counteroffer requiring the use of a different title insurance company, that counteroffer has the same legal effect as rejecting the buyer's offer.

Therefore, by submitting a counteroffer requesting a different title insurance company, the seller is risking the transaction in its entirety.

Question: What is the listing agent's duty to the seller when drafting such a counteroffer?
Answer: The listing agent has a fiduciary duty to the seller. Therefore, the listing agent should explain to the seller the possible adverse consequences of submitting a counteroffer requiring the use of a specific title insurance company.

Question: Is it a breach of fiduciary duty for a listing agent to advise a seller to demand a certain title insurance company when it is not in the seller's best interests?
Answer: Yes. The listing agent has a fiduciary duty to act in the best interests of the seller. Therefore, the listing agent should insure that any such counteroffer is for the benefit of the seller, rather than solely for the agent's purposes.

KEY POINTS TO REMEMBER

- A broker cannot accept any fee, kickback or "thing of value" for referrals to a settlement service provider.

- A prohibited "thing of value" under RESPA is interpreted very broadly and may include joint advertising if one settlement service provider is paying more than a pro-rata share, or any other item that would defray the broker's expenses.

- Generally, a broker cannot accept any portion of a settlement service charge other than for services rendered.

- Generally, a seller may not require as a condition of sale that the buyer purchase title insurance from any particular title company.

- Affiliated business arrangements are allowed under RESPA as long as certain requirements are met.

CHAPTER 21

· · · · · · · · · · · · · · · · · ·

Antitrust

Antitrust laws prohibit anticompetitive or unfair business practices. The penalties for antitrust violations can be substantial. New business models such as "minimum service" or "limited service" brokerages and "by owner" companies have resulted in a great deal of controversy and discussion. Given these discussions and the existing political climate, it is critical for brokers to understand and comply with the antitrust laws.

FEDERAL ANTITRUST LAW

The Sherman Antitrust Act was enacted in 1890 and was named for Senator John Sherman from Ohio. The term "antitrust" was used because the law was originally enacted to prohibit business trusts. A business trust was a form of business entity used in the late 19th century. A business trust was created when corporate leaders convinced shareholders of all companies in one industry to transfer their shares to a board of trustees in exchange for dividend-paying certificates. The board of trustees would then manage all the companies in trust and minimize competition in the process.

The Sherman Antitrust Act declared every contract, combination or conspiracy in restraint of trade illegal. The Act states in Section 1:

> Every contract, combination in the form of trust or otherwise, or conspiracy, in restraint of trade or commerce among the several States, or with foreign nations, is declared to be illegal. Every person who shall make any contract or engage in any combination or conspiracy hereby declared to be illegal shall be deemed guilty of a felony, and, on conviction thereof, shall be punished by fine not exceeding $10,000,000 if a corporation, or, if any other person, $350,000, or by imprisonment not exceeding three years, or by both said punishments, in the discretion of the court. 15 U.S.C. §1.

Thus, the Sherman Antitrust Act set forth two elements of a Section 1 violation: (1) a contract, combination, or conspiracy (2) that restrains trade. According to the *U.S. Department of Justice Antitrust Manual*, the most common violations of the Sherman Antitrust Act and the violations most likely to be prosecuted criminally are price fixing, bid rigging and territorial or customer allocation among competitors (horizontal agreements).

The U.S. Supreme Court has issued numerous opinions interpreting the act. In doing so, the court identified certain restraints, such as agreements to fix prices, agreements not to deal with a competitor or supplier, and agreements to allocate territories in order to minimize competition as *per se* violations, meaning that the agreements are assumed to be antitrust violations without further evidence. *See, United States v. Topco Associates, Inc.*, 405 U.S. 596 (1972).

ARIZONA ANTITRUST LAW

Arizona also has enacted statutes that mirror federal antitrust law. Pursuant to A.R.S. §44-1402 "[a] contract, combination or conspiracy between two or more persons in restraint of, or to monopolize, trade or commerce, any part of which is within this state, is unlawful." The Arizona Attorney General's office is charged with enforcing the state antitrust laws.

See, A.R.S. §44-1406. In an action in which a person or entity is found guilty of an antitrust violation, the court may assess a civil penalty of up to $150,000 for each violation. *See,* A.R.S. §44-1406. In addition, a person who is threatened with business injury due to an antitrust violation may bring a court action for damages. In such action, if the court finds a "flagrant" antitrust violation, it can award treble damages. *See, Western Waste Serv. Sys. v. Superior Court,* 120 Ariz. 90, 584 P.2d 554 (1978). *(Defining "flagrant" as conduct that is shocking, outrageous, or outstandingly bad).*

ASSOCIATION MEETINGS

Be especially aware of antitrust implications at REALTOR® association meetings because such meetings by their nature are groups of competitors who come together to promote common business interests. Therefore, association meetings are particularly vulnerable to antitrust allegations.

KEY POINTS TO REMEMBER

- Do not agree with another broker, explicitly or implicitly to:

  - charge sellers a certain commission amount

  - offer cooperating brokers a certain commission split

  - refuse to cooperate or deal with another brokerage firm

  - divide or allocate territory geographically, by price range, type of property, or by some other way

  - boycott or not use a certain service provider

- Establish commission amounts, brokerage fees and listing terms independently.

- Evidence decisions to focus on certain territory or property types with written marketing and demographic studies.

- Decide whether to deal with other real estate brokers or service providers based on individual judgments, goals, and experiences.

- Stop any discussions at meetings relating to any of the above.

CHAPTER 22

Leasing and Property Management

A lease is a valuable interest in real property. Single-family homes, apartments and mobile homes are leased as residences. Business offices, retail outlets, industrial buildings and agricultural land are leased for commercial purposes. Thus, a significant number of individuals are involved in the leasing of real property. Landlords, tenants and brokers should all understand and comply with the laws governing the leasing of property.

LANDLORD TENANT STATUTES

The relationship between a residential landlord and tenant is governed by the Arizona Residential Landlord and Tenant Act. A.R.S. §33-1301 *et. seq.* Commercial landlord tenant relationships are governed by a different set of landlord tenant statutes. A.R.S. §33-310 *et. seq.* Mobile home parks are governed by yet another set of statutes, the Arizona Mobile Home Parks Residential Landlord and Tenant Act. A.R.S. §33-1401 *et. seq.* There are significant differences in the laws governing residential, commercial, and mobile home landlord tenant relationships. The primary focus of this discussion is residential landlord tenant law.

LEASE AGREEMENTS

An agreement for leasing for a longer period than one year must be in writing to be enforceable. A.R.S. §44-101(6). A verbal rental agreement is generally considered to be a month-to-month tenancy. *See,* A.R.S. §33-1314. AAR produces a Residential Rental Agreement which is drafted to comply with the Residential Landlord and Tenant Act. A commercial lease is generally drafted by an attorney or by individual brokerage firms.

RESIDENTIAL RENTALS

Residential Landlord's Obligations

In general, residential tenants have a great deal of statutory protection. Pursuant to A.R.S. §33-1322, a landlord must disclose to the tenant in writing at or before the commencement of the rental agreement the name and address of the person authorized to manage the property and an owner or person authorized to act on behalf of the owner for the purpose of service of process and receiving notices and demands. Additionally, the statute requires the landlord to inform the tenant in writing that a free copy of the Arizona Residential Landlord and Tenant Act is available through the Arizona Secretary of State's office. If there is a written rental agreement, the landlord must deliver a signed copy of the rental agreement, with all blank spaces completed, to the tenant within a reasonable time after the agreement is executed.

The landlord must maintain a fit premises. A.R.S. §33-1324 requires a landlord to:

- comply with the requirements of applicable building codes materially affecting health and safety
- make all repairs and do whatever is necessary to put and keep the premises in a fit and habitable condition
- keep all common areas of the premises in a clean and safe condition
- maintain in good and safe working order and condition all electrical, plumbing, sanitary, heating, ventilating, air-conditioning

and other facilities and appliances, including elevators, supplied or required to be supplied by him

- provide and maintain appropriate receptacles and conveniences for the removal of ashes, garbage, rubbish and other waste incidental to the occupancy of the dwelling unit and arrange for their removal
- supply running water and reasonable amounts of hot water at all times, reasonable heat and with a few exceptions, supply reasonable air-conditioning or cooling

The handling of security deposits is also highly regulated. A.R.S. §33-1321 prohibits a landlord from demanding a security deposit, however denominated, including, but not limited to, prepaid rent, of more than one and one-half month's rent. Any fee or deposit not designated as nonrefundable is refundable. Further, the purpose of all nonrefundable fees or deposits must be stated in writing by the landlord. Upon move in, a landlord must provide the tenant with a move-in form for specifying any existing damages to the dwelling unit and written notification to the tenant that the tenant may be present at the move out inspection.

When the tenancy is terminated the prepaid rent and security may be applied to the payment of all rent, and subject to a landlord's duty to mitigate damages, all charges as specified in the lease agreement, including the amount of damages which the landlord has suffered by reason of the tenant's failure to maintain the property pursuant to A.R.S. §33-1341. Within 14 days (excluding Saturdays, Sundays or other legal holidays) after termination of the tenancy, the landlord must provide the tenant an itemized list of all deductions together with any amounts payable to the tenant. If the landlord fails to comply with these requirements, the tenant may recover twice the amount wrongfully withheld.

A landlord may adopt rules or regulations concerning the tenant's use and occupancy of the premises; however, pursuant to A.R.S. §33-1342, the rules or regulations are enforceable only if the rules or regulations:

- promote the convenience, safety or welfare of the tenants in the premises, preserve the landlord's property from abusive use or make a fair distribution of services and facilities held out for the tenants generally

- are reasonably related to the purpose for which adopted
- apply to all tenants in the premises in a fair manner
- are sufficiently explicit in prohibition, direction or limitation of the tenant's conduct to fairly inform the tenant of what the tenant must or must not do to comply
- are not for the purpose of evading the obligations of the landlord

If the landlord adopts a rule or regulation after the tenant enters into the rental agreement it will be enforceable if a 30-day notice of its adoption is given to the tenant, and it does not constitute a substantial modification of the tenant's rental agreement. If state, county, municipal or other governmental bodies adopt new ordinances, rules or other legal provisions affecting existing rental agreements, the landlord may make immediate amendments to lease agreements to bring them into compliance with the law. However, the landlord still must give the tenant written notice of the change.

Residential Tenant's Obligations

A residential tenant also has certain obligations. Pursuant to A.R.S. §33-1341, a tenant must:

- comply with all building codes materially affecting health and safety
- keep the premises as clean and safe as the condition of the premises permit
- dispose all ashes, rubbish, garbage and other waste in a clean and safe manner
- keep all plumbing fixtures as clean as their condition permits.
- use all electrical, plumbing, sanitary, heating, ventilating, air-conditioning and other facilities and appliances including elevators in a reasonable manner
- not destroy, deface, damage, impair or remove any part of the premises or knowingly permit any person to do so
- not disturb the neighbors' peaceful enjoyment of the premises

A tenant may not unreasonably withhold consent to the landlord to enter the property for inspections, to perform necessary or agreed repairs, decorations, alterations, improvements, and services, or to show the property to prospective or actual buyers, mortgagees, tenants, workmen or contractors. A.R.S. §33-1343. Except in case of emergency or if it is impracticable to do so, the landlord must give the tenant at least two days' notice of the intent to enter and enter only at reasonable times. A landlord may enter the property without consent in case of emergency.

Remedies

If either the landlord or the tenant fails to comply with their obligations, the act sets forth specific remedies. Generally, either party must give the other a notice and opportunity to cure the noncompliance before taking further action. *See,* A.R.S. §33-1361 through §33- 1377.

Rental Property Registration Requirements — Slumlord Abatement

A.R.S. §33-1902 requires an owner of residential rental property to provide the county assessor with the following information:
- the name, address and telephone number of the property owner
- if the property is owned by a corporation, limited liability company, partnership, limited partnership, trust or real estate investment trust, the name, address and telephone number of any of the following:
    - for a corporation, a corporate officer
    - for a partnership, a general partner
    - for a limited liability company, the managing or administrative member
    - for a limited partnership, a general partner
    - for a trust, a trustee
    - for a real estate investment trust, a general partner or an officer
- the street address and parcel number of the property
- the year the building was built

If the owner lives out of state, the owner must designate and record with the assessor a statutory agent who lives in this state and who will accept legal service on behalf of the owner.

Residential rental property is not to be occupied if the above information is not filed with the county assessor. If a tenant wishes to terminate a tenancy due to the landlord's failure to file this information with the county assessor, the tenant must give the landlord, owner or managing agent a written 10-day notice to comply. If the owner does not comply within 10 days after receipt of the notice, the tenant may terminate the rental agreement, and the landlord must return all prepaid rent to the tenant and security deposits in accordance with A.R.S. §33-1321(D). Further, failure to comply with the statute may subject the owner to civil penalties.

PROPERTY MANAGEMENT AGREEMENTS

Brokers involved in property management assist property owners in leasing their property. Generally speaking, property managers procure suitable tenants, collect rents, and assist in the maintenance of the property. A property management agreement between the broker and the owner set forth the property managers responsibilities and compensation. Pursuant to A.R.S. §32-2173 property management agreements must be written in clear, unambiguous language, and must:

- state all material terms and conditions of the property management firm's services, obligations, duties and responsibilities to the property owner
- be signed by both parties
- specify a beginning and an ending date
- contain agreeable cancellation provisions
- provide for the manner of disposition of all monies collected by the property management firm, including any tenant deposits
- specify the type and frequency of status reports to the owner

- state the amount and purpose of monies the property management firm holds as an operating reserve
- provide for the disposition and allocation of interest earned on trust account monies
- state the terms and conditions of compensation the property owner pays for services pursuant to the property management agreement
- not be assigned to another licensee or licensed entity without the express written consent of the property owner

A property management agreement may:

- contain an automatic renewal provision, if the property management firm sends the owner a reminder notice at least 30 days before the renewal date
- provide for reasonable liquidated damages or cancellation fees for early termination of the agreement
- allow the property management firm's broker to authorize a person to transfer monies from or to be a signatory on the property management trust account
- require more than one signature on checks written from a property management account
- contain any other agreed upon provisions that are not in conflict with the statutory requirements

When a property management agreement is terminated, the property management firm must immediately provide the owner with:

- all rental agreements or related documents in the property management firm's possession for current and previous tenants, such as any applications, property inventories, leases, pet permits, default notices, lease amendments or addenda in the property management firm's possession
- all building plans, environmental studies, conditions, covenants and restrictions, inspection reports, contracts, keys, warranties, personal property or other documents in the possession of the property management firm

Thereafter, the property management firm must provide the owner with a final accounting of the property's financial status that includes:

- within five days, a list of all tenant security obligations
- within 35 days, reimbursement for all monies remaining in the property accounts except for monies needed for unpaid obligations
- within 75 days, a final accounts receivable and payable list
- within 75 days, a final bank account reconciliation

PAYMENT OF FINDER FEES TO APARTMENT TENANTS

Pursuant to A.R.S. §32-2176 a property management firm or a property owner may pay a finder fee to a current tenant, for introducing or arranging an introduction of a potential apartment tenant in an apartment complex. The finder fee may not exceed a $100 credit toward or reduction in the tenant's monthly rent. A tenant may receive such a finder fee up to six times in any 12-month period.

LEASE/PURCHASE AND LEASE/OPTION AGREEMENTS[14]

A buyer may want to enter into a lease/purchase or lease/option agreement because the buyer is unable to obtain financing for some period of time. A seller may consider a lease/purchase or lease/option agreement if the seller has been marketing the property for some period of time without success. A lease/purchase or lease/option agreement can be complex, and if the parties are entering into such an agreement because of a potential buyer's inability to obtain financing, the chance for a default or breach of the agreement is increased. However, a carefully drafted agreement in which the rights and obligations of the parties are clearly stated can prevent unnecessary disputes.

---

[14] *Thanks once again to Christopher Combs, who originally co-authored this article with me.*

A lease/purchase agreement is an agreement in which the buyer and seller enter into both a lease agreement and a purchase contract at the same time. The buyer will lease the property, for example, for one year, and at the end of the one-year period the buyer will purchase the property by closing escrow.

Question: Should the parties execute both a lease agreement and a purchase contract?

Answer: Yes. In a lease/purchase agreement, the parties should enter into a lease agreement for the specified period of time. The AAR Residential Rental Agreement and Receipt for Deposit should be used for this purpose. The parties should also enter into an AAR Residential Resale Real Estate Purchase Contract. The rental agreement should reference the purchase contract and vice versa. Additionally, the rental agreement and purchase contract should have cross default clauses; in other words, a breach of one agreement constitutes a breach of both.

Question: During the term of the lease in the lease/purchase agreement, prior to close of escrow, is the relationship between the parties governed by the Arizona Residential Landlord and Tenant Act (Landlord/Tenant Act)?

Answer: Yes. The Landlord/Tenant Act applies during the lease period of a lease/purchase agreement. Although the Landlord/Tenant Act at A.R.S. §33-1308(2) excludes "[o]ccupancy under a contract of sale of a dwelling unit or the property of which it is a part, if the occupant is the purchaser or person who succeeds to his interest," this provision should be construed to exclude occupancy under an "agreement for sale" (also known as contract for deed, land contract, or installment contract), not a lease/purchase. Thus, the Landlord/Tenant Act should govern the rights of the parties in a lease/purchase agreement prior to close of escrow.

Question: What are the landlord/seller's rights if the tenant/buyer fails to make the rental payments as required under the lease/purchase agreement?

Answer: If the tenant/buyer fails to make the rental payments as required, such a breach of the lease agreement should also constitute a breach of the purchase contract, if the lease/purchase agreement contains a cross default clause. Therefore, if the tenant fails to pay the rental payments as required, the landlord/seller may institute a special entry and detainer action pursuant to A.R.S. §33-1368(A) to evict the tenant and terminate the purchase contract as a result of the breach.

In a lease/option agreement the buyer and seller enter into a lease agreement containing a clause that gives the tenant/buyer the right, but not the obligation, to purchase the property under specified conditions. The lease/option should be drafted to provide that a default in the lease agreement results in the termination of the tenant/buyer's option to purchase.

Question: *Should a lease/option require the tenant/buyer to purchase at a fixed price agreed upon at the time the lease/option is entered into?*
Answer: An option to purchase may be at a fixed price, based on fair market value established by an appraisal at the time the option is exercised, or the option may be drafted as a "first right of refusal" in which the tenant/buyer has an option to purchase the property on the same terms as an offer from a bona fide third party. There are benefits and risks associated with each method.

Question: *What are some other considerations in drafting a lease/option?*
Answer: A lease/option should be carefully drawn to document the understanding of the buyer and seller. Since you cannot predict future events or economic conditions, the option should be limited in time, and the price should be based on the anticipated fair market value of the property at the time the option is exercised. Additionally, the tenant/buyer should be required to take title to the property in the condition of the property at the time the option is exercised, rather than the condition that existed when the lease/option was executed. The lease/option should also provide that the option terminates with the expiration of the lease and can only be exercised if the tenant/buyer is not in default.

Question: *How should the lease/option agreement provide that the option be exercised?*

Answer: The lease/option agreement should set forth (1) the period during which the option can be exercised: for example, 90 days prior to the expiration of the lease; (2) the manner in which it can be exercised: i.e., written notice; (3) to whom notice must be given, normally the seller; (4) how soon after the option is exercised the closing must occur; and (5) the manner of determining the purchase price: i.e., appraisal or fixed price.

Question: *What are some additional considerations if the option is a "first right of refusal"?*

Answer: When in writing an option as a "first right of refusal" the agreement should provide that the tenant/buyer must be given written notice of the proposed offer or a copy of the offer, all terms of the proposed sale, and the specific time period and manner within which to respond.

KEY POINTS TO REMEMBER

- Residential rental agreements are highly regulated by the Residential Landlord and Tenant Act.

- Commercial leasing and mobile home parks are governed by specific statutes that vary dramatically from the statutes governing residential rentals.

- Residential rental property must be registered with the county assessor's office.

- Property management agreements must comply with ADRE rules.

- Lease/purchase and lease/option agreements must be carefully drafted and should certain cross-default clauses.

CHAPTER 23

Miscellaneous Real Estate Issues

This chapter briefly addresses a variety of topics that are common issues in the transfer of real estate, but have not been covered in the previous chapters.

LISTING OF A HOME BUILT BY AN OWNER-BUILDER

Pursuant to A.R.S. §32-1151, it is unlawful for any person to act in the capacity of a contractor without a contractor's license. However, under the owner-builder exception, property owners who build or improve their own property and who do the work themselves, with their own employees or with duly licensed contractors, need not be licensed if the structure is intended for occupancy solely by the owner and is not intended for sale or for rent. Proof of the sale or rent or the offering for sale or rent of the structure by the owner-builder within one year after completion or issuance of a certificate of occupancy is *prima facie* evidence that such project was undertaken for the purpose of sale or rent. A.R.S. §32-1121(A)(5). This one-year "safe harbor" is only a presumption, however, which can be rebutted by a change in circumstances.

Therefore, a listing broker should advise an owner-builder who seeks to list a property within one year of completion to seek legal counsel regarding any potential liability. Further, the fact that the property was constructed by the owner should be disclosed in writing to any potential buyer. A buyer's broker should advise a buyer interested in purchasing such a property, to have the property thoroughly inspected during the buyer's inspection or due diligence period.

HOMESTEAD EXEMPTION

Every person or married couple over 18 who resides in Arizona is entitled to a homestead exemption. Homeowners do not need to take any action to assert the homestead exemption because the exemption attaches by law. A.R.S. §33-1102. The homestead exempts a single-family home, condominium, cooperative or mobile home in which the person resides, from attachment, execution and forced sale due to a nonconsensual judgment or lien, up to $150,000 in value or equity. A.R.S. §33-1101 *et. seq.* Consensual liens (liens that the person allows to be recorded against the home), such as a mortgage or deed of trust are not affected by the homestead exemption. A.R.S. §33-1103; A.R.S. §33-1104. In other words, a mortgage or deed of trust encumbering the home may be foreclosed for nonpayment and the homestead exemption will not protect the homeowner. The homestead exemption only prevents certain creditors, such as judgment creditors, from taking the first $150,000 of equity in a person's home to satisfy a debt. A person can voluntarily waive the homestead protection by signing a declaration of waiver and recording the waiver in the county in which the home is located. A.R.S. §33-1104 (B).

BOUNDARY DISPUTES

Adverse Possession/Prescriptive Easement

Adverse possession is based on the hostile possession of land and results in the acquisition of fee title to the land. Adverse possession is defined as "an actual and visible appropriation of the land, commenced and continued under a claim of right inconsistent with and hostile to the claim of another." A.R.S. §12-521(A). To acquire title by adverse possession, a person must demonstrate that the person (or the person's predecessors in interest) had exclusive possession over the property for a total of 10 years. *See, Overson v. Cowley,* 136 Ariz. 60, 664 P.2d 210 (App. 1982).

A prescriptive easement is based on the hostile use of land, and results in the acquisition of a nonexclusive right to continue to use it. To establish a prescriptive easement, a person must demonstrate that the land was actually and visibly used for a specific purpose for 10 years, and that the use was commenced and continued under a claim of right inconsistent with and hostile to the claim of the owner of land. *See, Ammer v. Arizona Water Co.,* 169 Ariz. 205, 818 P.2d 190 (App. 1991); A.R.S. §12-521(A) and 12-526(A).

Generally speaking, a person claiming rights by adverse possession or prescriptive may be required to file a quiet title action to obtain title to the property at issue if there is a dispute. Also, an adverse possession or prescriptive easement claim may be a covered risk under an owner's title insurance policy.

Boundary by Acquiescence

Boundary by acquiescence was defined by the Arizona Court of Appeals in 2003. Generally, to establish the doctrine of boundary by acquiescence, the party asserting the claim must prove: (1) occupation or possession of property up to a clearly defined line; (2) mutual acquiescence by the adjoining landowners in that line as the dividing line between their properties; and (3) continued acquiescence for 10 years. A.R.S. §12-526(A). *See, Mealey v. Arndt,* 206 Ariz. 218, 76 P.3d 892 (App. 2003).

QUIET TITLE ACTION

A quiet title action is a lawsuit to settle a dispute about who owns a parcel of property, for example in an adverse possession claim. A quiet title action may also be pursued if there is a cloud on the title, meaning that there may be a person who may assert some kind of interest in a property. Such an action may be brought by anyone having or claiming an interest in a parcel of real property against any person who claims an adverse interest. A.R.S. §12-1101(A).

Before filing a quiet title action, the party asserting the claim should send the adverse party a quit claim deed along with $5 (or a larger sum to encourage the party to relinquish the claim) and request that the adverse party execute the quit claim deed. If the adverse party does not execute the quit claim deed, the party asserting the claim may recover the attorney's fees incurred in the quiet title action if the party prevails. A.R.S. §12-1103(B). The purpose of this requirement is to avoid needless litigation. *See, Mariposa Development Co. v. Stoddard,* 147 Ariz. 561, 711 P.2d 1234 (App. 1985)

TREES AND VEGETATION ACROSS BOUNDARY LINES

Trees and other vegetation often grow across boundary lines. In the case of *Cannon v. Dunn,* 145 Ariz. 115, 700 P.2d 502 (App. 1985), the roots of a eucalyptus tree in the adjoining landowner's yard invaded the subsurface of the neighbor's land. The neighbor sued the adjoining landowner for trespass or the abatement of the nuisance and asked the court for an injunction and damages. The court denied the neighbor's request for damages and injunctive relief because the neighbor did not sustain any actual damage from the growth of the roots. However, the court stated that a landowner who sustains injury by the branches or roots of a tree or plant on adjoining land intruding into the landowner's property may, without notice, cut off the offending branches or roots at the property line. If some "actual and sensible or substantial damage" is sustained, the injured landowner may maintain an action in trespass and an action for injunctive relief to abate the nuisance.

LIS PENDENS

Lis pendens means a pending suit and is a document that is recorded against real property to give notice that title to the property is the subject of a lawsuit. *See, Tucson Estates, Inc. v. Superior Court,* 151 Ariz. 600, 729 P.2d 954 (App. 1986). On occasion, a broker will consider filing a *lis pendens* on a property because of a commission dispute. However, a *lis pendens* is not authorized in a commission dispute. A.R.S. §12-1191(A) provides in pertinent part:

> In an action affecting title to real property, the plaintiff at the time of filing the complaint, or thereafter, and the defendant at the time of filing the defendant's pleading when affirmative relief is claimed in such pleading, or thereafter, may file in the office of the recorder of the county in which the property is situated a notice of the pendency of the action or defense.

If a *lis pendens* is filed in a lawsuit that does not affect title to real property, the *lis pendens* is groundless. *Richey v. Western Pacific Development Corp.* 140 Ariz. 597, 684 P.2d 169 (App. 1984). In the *Richey* case, a broker sued to collect an $8,000 real estate commission and recorded a *lis pendens* on the property that had been sold. The defendant counterclaimed for damages pursuant to A.R.S. §33-420 for a groundless *lis pendens*.

A.R.S. §33-420 states in pertinent part:

A. A person purporting to claim an interest in, or a lien or encumbrance against, real property, who causes a document asserting such claim to be recorded in the office of the county recorder, knowing or having reason to know that the document is forged, groundless, contains a material misstatement or false claim or is otherwise invalid is liable to the owner or beneficial title holder of the real property for the sum of not less than $5,000, or for treble the actual damages caused by the recording, whichever is greater, and reasonable attorney fees and costs of the action.

B. A person who is named in a document that purports to create an interest in, or a lien or encumbrance against, real property and who knows that the document is forged, groundless, contains a material misstatement or false claim or is otherwise invalid shall be liable to the owner or title holder for the sum of not less than $1,000, or for treble actual damages, whichever is greater, and reasonable attorney fees and costs as provided in this section, if he willfully refuses to release or correct such document of record within 20 days from the date of a written request from the owner or beneficial title holder of the real property.

Because the commission claim did not affect title to real property, but was simply a money claim, the *lis pendens* was groundless. The defendant was awarded $1,000 statutory damages plus attorney's fees, even though the *lis pendens* was removed before any actual damages were incurred.

KEY POINTS TO REMEMBER

- An owner-builder who wants to sell the property within one year after completion of construction or issuance of a certificate of occupancy should be referred to legal counsel.

- The homestead exemption prevents certain creditors from taking the first $150,000 of equity in a person's home to satisfy a debt.

- Possession or use of another's land for 10 years or more may result in the continued right to possess or use the land.

- A landowner may generally cut the branches of a tree on adjoining land at the property line.

- A *lis pendens* is a recorded notice of a pending lawsuit that affects title to a property and should never be recorded in a commission dispute.

CHAPTER 24

Serving a Nonprofit Association/Board of Realtors® as an Officer or Director[15]

AAR and the local REALTOR® associations depend on association members to volunteer their time and expertise to accomplish association objectives. These associations could not make a contribution to the real estate industry without these individuals, who serve on workgroups, committees, Key Result Areas (KRAs), and in leadership positions. State and local leaders, who serve as association directors and association officers, are often called upon to make difficult decisions involving significant expenditure of funds. However, these leaders of the industry are not exposed to a great deal of liability as long as they act in good faith and exercise ordinary care.

AAR and most local associations are nonprofit corporations. A nonprofit corporation is governed by its Articles of Incorporation, Bylaws, Policy Statements and the Arizona Nonprofit Corporation Act (NCA), A.R.S. §10-3101 *et. seq.* These governing documents and Arizona law define the scope of the duties and liabilities associated with serving as an

---

[15] *This discussion is applicable to an association that is formed as a nonprofit corporation. To determine whether an association is a nonprofit corporation, check the association's governing documents or contact the Arizona Corporation Commission.*

officer or director and may modify or supplement the NCA. Therefore, an officer or director should review the association's governing documents.

STANDARDS OF CONDUCT FOR OFFICERS AND DIRECTORS OF A NONPROFIT CORPORATION

The NCA sets forth the standards of conduct for officers and directors of a nonprofit corporation. The NCA provides that an officer or director's duties must be discharged:

- in good faith
- with the care an ordinarily prudent person in a like position would exercise under similar circumstances
- in a manner the director reasonably believes to be in the best interests of the corporation

See, A.R.S. §10-3830 (directors); A.R.S. §10-3842 (officers).

In discharging these duties, an officer or director is entitled to rely on information, opinions, reports or statements, including financial statements and other financial data, if prepared or presented by:

- officers or employees of the association whom the officer or director reasonably believes are reliable and competent in the matters presented
- legal counsel, public accountants or other persons as to matters the officer or director reasonably believes are within the person's professional or expert competence
- a committee of or appointed by the board of directors of which the director is not a member if the director reasonably believes the committee merits confidence

The NCA also provides that a director is presumed in all cases to have acted, failed to act or otherwise discharged such director's duties in good faith, with prudent care and in the corporation's best interests. A person challenging a director's action, failure to act or other discharge of duties has the burden to establish by clear and convincing evidence facts rebutting this presumption.

ASSOCIATION GOVERNING DOCUMENT PROVISIONS

By way of example, the AAR governing documents contain various provisions relating to the duties and liability of AAR officers and directors. AAR was incorporated in 1953 as a 501(c)(6) nonprofit corporation.

The AAR Articles of Incorporation provide that:

- management and control of AAR is vested in the board of directors
- the directors and any person that serves on a board or council in an advisory capacity shall not be subject to suit for acts or omissions made in good faith within the scope of their official capacity
- the directors and any person who serves on a board or council in an advisory capacity shall not be subject to personal liability for breach of fiduciary duty to maximum extent provided by law
- AAR shall indemnify any person who incurs expenses by reason of the fact that the person is or was an AAR officer, director, employee or agent to the maximum extent provided by law

The AAR Bylaws provide that:

- AAR business is managed by the board of directors and the executive committee *(AAR Executive Committee officers are president, president-elect, first vice president, treasurer and five regional vice presidents)*
- every officer shall be indemnified against all expenses and liabilities reasonably incurred in conjunction with any proceeding in which that officer is involved by reason of being or having been an AAR officer, except in such cases wherein the officer is adjudged guilty of willful misfeasance or malfeasance in the performance of such officer's duties or shall have acted in such a manner as has exceeded such officer's authority

The AAR Policy Statements and Official Statements:

- contain guidelines for internal AAR operations
- require the executive committee to insure that AAR is strategically focused, to monitor but avoid conducting day-to-day AAR

operations, to conduct business in a timely and honest fashion, and to observe the internal and external chain of command.

Question: *Can an individual be held personally liable for actions taken as an association officer or director?*
Answer: Officers and directors of a nonprofit corporation are largely shielded from personal civil liability for actions taken as officers or directors provided that they act in good faith and within the scope of their official duties. However, an officer or director can be held personally liable in certain circumstances. For example, an officer or director may be held personally liable for directly injuring someone or intentionally taking a fraudulent or illegal action.

Question: *If an officer or director is named in a lawsuit, will the association indemnify the individual for any expenses?*
Answer: An officer or director of a nonprofit corporation probably has a right to be indemnified for reasonable expenses incurred as a result of a lawsuit the officer/director was involved in due to the individual's position in the association. The NCA provides that a corporation may indemnify an individual made a party to a proceeding because the individual is or was an officer or director if:
- the individual's conduct was in good faith
- the individual reasonably believed:
    - in the case of conduct in an official capacity with the corporation, that the conduct was in its best interests
    - in all other cases, that the conduct was at least not opposed to its best interests
- in the case of any criminal proceedings, the individual had no reasonable cause to believe the conduct was unlawful

However, an officer or director may not be indemnified under this statute if the officer or director was adjudged liable to the corporation or in connection with any other proceeding in which the director was adjudged liable on the basis that personal benefit was improperly received. A.R.S. §10-3851.

Further, absent wrongdoing, and unless limited by its articles of incorporation, an association formed as a nonprofit corporation must indemnify an individual for expenses if the individual was the prevailing party in the defense of any proceeding to which the individual was a party because the individual is or was an officer or director of the corporation. In most cases the association, absent wrongdoing and subject to its articles of incorporation, must also indemnify an officer or director against liability. A.R.S. §10-3852.

Question: Does the Association have liability insurance?

Answer: Provided that a REALTOR® association maintains its governing documents in full compliance with the NAR Constitution, Bylaws and Policies, and adheres to NAR policies, procedures and requirements in its day-to-day activities as required, the association and its officers and directors should be insured by the NAR Professional Liability Insurance Policy. This policy generally covers claims relating to negligent acts, errors, omissions, misstatements, misleading statements or breaches of fiduciary duty as described in the policy. The policy also includes a number of exceptions. An officer or director may want to become familiar with this insurance policy and to explore whether an individual personal umbrella policy may provide additional protection. Note: Associations should submit all governing documents to NAR's Policy Division for compliance review a minimum of every two years. Changes to governing documents should be submitted for review when proposed.

Question: Should an officer or director be concerned about conflicts of interest?

Answer: Yes. Although conflicts are rare, it is important as an association officer or director to recognize a potential conflict of interest with the association so that it can be handled appropriately.

Question: What constitutes a conflict of interest?

Answer: "Conflicting interest" is defined in the NCA as an interest respecting a transaction or proposed transaction involving the association, its subsidiary or any other entity in which the association has a controlling interest if the officer or director or a related person[16] is either:

- a party to the transaction, or
- has a beneficial financial interest in or is so closely linked to the transaction and of such financial significance to the director or a related person that the interest would reasonably be expected to exert an influence on the director's judgment if called on to vote on the transaction.

A conflict of interest may also exist if the officer or director knows that any of the following persons is either a party to the transaction or has a beneficial financial interest in or is so closely linked to the transaction, and it is of such financial significance to the person that the interest would reasonably be expected to exert an influence on the officer or director's judgment if called on to vote on the transaction:

- an entity, other than the corporation, of which the officer or director is a director, general partner, agent or employee
- a person who controls one or more of the above or an entity that is controlled by or is under common control with one or more of the above entities
- a general partner, principal or employer of the officer or director.

Question: *What should an officer or director do if a conflict of interest arises?*
Answer: The officer or director should immediately disclose the existence and nature of the conflicting interest and disclose all facts reasonably material to a judgment about whether or not to proceed with the transaction. Consult the association's governing documents for further guidance.

---

[16]The spouse, or a parent or sibling of the spouse, of the director; a child, grandchild, sibling, parent or spouse of a child, grandchild, sibling or parent, of the director; an individual having the same home as the director; or a trust or estate of which an individual specified in this subdivision is a substantial beneficiary. A trust, estate, incompetent, conservatee or minor of which the director is a fiduciary.

KEY POINTS TO REMEMBER

When acting as an officer or director of a nonprofit association:

- Act in good faith with prudent care and in the association's best interests.

- Be prepared for meetings and review advance materials.

- Ask questions and participate in meeting discussions.

- Be aware of any potential conflicts of interest and act accordingly.

- Do not use the position to further private interests.

CHAPTER 25

Broker Risk Reduction

Minimizing risk is a legitimate goal in any situation. The following tips should assist a broker in better serving the client and reducing the possibility of costly and time-consuming litigation.

RISK REDUCTION TIPS

- *Get to Know Your Client:* the disclosures, advice and counsel required of the broker, depend upon:
  - the facts of each transaction
  - the knowledge and the experience of the client
  - the questions asked by the client
  - the nature of the property
  - the terms of sale
- *Read & Understand the Purchase Contract & Related Forms:* understanding these documents is pivotal to giving competent advice
- *Educate Your Client:* on the contract, CC&Rs, title report, public report and any other important matters

- *Avoid Shortcuts:* shortcuts such as incorporating the MLS or listing form into the contract, giving buyer a list of properties to see at open houses unaccompanied and failing to write contingencies out completely all lead to ambiguity and the potential for disputes
- *Handle Offers Properly:* and submit all offers promptly
- *Practice Within Your Area of Expertise:* both in practice area and geographically
- *When in Doubt, Disclose:* if you have actual knowledge of a material defect, disclose it — if you notice a suspicious condition, point it out to the client and recommend the appropriate technical or professional investigation
- *Assist Your Client with Disclosures and Due Diligence:* insist on inspections and attend the inspections and walkthroughs — supply the buyer with the tools to obtain information
- *Think Before You Speak:* don't speculate or guess — identify the source of any information provided and direct your client to the source if possible
- *Verify Information:* if you have reason to question the accuracy of information being provided in a transaction or where the client has questioned the accuracy of the information
- *Follow Through:* get buyer pre-approved for financing — review the title report and all other pertinent documents
- *Document the Transaction:* take contemporaneous notes, confirm important issues in writing, maintain a fax/e-mail/phone log, keep a complete and organized file
- *Communicate:* promptly return calls to clients and the other broker, provide updates even if nothing is happening, handle complaints promptly

RISK MANAGEMENT AND DISPUTE RESOLUTION TOOLS PROVIDED BY AAR

AAR provides risk management and dispute resolution tools for both members and consumers, such as:

AAR's Dispute Resolution System (mediation) assists buyers and sellers resolve their disputes. AAR also has informal dispute-resolving processes available to consumers (e.g., ombudsmen). Visit AAR's Web site or contact AAR to speak directly to someone about these processes.

The REALTOR® arbitration system is available to resolve complaints within AAR's jurisdiction. More information about REALTOR® arbitration is available on the Web site or by calling the association.

The Buyer Advisory, available on AAR's Web site provides buyers with information about important issues, explains why certain issues are important, and directs buyers, via hyperlink in the electronic version, to sources of additional information.

The AAR Legal Hotline, which allows designated REALTORS® (who can also give access to one REALTOR® per office or branch) to consult with a hotline attorney about problems as they arise. (Available to AAR members only.)

The Legal Information Section of AAR's Web site has legal Q&As and other articles covering numerous legal topics.

CHAPTER 26

Definitions and Resources

DEFINITIONS

Every industry has its own terminology, and real estate is no different. However, some real estate terms are often misunderstood. The following are some common real estate terms and their meanings.

AAR: Arizona Association of REALTORS®, the largest trade association in Arizona, representing over 53,000 Arizona REALTORS® belonging to 21 local associations. Members are active real estate licensees from all areas of real estate, including residential, commercial, property management, land, appraisal and relocation.

ADRE: Arizona Department of Real Estate, the state department that licenses and regulates real estate brokers.

AGENCY: Agency is the relationship that occurs when a broker represents a buyer or seller in a real estate transaction. An agent has fiduciary duties to the client, such as confidentiality, accounting, reasonable care, loyalty, obedience, advocacy and disclosure.

AS IS: A provision in a contract indicating that the property will be sold in its existing physical condition.

BUYER-BROKER AGREEMENT: A buyer-broker agreement is an employment agreement between a buyer and a broker that employs the broker to locate property and negotiate terms and conditions acceptable to the buyer for the purchase of a home. The buyer usually agrees to work exclusively with the broker, and the compensation that the buyer is obligated to pay is often offset by any compensation the broker receives from the listing agent.

CONDITIONS, COVENANTS & RESTRICTIONS (CC&Rs): CC&Rs are recorded against the home and are an enforceable contract. The CC&Rs empower the homeowner's association, if there is one, to control certain aspects of the home. If there is no homeowner's association, the CC&Rs can be enforced by the other homeowners.

CONTINGENCY: A contingency is a clause in a contract that requires the completion of a certain act before the parties are obligated to perform their contractual obligations. The most common contingencies are financing, acceptable property condition, and condition of title.

CONTRACT: A contract is an agreement to do or not to do something. A contract for the sale of a home must be in a signed writing to be enforceable. The Arizona Association of REALTORS® (AAR) Residential Resale Real Estate Purchase Contract is the most common form of contract for the transfer of resale residential real property in Arizona.

DUAL REPRESENTATION (Dual Agency): Where one broker either individually, or two salespeople working for the same broker, represent both the buyer and seller in a real estate transaction.

EASEMENT: An easement gives persons other than the owner access to or a right of way over the homeowner's property. Common easements include utility easements and roadway easements.

ESCROW INSTRUCTIONS: Escrow instructions are instructions to the escrow company on how to carry out the terms of a contract. The contract is often used as escrow instructions. Other times, the escrow instructions are preprinted forms from the escrow company with any necessary additional or supplemental instructions.

FIXTURE: A fixture is an item that was once personal property, but is affixed to the home in such a manner as to become a part of the home itself. A buyer purchases the fixtures affixed to the home.

KRA: An AAR committee called a key result area. AAR has five key result areas: Operations, Information Management, Professional Development, Industry Issues, and Governmental. Each area establishes work groups, committees, and forums as needed. An officer of the association serves as a liaison to each key result area.

LATENT: Something that is concealed or hidden from view.

LISTING AGREEMENT: An employment contract between a seller and a listing broker. The agreement establishes the duties of the broker and the terms under which the broker will earn a commission.

LICENSEE: A person licensed by the ADRE.

MATERIAL: Something that is important or significant.

MLS: The Multiple Listing Service (MLS) is a repository of information on homes for sale. The MLS is also a means by which broker participants make offers of compensation to other broker participants for bringing a ready, willing and able buyer for the property. There are many regional and local Multiple Listing Service companies in Arizona, none of which are owned or operated by AAR.

NAR: NATIONAL ASSOCIATION OF REALTORS®, the world's largest professional association. Members belong to one or more of 1,700 local associations/boards and 54 state and territory associations of REALTORS®.

REALTOR: The term REALTOR® is a federally registered membership mark used by real estate licensees who are members of the NATIONAL ASSOCIATION OF REALTORS® and agree to abide by its strict Code of Ethics. Not all real estate licensees are REALTORS®.

RIGHT OF FIRST REFUSAL: A right of first refusal is a provision in a contract that requires the owner of a home to give another party (usually a tenant) the first opportunity to purchase or lease the property.

TITLE COMMITMENT: The title commitment reflects the condition of the title to a property, whether the taxes and assessments are paid, whether there are deed restrictions, liens and easements on the property, and what the requirements are for the issuance of title insurance.

TITLE INSURANCE: There are generally two title insurance policies issued at close of escrow, the owner's policy and the lender's policy.

The owner's policy is an insurance policy that protects a homeowner from defects in the title to the home, such as a forged deed. The lender's policy protects the lender against the same sort of title defects until the loan is paid.

VOIDABLE: A contract that is subject to rescission by one of the parties who acted under a disability, such as being a minor. A voidable contract may avoided or adjudged void but is not, in and of itself, void.

WRAPAROUND FINANCING: Wraparound financing occurs when a seller sells property that is already subject to an existing loan and takes back a loan for a purchase price that exceeds the existing first loan.

INDUSTRY RESOURCES

REALTOR® Associations

NATIONAL ASSOCIATION OF REALTORS® (NAR): *www.realtor.com*

Arizona Association of REALTORS® (AAR): *www.aaronline.com*

Local REALTOR® Associations: *www.aaronline.com/documents/AllAssnNames.aspx*

- Bullhead City/Mohave Valley Association of REALTORS®
- Central Arizona Board of REALTORS®
- Douglas Association of REALTORS®
- Graham/Greenlee Board of REALTORS®
- Green Valley Association of REALTORS®
- Kingman/Golden Valley Association of REALTORS®
- Lake Havasu Association of REALTORS®
- La Paz Association of REALTORS®
- Northern Arizona Association of REALTORS®
- Phoenix Association of REALTORS®
- Prescott Area Association of REALTORS®
- Santa Cruz County Board of REALTORS®

- Scottsdale Area Association of REALTORS®
- Sedona/Verde Valley Association of REALTORS®
- Southeast Arizona Association of REALTORS®
- Southeast Valley Regional Association of REALTORS®
- Tucson Association of REALTORS®
- West Maricopa County Regional Association of REALTORS®
- Western Pinal Association of REALTORS®
- White Mountain Association of REALTORS®
- Yuma Association of REALTORS®

Arizona Commercial Information Exchange (AZCiE): *www.azcie.com*

Legal Information

Arizona Courts: *www.supreme.state.az.us/nav2/appeals.htm*

Arizona State Legislature: *www.azleg.gov/*

State Bar of Arizona: *www.azbar.org/*

Arizona Revised Statutes (A.R.S.): *www.azleg.state.az.us/ArizonaRevised Statutes.asp*

State Agencies

State of Arizona: *az.gov/webapp/portal/*

Board of Appraisal: *www.appraisal.state.az.us/*

Attorney General: *www.azag.gov/*

Registrar of Contractors: *www.azroc.gov/*

Department of Environmental Quality: *www.azdeq.gov/*

Department of Financial Institutions (Formerly State Banking): *azdfi.gov/*

Department of Insurance: *www.id.state.az.us/*

Office of Manufactured Housing: *www.dbfs.state.az.us/OMH/index_omh.html*

Department of Real Estate (ADRE): *www.re.state.az.us*

Structural Pest Control Commission: *www.sb.state.az.us/*

Board of Technical Registration: *www.btr.state.az.us/*

Department of Water Resources: *www.azwater.gov/dwr/*

Federal Law & Agencies

Do Not Call Registry: *www.telemarketing.donotcall.gov*

Lead-based Paint, Housing and Urban Development (HUD): *www.hud.gov/offices/lead/index.cfm*

Lead-based Paint, Environmental Protection Agency (EPA): *www.epa.gov/opptintr/lead/*

RESPA, Housing and Urban Development (HUD): *www.hud.gov/offices/hsg/sfh/res/respa_hm.cfm*

Polybutylene Class Action Settlements:

Cox Class Settlement: *www.pbpipe.com/index1.htm*

Spencer Class Settlement: *www.spencerclass.com/*

Crime Statistics & Sex Offender Registry:

Phoenix, Tempe, Glendale, Mesa, Scottsdale, Chandler, Gilbert and Peoria: *www.faxnet1.org*

Sex Offender Registry: *www.azsexoffender.org*

CHAPTER 27

NAR Code of Ethics

All REALTORS® must adhere to the NAR Code of Ethics, therefore, the entire 2006 Code follows in its entirety. The NAR Code of Ethics was referenced in one Arizona case, *Baker v. Leight*, 370 P.2d 268 (Ariz. 1962). In this case the buyers brought a claim for fraud, rescission of contract and unjust enrichment against a seller and the seller's broker, who was not a REALTOR®. The Arizona Supreme Court stated: "It is immaterial as to whether the broker is a member of the National Association if it is established that this Association Code of Ethics is applicable to those in the real estate profession in this state." The court further stated that NAR's Code of Ethics "is regarded as the standard of conduct by real estate [brokers] throughout the United States and shall be regarded as such in the State of Arizona." However, no case subsequent to *Baker v. Leight* has referred to the NAR Code of Ethics.

NAR promotes consumer protection, but NAR does not encourage or endorse incorporation of the Code of Ethics into statute, rule or case law. *See, NAR Code of Ethics and Arbitration Manual, Ethics — Statements of Professional Standards Policy14 (2005).* The Code of Ethics is copyrighted by NAR, subject to interpretation only by the NAR Professional

Standards Committee and REALTOR® associations have the responsibility for its enforcement. The Code's high standards are adopted voluntarily by REALTOR® members.

Code of Ethics and Standards of Practice
of the NATIONAL ASSOCIATION OF REALTORS®
Effective January 1, 2006

Where the word REALTORS® is used in this Code and Preamble, it shall be deemed to include REALTOR-ASSOCIATE®s.

While the Code of Ethics establishes obligations that may be higher than those mandated by law, in any instance where the Code of Ethics and the law conflict, the obligations of the law must take precedence.

Preamble

Under all is the land. Upon its wise utilization and widely allocated ownership depend the survival and growth of free institutions and of our civilization. REALTORS® should recognize that the interests of the nation and its citizens require the highest and best use of the land and the widest distribution of land ownership. They require the creation of adequate housing, the building of functioning cities, the development of productive industries and farms, and the preservation of a healthful environment.

Such interests impose obligations beyond those of ordinary commerce. They impose grave social responsibility and a patriotic duty to which REALTORS® should dedicate themselves, and for which they should be diligent in preparing themselves. REALTORS®, therefore, are zealous to maintain and improve the standards of their calling and share with their fellow REALTORS® a common responsibility for its integrity and honor.

In recognition and appreciation of their obligations to clients, customers, the public, and each other, REALTORS® continuously strive to become and remain informed on issues affecting real estate and, as knowledgeable professionals, they willingly share the fruit of their experience and study with others. They identify and take steps, through enforcement of this Code of Ethics and by assisting appropriate regulatory bodies, to eliminate practices which may damage the public or which might discredit or bring dishonor to the real estate profession. REALTORS® having direct personal knowledge of conduct that may violate the Code of Ethics involving misappropriation of client or customer funds or property, willful discrimination, or fraud resulting in substantial economic harm, bring such matters to the attention of the appropriate Board or Association of REALTORS®. (Amended 1/00)

Realizing that cooperation with other real estate professionals promotes the best interests of those who utilize their services, REALTORS® urge exclusive representation of clients; do not attempt to gain any unfair advantage over their competitors; and they refrain from making unsolicited comments about other practitioners. In instances where their opinion is sought, or where REALTORS® believe that comment is necessary, their opinion is offered in an objective, professional manner, uninfluenced by any personal motivation or potential advantage or gain.

The term REALTOR® has come to connote competency, fairness, and high integrity resulting from adherence to a lofty ideal of moral conduct in business relations. No inducement of profit and no instruction from clients ever can justify departure from this ideal.

In the interpretation of this obligation, REALTORS® can take no safer guide than that which has been handed down through the centuries, embodied in the Golden Rule, "Whatsoever ye would that others should do to you, do ye even so to them."

Accepting this standard as their own, REALTORS® pledge to observe its spirit in all of their activities and to conduct their business in accordance with the tenets set forth below.

Duties to Clients and Customers

Article I

When representing a buyer, seller, landlord, tenant, or other client as an agent, REALTORS® pledge themselves to protect and promote the interests of their client. This obligation to the client is primary, but it does not relieve REALTORS® of their obligation to treat all parties honestly.

When serving a buyer, seller, landlord, tenant or other party in a non-agency capacity, REALTORS® remain obligated to treat all parties honestly. (Amended 1/01)

• Standard of Practice 1-1

REALTORS®, when acting as principals in a real estate transaction, remain obligated by the duties imposed by the Code of Ethics. (Amended 1/93)

• Standard of Practice 1-2

The duties the Code of Ethics imposes are applicable whether REALTORS® are acting as agents or in legally recognized non-agency capacities except that any duty imposed exclusively on agents by law or regulation shall not be imposed by this Code of Ethics on REALTORS® acting in non-agency capacities.

As used in this Code of Ethics, "client" means the person(s) or entity(ies) with whom a REALTOR® or a REALTOR®'s firm has an agency or legally recognized non-agency relationship; "customer" means a party to a real estate transaction who receives information, services, or benefits but has no contractual relationship with the REALTOR® or the REALTORS®'s firm; "prospect" means a purchaser, seller, tenant, or landlord who is not subject to a representation relationship with the REALTOR® or REALTOR®'s firm; "agent" means a real estate licensee (including brokers and sales ASSOCIATEs) acting in an agency relationship as defined by state law or regulation; and "broker" means a real estate licensee (including brokers and sales ASSOCIATEs) acting as an agent or in a legally recognized non-agency capacity. (Adopted 1/95, Amended 1/04)

• Standard of Practice 1-3

REALTORS®, in attempting to secure a listing, shall not deliberately mislead the owner as to market value.

• Standard of Practice 1-4

REALTORS®, when seeking to become a buyer/tenant representative, shall not mislead buyers or tenants as to savings or other benefits that might be realized through use of the REALTOR®'s services. (Amended 1/93)

• Standard of Practice 1-5

REALTORS® may represent the seller/landlord and buyer/tenant in the same transaction only after full disclosure to and with informed consent of both parties. (Adopted 1/93)

• Standard of Practice 1-6

REALTORS® shall submit offers and counter-offers objectively and as quickly as possible. (Adopted 1/93, Amended 1/95)

• Standard of Practice 1-7

When acting as listing brokers, REALTORS® shall continue to submit to the seller/landlord all offers and counter-offers until closing or execution of a lease unless the seller/landlord has waived this obligation in writing. REALTORS® shall not be obligated to continue to market the property after an offer has been accepted by the seller/landlord. REALTORS® shall recommend that sellers/ landlords obtain the advice of legal counsel prior to acceptance of a subsequent offer except where the acceptance is contingent on the termination of the pre-existing purchase contract or lease. (Amended 1/93)

• Standard of Practice 1-8

REALTORS®, acting as agents or brokers of buyers/tenants, shall submit to buyers/tenants all offers and counter-offers until acceptance but have no obligation to continue to show properties to their clients after an offer has been accepted unless otherwise agreed in writing. REALTORS®, acting as agents or brokers of buyers/tenants, shall recommend that buyers/tenants obtain the advice of legal counsel if there is a question as to whether a pre-existing contract has been terminated. (Adopted 1/93, Amended 1/99)

• Standard of Practice 1-9

The obligation of REALTORS® to preserve confidential information (as defined by state law) provided by their clients in the course of any agency relationship or non-agency relationship recognized by law continues after termination of agency relationships or any non-agency relationships recognized by law. REALTORS® shall not knowingly, during or following the termination of professional relationships with their clients:

1) reveal confidential information of clients; or
2) use confidential information of clients to the disadvantage of clients; or
3) use confidential information of clients for the REALTOR®'s advantage or the advantage of third parties unless:
   a) clients consent after full disclosure; or
   b) REALTORS® are required by court order; or
   c) it is the intention of a client to commit a crime and the information is necessary to prevent the crime; or
   d) it is necessary to defend a REALTOR® or the REALTOR®'s employees or ASSOCIATEs against an accusation of wrongful conduct

Information concerning latent material defects is not considered confidential information under this Code of Ethics. (Adopted 1/93, Amended 1/01)

• Standard of Practice 1-10

REALTORS® shall, consistent with the terms and conditions of their real estate licensure and their property management agreement, competently manage the property of clients with due regard for the rights, safety and health of tenants and others lawfully on the premises. (Adopted 1/95, Amended 1/00)

• Standard of Practice 1-11

REALTORS® who are employed to maintain or manage a client's property shall exercise due diligence and make reasonable efforts to protect it against reasonably foreseeable contingencies and losses. (Adopted 1/95)

• Standard of Practice 1-12

When entering into listing contracts, REALTORS® must advise sellers/landlords of:

1) the REALTOR®'s company policies regarding cooperation and the amount(s) of any compensation that will be offered to subagents,

buyer/tenant agents, and/or brokers acting in legally recognized non-agency capacities;

2) the fact that buyer/tenant agents or brokers, even if compensated by listing brokers, or by sellers/landlords may represent the interests of buyers/tenants; and

3) any potential for listing brokers to act as disclosed dual agents, e.g. buyer/tenant agents. (Adopted 1/93, Renumbered 1/98, Amended 1/03)

• Standard of Practice 1-13

When entering into buyer/tenant agreements, REALTORS® must advise potential clients of:

1) the REALTOR®'s company policies regarding cooperation;

2) the amount of compensation to be paid by the client;

3) the potential for additional or offsetting compensation from other brokers, from the seller or landlord, or from other parties;

4) any potential for the buyer/tenant representative to act as a disclosed dual agent, e.g. listing broker, subagent, landlord's agent, etc., and

5) the possibility that sellers or sellers' representatives may not treat the existence, terms, or conditions of offers as confidential unless confidentiality is required by law, regulation, or by any confidentiality agreement between the parties. (Adopted 1/93, Renumbered 1/98, Amended 1/06)

• Standard of Practice 1-14

Fees for preparing appraisals or other valuations shall not be contingent upon the amount of the appraisal or valuation. (Adopted 1/02)

• Standard of Practice 1-15

REALTORS®, in response to inquiries from buyers or cooperating brokers shall, with the sellers' approval, disclose the existence of offers on the property. Where disclosure is authorized, REALTORS® shall also disclose whether offers were obtained by the listing licensee, another licensee in the listing firm, or by a cooperating broker. (Adopted 1/03, Amended 1/06)

Article 2

REALTORS® shall avoid exaggeration, misrepresentation, or concealment of pertinent facts relating to the property or the transaction. REALTORS® shall not, however, be obligated to discover latent defects in the property, to advise on matters outside the scope of their real estate license, or to disclose facts which are confidential under the scope of agency or non-agency relationships as defined by state law. (Amended 1/00)

• Standard of Practice 2-1

REALTORS® shall only be obligated to discover and disclose adverse factors reasonably apparent to someone with expertise in those areas required by their real estate licensing authority. Article 2 does not impose upon the REALTOR® the obligation of expertise in other professional or technical disciplines. (Amended 1/96)

• Standard of Practice 2-2

(Renumbered as Standard of Practice 1-12 1/98)

• Standard of Practice 2-3

(Renumbered as Standard of Practice 1-13 1/98)

• Standard of Practice 2-4

REALTORS® shall not be parties to the naming of a false consideration in any document, unless it be the naming of an obviously nominal consideration.

• Standard of Practice 2-5

Factors defined as "non-material" by law or regulation or which are expressly referenced in law or regulation as not being subject to disclosure are considered not "pertinent" for purposes of Article 2. (Adopted 1/93)

Article 3

REALTORS® shall cooperate with other brokers except when cooperation is not in the client's best interest. The obligation to cooperate does not include the obligation to share commissions, fees, or to otherwise compensate another broker. (Amended 1/95)

• **Standard of Practice 3-1**

REALTORS®, acting as exclusive agents or brokers of sellers/ landlords, establish the terms and conditions of offers to cooperate. Unless expressly indicated in offers to cooperate, cooperating brokers may not assume that the offer of cooperation includes an offer of compensation. Terms of compensation, if any, shall be ascertained by cooperating brokers before beginning efforts to accept the offer of cooperation. (Amended 1/99)

• **Standard of Practice 3-2**

REALTORS® shall, with respect to offers of compensation to another REALTOR®, timely communicate any change of compensation for cooperative services to the other REALTOR® prior to the time such REALTOR® produces an offer to purchase/lease the property. (Amended 1/94)

• **Standard of Practice 3-3**

Standard of Practice 3-2 does not preclude the listing broker and cooperating broker from entering into an agreement to change cooperative compensation. (Adopted 1/94)

• **Standard of Practice 3-4**

REALTORS®, acting as listing brokers, have an affirmative obligation to disclose the existence of dual or variable rate commission arrangements (i.e., listings where one amount of commission is payable if the listing broker's firm is the procuring cause of sale/lease and a different amount of commission is payable if the sale/lease results through the efforts of the seller/landlord or a cooperating broker). The listing broker shall, as soon as practical, disclose the existence of such arrangements to potential cooperating brokers and shall, in response to inquiries from cooperating brokers, disclose the differential that would result in a cooperative transaction or in a sale/lease that results through the efforts of the seller/landlord. If the cooperating broker is a buyer/tenant representative, the buyer/tenant representative must disclose such information to their client before the client makes an offer to purchase or lease. (Amended 1/02)

• **Standard of Practice 3-5**

It is the obligation of subagents to promptly disclose all pertinent facts to the principal's agent prior to as well as after a purchase or lease agreement is executed. (Amended 1/93)

• **Standard of Practice 3-6**

REALTORS® shall disclose the existence of accepted offers, including offers with unresolved contingencies, to any broker seeking cooperation. (Adopted 5/86, Amended 1/04)

• **Standard of Practice 3-7**

When seeking information from another REALTOR® concerning property under a management or listing agreement, REALTORS® shall disclose their REALTOR® status and whether their interest is personal or on behalf of a client and, if on behalf of a client, their representational status. (Amended 1/95)

• **Standard of Practice 3-8**

REALTORS® shall not misrepresent the availability of access to show or inspect a listed property. (Amended 11/87)

Article 4

REALTORS® shall not acquire an interest in or buy or present offers from themselves, any member of their immediate families, their firms or any member thereof, or any entities in which they have any ownership interest, any real property without making their true position known to the owner or the owner's agent or broker. In selling property they own, or in which they have any interest, REALTORS® shall reveal their ownership or interest in writing to the purchaser or the purchaser's representative. (Amended 1/00)

• **Standard of Practice 4-1**

For the protection of all parties, the disclosures required by Article 4 shall be in writing and provided by REALTORS® prior to the signing of any contract. (Adopted 2/86)

Article 5

REALTORS® shall not undertake to provide professional services concerning a property or its value where they have a present or contemplated interest unless such interest is specifically disclosed to all affected parties.

Article 6

REALTORS® shall not accept any commission, rebate, or profit on expenditures made for their client, without the client's knowledge and consent.

When recommending real estate products or services (e.g., homeowner's insurance, warranty programs, mortgage financing, title insurance, etc.), REALTORS® shall disclose to the client or customer to whom the recommendation is made any financial benefits or fees, other than real estate referral fees, the REALTOR® or REALTOR®'s firm may receive as a direct result of such recommendation. (Amended 1/99)

• Standard of Practice 6-1

REALTORS® shall not recommend or suggest to a client or a customer the use of services of another organization or business entity in which they have a direct interest without disclosing such interest at the time of the recommendation or suggestion. (Amended 5/88)

Article 7

In a transaction, REALTORS® shall not accept compensation from more than one party, even if permitted by law, without disclosure to all parties and the informed consent of the REALTOR®'s client or clients. (Amended 1/93)

Article 8

REALTORS® shall keep in a special account in an appropriate financial institution, separated from their own funds, monies coming into their possession in trust for other persons, such as escrows, trust funds, clients' monies, and other like items.

Article 9

REALTORS®, for the protection of all parties, shall assure whenever possible that all agreements related to real estate transactions including, but not limited to, listing and representation agreements, purchase contracts, and leases are in writing in clear and understandable language expressing the specific terms, conditions, obligations and commitments of the parties. A copy of each agreement shall be furnished to each party to such agreements upon their signing or initialing. (Amended 1/04)

• Standard of Practice 9-1

For the protection of all parties, REALTORS® shall use reasonable care to ensure that documents pertaining to the purchase, sale, or lease of real estate are kept current through the use of written extensions or amendments. (Amended 1/93)

Duties to the Public

Article 10

REALTORS® shall not deny equal professional services to any person for reasons of race, color, religion, sex, handicap, familial status, or national origin. REALTORS® shall not be parties to any plan or agreement to discriminate against a person or persons on the basis of race, color, religion, sex, handicap, familial status, or national origin. (Amended 1/90)

REALTORS®, in their real estate employment practices, shall not discriminate against any person or persons on the basis of race, color, religion, sex, handicap, familial status, or national origin. (Amended 1/00)

• Standard of Practice 10-1

When involved in the sale or lease of a residence, REALTORS® shall not volunteer information regarding the racial, religious or ethnic composition of any neighborhood nor shall they engage in any activity which may result in panic selling, however, REALTORS® may provide other demographic information. (Adopted 1/94, Amended 1/06)

• **Standard of Practice 10-2**

When not involved in the sale or lease of a residence, REALTORS® may provide demographic information related to a property, transaction or professional assignment to a party if such demographic information is (a) deemed by the REALTOR® to be needed to assist with or complete, in a manner consistent with Article 10, a real estate transaction or professional assignment; and (b) is obtained or derived from a recognized, reliable, independent, and impartial source. The source of such information and any additions, deletions, modifications, interpretations, or other changes shall be disclosed in reasonable detail. (Adopted 1/05, Renumbered 1/06)

• **Standard of Practice 10-3**

REALTORS® shall not print, display or circulate any statement or advertisement with respect to selling or renting of a property that indicates any preference, limitations or discrimination based on race, color, religion, sex, handicap, familial status, or national origin. (Adopted 1/94, Renumbered 1/05 and 1/06)

• **Standard of Practice 10-4**

As used in Article 10 "real estate employment practices" relates to employees and independent contractors providing real estate-related services and the administrative and clerical staff directly supporting those individuals. (Adopted 1/00, Renumbered 1/05 and 1/06)

Article II

The services which REALTORS® provide to their clients and customers shall conform to the standards of practice and competence which are reasonably expected in the specific real estate disciplines in which they engage; specifically, residential real estate brokerage, real property management, commercial and industrial real estate brokerage, real estate appraisal, real estate counseling, real estate syndication, real estate auction, and international real estate.

REALTORS® shall not undertake to provide specialized professional services concerning a type of property or service that is outside their field of competence unless they engage the assistance of one who is competent on such types of property or service, or unless the facts are fully disclosed to the client. Any persons engaged to provide such assistance shall be so identified to the client and their contribution to the assignment should be set forth. (Amended 1/95)

• Standard of Practice 11-1

When REALTORS® prepare opinions of real property value or price, other than in pursuit of a listing or to assist a potential purchaser in formulating a purchase offer, such opinions shall include the following:
1) identification of the subject property
2) date prepared
3) defined value or price
4) limiting conditions, including statements of purpose(s) and intended user(s)
5) any present or contemplated interest, including the possibility of representing the seller/landlord or buyers/tenants
6) basis for the opinion, including applicable market data
7) if the opinion is not an appraisal, a statement to that effect (Amended 1/01)

• Standard of Practice 11-2

The obligations of the Code of Ethics in respect of real estate disciplines other than appraisal shall be interpreted and applied in accordance with the standards of competence and practice which clients and the public reasonably require to protect their rights and interests considering the complexity of the transaction, the availability of expert assistance, and, where the REALTOR® is an agent or subagent, the obligations of a fiduciary. (Adopted 1/95)

• Standard of Practice 11-3

When REALTORS® provide consultive services to clients which involve advice or counsel for a fee (not a commission), such advice shall be rendered in an objective manner and the fee shall not be contingent on the substance of the advice or counsel given. If brokerage or transaction services are to be provided in addition to consultive services, a separate compensation may be paid with prior agreement between the client and REALTOR®. (Adopted 1/96)

• Standard of Practice 11-4

The competency required by Article 11 relates to services contracted for between REALTORS® and their clients or customers; the duties expressly imposed by the Code of Ethics; and the duties imposed by law or regulation. (Adopted 1/02)

Article 12

REALTORS® shall be careful at all times to present a true picture in their advertising and representations to the public. REALTORS® shall also ensure that their professional status (e.g., broker, appraiser, property manager, etc.) or status as REALTORS® is clearly identifiable in any such advertising. (Amended 1/93)

• Standard of Practice 12-1

REALTORS® may use the term "free" and similar terms in their advertising and in other representations provided that all terms governing availability of the offered product or service are clearly disclosed at the same time. (Amended 1/97)

• Standard of Practice 12-2

REALTORS® may represent their services as "free" or without cost even if they expect to receive compensation from a source other than their client provided that the potential for the REALTOR® to obtain a benefit from a third party is clearly disclosed at the same time. (Amended 1/97)

• Standard of Practice 12-3

The offering of premiums, prizes, merchandise discounts or other inducements to list, sell, purchase, or lease is not, in itself, unethical even if receipt of the benefit is contingent on listing, selling, purchasing, or leasing through the REALTOR® making the offer. However, REALTORS®

must exercise care and candor in any such advertising or other public or private representations so that any party interested in receiving or otherwise benefiting from the REALTOR®'s offer will have clear, thorough, advance understanding of all the terms and conditions of the offer. The offering of any inducements to do business is subject to the limitations and restrictions of state law and the ethical obligations established by any applicable Standard of Practice. (Amended 1/95)

• Standard of Practice 12-4

REALTORS® shall not offer for sale/lease or advertise property without authority. When acting as listing brokers or as subagents, REALTORS® shall not quote a price different from that agreed upon with the seller/landlord. (Amended 1/93)

• Standard of Practice 12-5

REALTORS® shall not advertise nor permit any person employed by or affiliated with them to advertise listed property without disclosing the name of the firm. (Adopted 11/86)

• Standard of Practice 12-6

REALTORS®, when advertising unlisted real property for sale/lease in which they have an ownership interest, shall disclose their status as both owners/landlords and as REALTORS® or real estate licensees. (Amended 1/93)

• Standard of Practice 12-7

Only REALTORS® who participated in the transaction as the listing broker or cooperating broker (selling broker) may claim to have "sold" the property. Prior to closing, a cooperating broker may post a "sold" sign only with the consent of the listing broker. (Amended 1/96)

Article 13

REALTORS® shall not engage in activities that constitute the unauthorized practice of law and shall recommend that legal counsel be obtained when the interest of any party to the transaction requires it.

Article 14

If charged with unethical practice or asked to present evidence or to cooperate in any other way, in any professional standards proceeding or investigation, REALTORS® shall place all pertinent facts before the proper tribunals of the Member Board or affiliated institute, society, or council in which membership is held and shall take no action to disrupt or obstruct such processes. (Amended 1/99)

• Standard of Practice 14-1

REALTORS® shall not be subject to disciplinary proceedings in more than one Board of REALTORS® or affiliated institute, society or council in which they hold membership with respect to alleged violations of the Code of Ethics relating to the same transaction or event. (Amended 1/95)

• Standard of Practice 14-2

REALTORS® shall not make any unauthorized disclosure or dissemination of the allegations, findings, or decision developed in connection with an ethics hearing or appeal or in connection with an arbitration hearing or procedural review. (Amended 1/92)

• Standard of Practice 14-3

REALTORS® shall not obstruct the Board's investigative or professional standards proceedings by instituting or threatening to institute actions for libel, slander or defamation against any party to a professional standards proceeding or their witnesses based on the filing of an arbitration request, an ethics complaint, or testimony given before any tribunal. (Adopted 11/87, Amended 1/99)

• Standard of Practice 14-4

REALTORS® shall not intentionally impede the Board's investigative or disciplinary proceedings by filing multiple ethics complaints based on the same event or transaction. (Adopted 11/88)

Duties to REALTORS®

Article 15

REALTORS® shall not knowingly or recklessly make false or misleading statements about competitors, their businesses, or their business practices. (Amended 1/92)

• Standard of Practice 15-1

REALTORS® shall not knowingly or recklessly file false or unfounded ethics complaints. (Adopted 1/00)

Article 16

REALTORS® shall not engage in any practice or take any action inconsistent with exclusive representation or exclusive brokerage relationship agreements that other REALTORS® have with clients. (Amended 1/04)

• Standard of Practice 16-1

Article 16 is not intended to prohibit aggressive or innovative business practices which are otherwise ethical and does not prohibit disagreements with other REALTORS® involving commission, fees, compensation or other forms of payment or expenses. (Adopted 1/93, Amended 1/95)

• Standard of Practice 16-2

Article 16 does not preclude REALTORS® from making general announcements to prospects describing their services and the terms of their availability even though some recipients may have entered into agency agreements or other exclusive relationships with another REALTOR®. A general telephone canvass, general mailing or distribution addressed to all prospects in a given geographical area or in a given profession, business, club, or organization, or other classification or group is deemed "general" for purposes of this standard. (Amended 1/04)

Article 16 is intended to recognize as unethical two basic types of solicitations:

First, telephone or personal solicitations of property owners who have been identified by a real estate sign, multiple listing compilation, or other information service as having exclusively listed their property with another REALTOR®; and

Second, mail or other forms of written solicitations of prospects whose properties are exclusively listed with another REALTOR® when such solicitations are not part of a general mailing but are directed specifically to property owners identified through compilations of current listings, "for sale" or "for rent" signs, or other sources of information required by Article 3 and Multiple Listing Service rules to be made available to other REALTORS® under offers of subagency or cooperation. (Amended 1/04)

• Standard of Practice 16-3

Article 16 does not preclude REALTORS® from contacting the client of another broker for the purpose of offering to provide, or entering into a contract to provide, a different type of real estate service unrelated to the type of service currently being provided (e.g., property management as opposed to brokerage) or from offering the same type of service for property not subject to other brokers' exclusive agreements. However, information received through a Multiple Listing Service or any other offer of cooperation may not be used to target clients of other REALTORS® to whom such offers to provide services may be made. (Amended 1/04)

• Standard of Practice 16-4

REALTORS® shall not solicit a listing which is currently listed exclusively with another broker. However, if the listing broker, when asked by the REALTOR®, refuses to disclose the expiration date and nature of such listing; i.e., an exclusive right to sell, an exclusive agency, open listing, or other form of contractual agreement between the listing broker and the client, the REALTOR® may contact the owner to secure such information and may discuss the terms upon which the REALTOR® might take a future listing or, alternatively, may take a listing to become effective upon expiration of any existing exclusive listing. (Amended 1/94)

• Standard of Practice 16-5

REALTORS® shall not solicit buyer/tenant agreements from buyers/ tenants who are subject to exclusive buyer/tenant agreements. However, if asked by a REALTOR®, the broker refuses to disclose the expiration date of the exclusive buyer/tenant agreement, the REALTOR® may contact the buyer/tenant to secure such information and may discuss the terms upon which the REALTOR® might enter into a future buyer/tenant agreement or, alternatively, may enter into a buyer/tenant agreement to become effective upon the expiration of any existing exclusive buyer/tenant agreement. (Adopted 1/94, Amended 1/98)

• Standard of Practice 16-6

When REALTORS® are contacted by the client of another REALTOR® regarding the creation of an exclusive relationship to provide the same type of service, and REALTORS® have not directly or indirectly initiated such discussions, they may discuss the terms upon which they might enter into a future agreement or, alternatively, may enter into an agreement which becomes effective upon expiration of any existing exclusive agreement. (Amended 1/98)

• Standard of Practice 16-7

The fact that a prospect has retained a REALTOR® as an exclusive representative or exclusive broker in one or more past transactions does not preclude other REALTORS® from seeking such prospect's future business. (Amended 1/04)

• Standard of Practice 16-8

The fact that an exclusive agreement has been entered into with a REALTOR® shall not preclude or inhibit any other REALTOR® from entering into a similar agreement after the expiration of the prior agreement. (Amended 1/98)

• Standard of Practice 16-9

REALTORS®, prior to entering into a representation agreement, have an affirmative obligation to make reasonable efforts to determine whether the prospect is subject to a current, valid exclusive agreement to provide the same type of real estate service. (Amended 1/04)

• Standard of Practice 16-10

REALTORS®, acting as buyer or tenant representatives or brokers, shall disclose that relationship to the seller/landlord's representative or broker at first contact and shall provide written confirmation of that disclosure to the seller/ landlord's representative or broker not later than execution of a purchase agreement or lease. (Amended 1/04)

• Standard of Practice 16-11

On unlisted property, REALTORS® acting as buyer/tenant representatives or brokers shall disclose that relationship to the seller/landlord at first contact for that buyer/tenant and shall provide written confirmation of such disclosure to the seller/landlord not later than execution of any purchase or lease agreement. (Amended 1/04)

REALTORS® shall make any request for anticipated compensation from the seller/landlord at first contact. (Amended 1/98)

• Standard of Practice 16-12

REALTORS®, acting as representatives or brokers of sellers/landlords or as subagents of listing brokers, shall disclose that relationship to buyers/ tenants as soon as practicable and shall provide written confirmation of such disclosure to buyers/tenants not later than execution of any purchase or lease agreement. (Amended 1/04)

• Standard of Practice 16-13

All dealings concerning property exclusively listed, or with buyers/ tenants who are subject to an exclusive agreement shall be carried on with the client's representative or broker, and not with the client, except with the consent of the client's representative or broker or except where such dealings are initiated by the client.

Before providing substantive services (such as writing a purchase offer or presenting a CMA) to prospects, REALTORS® shall ask prospects whether they are a party to any exclusive representation agreement. REALTORS® shall not knowingly provide substantive services concerning a prospective transaction to prospects who are parties to exclusive representation agreements, except with the consent of the prospects' exclusive representatives or at the direction of prospects. (Adopted 1/93, Amended 1/04)

• **Standard of Practice 16-14**

REALTORS® are free to enter into contractual relationships or to negotiate with sellers/landlords, buyers/tenants or others who are not subject to an exclusive agreement but shall not knowingly obligate them to pay more than one commission except with their informed consent. (Amended 1/98)

• **Standard of Practice 16-15**

In cooperative transactions REALTORS® shall compensate cooperating REALTORS® (principal brokers) and shall not compensate nor offer to compensate, directly or indirectly, any of the sales licensees employed by or affiliated with other REALTORS® without the prior express knowledge and consent of the cooperating broker.

• **Standard of Practice 16-16**

REALTORS®, acting as subagents or buyer/tenant representatives or brokers, shall not use the terms of an offer to purchase/lease to attempt to modify the listing broker's offer of compensation to subagents or buyer/tenant representatives or brokers nor make the submission of an executed offer to purchase/lease contingent on the listing broker's agreement to modify the offer of compensation. (Amended 1/04)

• **Standard of Practice 16-17**

REALTORS®, acting as subagents or as buyer/tenant representatives or brokers, shall not attempt to extend a listing broker's offer of cooperation and/or compensation to other brokers without the consent of the listing broker. (Amended 1/04)

• **Standard of Practice 16-18**

REALTORS® shall not use information obtained from listing brokers through offers to cooperate made through multiple listing services or through other offers of cooperation to refer listing brokers' clients to other brokers or to create buyer/tenant relationships with listing brokers' clients, unless such use is authorized by listing brokers. (Amended 1/02)

• Standard of Practice 16-19

Signs giving notice of property for sale, rent, lease, or exchange shall not be placed on property without consent of the seller/landlord. (Amended 1/93)

• Standard of Practice 16-20

REALTORS®, prior to or after terminating their relationship with their current firm, shall not induce clients of their current firm to cancel exclusive contractual agreements between the client and that firm. This does not preclude REALTORS® (principals) from establishing agreements with their ASSOCIATED licensees governing assignability of exclusive agreements. (Adopted 1/98)

Article 17

In the event of contractual disputes or specific non-contractual disputes as defined in Standard of Practice 17-4 between REALTORS® (principals) ASSOCIATED with different firms, arising out of their relationship as REALTORS®, the REALTORS® shall submit the dispute to arbitration in accordance with the regulations of their Board or Boards rather than litigate the matter.

In the event clients of REALTORS® wish to arbitrate contractual disputes arising out of real estate transactions, REALTORS® shall arbitrate those disputes in accordance with the regulations of their Board, provided the clients agree to be bound by the decision.

The obligation to participate in arbitration contemplated by this Article includes the obligation of REALTORS® (principals) to cause their firms to arbitrate and be bound by any award. (Amended 1/01)

• Standard of Practice 17-1

The filing of litigation and refusal to withdraw from it by REALTORS® in an arbitrable matter constitutes a refusal to arbitrate. (Adopted 2/86)

• **Standard of Practice 17-2**

Article 17 does not require REALTORS® to arbitrate in those circumstances when all parties to the dispute advise the Board in writing that they choose not to arbitrate before the Board.

(Amended 1/93)

• **Standard of Practice 17-3**

REALTORS®, when acting solely as principals in a real estate transaction, are not obligated to arbitrate disputes with other REALTORS® absent a specific written agreement to the contrary. (Adopted 1/96)

• **Standard of Practice 17-4**

Specific non-contractual disputes that are subject to arbitration pursuant to Article 17 are:

1) Where a listing broker has compensated a cooperating broker and another cooperating broker subsequently claims to be the procuring cause of the sale or lease. In such cases the complainant may name the first cooperating broker as respondent and arbitration may proceed without the listing broker being named as a respondent. Alternatively, if the complaint is brought against the listing broker, the listing broker may name the first cooperating broker as a third-party respondent. In either instance the decision of the hearing panel as to procuring cause shall be conclusive with respect to all current or subsequent claims of the parties for compensation arising out of the underlying cooperative transaction. (Adopted 1/97)

2) Where a buyer or tenant representative is compensated by the seller or landlord, and not by the listing broker, and the listing broker, as a result, reduces the commission owed by the seller or landlord and, subsequent to such actions, another cooperating broker claims to be the procuring cause of sale or lease. In such cases the complainant may name the first cooperating broker as respondent and arbitration may proceed without the listing broker being named as a respondent. Alternatively, if the complaint

is brought against the listing broker, the listing broker may name the first cooperating broker as a third-party respondent. In either instance the decision of the hearing panel as to procuring cause shall be conclusive with respect to all current or subsequent claims of the parties for compensation arising out of the underlying cooperative transaction. (Adopted 1/97)

3) Where a buyer or tenant representative is compensated by the buyer or tenant and, as a result, the listing broker reduces the commission owed by the seller or landlord and, subsequent to such actions, another cooperating broker claims to be the procuring cause of sale or lease. In such cases the complainant may name the first cooperating broker as respondent and arbitration may proceed without the listing broker being named as a respondent. Alternatively, if the complaint is brought against the listing broker, the listing broker may name the first cooperating broker as a third-party respondent. In either instance the decision of the hearing panel as to procuring cause shall be conclusive with respect to all current or subsequent claims of the parties for compensation arising out of the underlying cooperative transaction. (Adopted 1/97)

4) Where two or more listing brokers claim entitlement to compensation pursuant to open listings with a seller or landlord who agrees to participate in arbitration (or who requests arbitration) and who agrees to be bound by the decision. In cases where one of the listing brokers has been compensated by the seller or landlord, the other listing broker, as complainant, may name the first listing broker as respondent and arbitration may proceed between the brokers. (Adopted 1/97)

5) Where a buyer or tenant representative is compensated by the seller or landlord, and not by the listing broker, and the listing broker, as a result, reduces the commission owed by the seller or landlord and, subsequent to such actions, claims to be the procuring cause of sale or lease. In such cases arbitration shall

be between the listing broker and the buyer or tenant representative and the amount in dispute is limited to the amount of the reduction of commission to which the listing broker agreed. (Adopted 1/05)

The Code of Ethics was adopted in 1913. Amended at the Annual Convention in 1924, 1928, 1950, 1951, 1952, 1955, 1956, 1961, 1962, 1974, 1982, 1986, 1987, 1989, 1990, 1991, 1992, 1993, 1994, 1995, 1996, 1997, 1998, 1999, 2000, 2001, 2002, 2003, 2004 and 2005.

Explanatory Notes:

The reader should be aware of the following policies which have been approved by the Board of Directors of the National Association:

In filing a charge of an alleged violation of the Code of Ethics by a REALTOR®, the charge must read as an alleged violation of one or more Articles of the Code. Standards of Practice may be cited in support of the charge.

The Standards of Practice serve to clarify the ethical obligations imposed by the various Articles and supplement, and do not substitute for, the Case Interpretations in Interpretations of the Code of Ethics.

Modifications to existing Standards of Practice and additional new Standards of Practice are approved from time to time. Readers are cautioned to ensure that the most recent publications are utilized.

AAR RESIDENTIAL RESALE PURCHASE CONTRACT

 ## BUYER ATTACHMENT

This attachment should be given to the Buyer prior to the submission of any offer and is not a part of the Residential Resale Real Estate Purchase Contract's terms.

ATTENTION BUYER!

You are entering into a legally binding agreement.

1. **Read the entire contract before you sign it.**

2. **Review the Seller's Property Disclosure Statement (See Section 4a).**
   • This information comes directly from the Seller.
   • Investigate any blank spaces, unclear answers or any other information that is important to you.

3. **Review the Inspection Paragraph (see Section 6a).**
   If important to you, hire a qualified:
   • Mold inspector
   • Roof inspector
   • Pest inspector
   • Pool inspector
   • Heating/cooling inspector
   Verify square footage (see Section 6b)
   Verify the property is on sewer or septic (see Section 6f)

4. **Confirm your ability to obtain insurance and insurability of the property during the inspection period with your insurance agent (see Sections 6a and 6e).**

5. **Apply for your home loan now, if you have not done so already, and provide your lender with all requested information (see Section 2e).** It is your responsibility to make sure that you and your lender deliver the necessary funds to escrow in sufficient time to allow escrow to close on the agreed upon date. Otherwise, the Seller may cancel the contract.

6. **Read the title commitment within five days of receipt (see Section 3c).**

7. **Read the CC&R's and all other governing documents within five days of receipt (see Section 3c), especially if the home is in a homeowner's association.**

8. **Conduct a thorough final walkthrough (see Section 6m).** If the property is unacceptable, speak up. After the closing may be too late.

You can obtain information through the Buyer's Advisory at http://www.aaronline.com. **Remember, you are urged to consult with an attorney, inspectors, and experts of your choice in any area of interest or concern in the transaction.** Be cautious about verbal representations, advertising claims, and information contained in a listing. Verify anything important to you.

RESIDENTIAL RESALE REAL ESTATE

PURCHASE CONTRACT

The printed portion of this contract has been approved by the Arizona Association of REALTORS® ("AAR"). This is intended to be a binding contract. No representation is made as to the legal validity or adequacy of any provision or the tax consequences thereof. If you desire legal, tax or other professional advice, consult your attorney, tax advisor, insurance agent or professional consultant.

REALTOR®

EQUAL HOUSING OPPORTUNITY

---

1. PROPERTY

1a. 1. **BUYER:** _____
BUYER'S NAME(S)

2. **SELLER:** _____ or ☐ as identified in section 9c.
SELLER'S NAME(S)

3. Buyer agrees to buy and Seller agrees to sell the real property with all improvements, fixtures, and appurtenances thereon
4. or incidental thereto, plus the personal property described herein (collectively the "Premises").

1b. 5. Premises Address: _____ Assessor's #: _____

6. City: _____ County: _____ AZ, Zip Code: _____

7. Legal Description: _____

1c. 8. $ _____ Full Purchase Price, paid as outlined below

9. $ _____ Earnest money _____

10. $ _____

11. $ _____

12. _____

1d. 13. **Close of Escrow:** Close of Escrow ("COE") shall occur when the deed is recorded at the appropriate county recorder's office.
14. Buyer and Seller shall comply with all terms and conditions of this Contract, execute and deliver to Escrow Company all
15. closing documents, and perform all other acts necessary in sufficient time to allow COE to occur on
16. _____, 20 ____ ("COE Date"). If Escrow Company or recorder's office is closed on
MONTH   DAY   YEAR
17. COE Date, COE shall occur on the next day that both are open for business.

18. Buyer shall deliver to Escrow Company a cashier's check, wired funds or other immediately available funds to pay any down
19. payment, additional deposits or Buyer's closing costs, and instruct the lender, if applicable, to deliver immediately available funds
20. to Escrow Company, in a sufficient amount and in sufficient time to allow COE to occur on COE Date.

1e. 21. **Possession:** Seller shall deliver possession, occupancy, access to keys and/or means to operate all locks, mailbox,
22. security system/alarms, and all common area facilities to Buyer at COE or ☐ _____.
23. Broker(s) recommend that the parties seek appropriate counsel from insurance, legal, tax, and accounting professionals
24. regarding the risks of pre-possession or post-possession of the Premises.

1f. 25. **Addenda Incorporated:** ☐ Assumption and Carryback ☐ Buyer Contingency ☐ Domestic Water Well ☐ HUD forms
26. ☐ H.O.A. ☐ Lead-Based Paint Disclosure ☐ Additional Clause ☐ On-site Wastewater Treatment Facility
27. ☐ Other: _____

1g. 28. **Fixtures and Personal Property:** Seller agrees that all existing fixtures on the Premises, and any existing personal
29. property specified herein, shall be included in this sale, including the following:

30. • free-standing range/oven   • flush-mounted speakers   • outdoor landscaping, fountains, and lighting
31. • built-in appliances   • attached fireplace equipment   • water-misting systems
32. • light fixtures   • window and door screens, sun screens • solar systems
33. • ceiling fans   • storm windows and doors   • pellet, wood-burning or gas-log stoves
34. • towel, curtain and drapery rods   • shutters and awnings   • timers
35. • draperies and other window coverings • garage door openers and controls • mailbox
36. • attached floor coverings   • attached TV/media antennas/satellite dishes • storage sheds

---

Initials: **SAMPLE/ SAMPLE**
SELLER   SELLER

©ARIZONA ASSOCIATION OF REALTORS® Form RPC 5/05

Initials: **SAMPLE/ SAMPLE**
BUYER   BUYER

PAGE 1 of 9

AAR Residential Resale Purchase Contract

37. If owned by the Seller, the following items also are included in this sale:

38.   • pool and spa equipment (including any   • security and/or fire systems   • water softeners
39.   mechanical or other cleaning systems)   and/or alarms   • water purification systems

40. **Additional existing personal property included in this sale (if checked):** ☐ refrigerator ☐ washer ☐ dryer

41.   As described: _____

42.   _____

43.   ☐ Other: _____

44.   _____

45.   _____

46. Additional existing personal property included shall not be considered part of the Premises and shall be transferred with no
47. monetary value, and free and clear of all liens or encumbrances.

48. Fixtures and leased items NOT included: _____

49. **IF THIS IS AN ALL CASH SALE, GO TO SECTION 3.**

2. FINANCING

2a.
50. **Loan Contingency:** Buyer's obligation to complete this sale is contingent upon Buyer obtaining loan approval for the loan described
51. in the AAR Loan Status Report without conditions no later than COE Date. If Buyer is unable to obtain loan approval without
52. conditions by COE Date, Buyer shall deliver a notice of the inability to obtain loan approval without conditions to Seller or Escrow
53. Company no later than COE Date.

2b.
54. **Unfulfilled Loan Contingency:** This Contract shall be cancelled and Buyer shall be entitled to a return of the Earnest Money if
55. after diligent and good faith effort, Buyer is unable to obtain loan approval without conditions by COE Date. Buyer is aware that
56. failure to have the down payment or other funds due from Buyer necessary to obtain the loan approval without conditions and
57. close this transaction is not an unfulfilled loan contingency. Buyer acknowledges that prepaid items paid separately from earnest
58. money are not refundable.

2c.
59. **Appraisal Contingency:** Buyer's obligation to complete this sale is contingent upon an appraisal of the Premises by an appraiser
60. acceptable to lender for at least the sales price. If the Premises fails to appraise for the sales price, Buyer has five (5) days after notice
61. of the appraised value to cancel this Contract and receive a refund of the Earnest Money or the appraisal contingency shall be waived.

2d.
62. **Loan Status Report:** The AAR Loan Status Report ("LSR") with, at a minimum, the Buyer's Loan Information section
63. completed, describing the current status of the Buyer's proposed loan, is attached hereto and incorporated herein by reference.

2e.
64. **Loan Application:** Unless previously completed within five (5) days, after Contract acceptance, Buyer shall: (i) complete,
65. sign and deliver to the lender a loan application with requested disclosures and documentation; (ii) grant lender
66. permission to access Buyer's Trimerged Residential Credit Report; and (iii) pay all required loan application fees.

2f.
67. **Loan Processing During Escrow:** Buyer agrees to diligently work to obtain the loan and will promptly provide the lender with
68. all additional documentation required. Buyer instructs the lender to provide loan status updates to Broker(s) and Seller. **Buyer**
69. **shall sign all loan documents no later than three (3) days prior to the COE Date.**

2g.
70. **Type of Financing:** ☐ Conventional ☐ FHA ☐ VA ☐ Assumption ☐ Seller Carryback ☐ _____
71. (If financing is to be other than new financing, see attached addendum.)

2h.
72. **Loan Costs:** Private Mortgage Insurance is required for certain types of loans and shall be paid by Buyer at COE in a
73. manner acceptable to lender. The following may be paid by either party:

74. Discount points shall be paid by: ☐ Buyer ☐ Seller ☐ Other _____

75. Discount points shall not exceed: _____ total points (Does not include loan origination fee)

76. A.L.T.A. Lender Title Insurance Policy shall be paid by ☐ Buyer ☐ Seller

77. Loan Origination Fee (Not to exceed _____ % of loan amount) shall be paid by ☐ Buyer ☐ Seller

78. Appraisal Fee, when required by lender, shall be paid by ☐ Buyer ☐ Seller ☐ Other _____

2i.
79. **Other Loan Costs:** In the event of an FHA or VA loan, Seller agrees to pay up to $ _____ of loan
80. costs not permitted to be paid by the Buyer, in addition to the other costs Seller has agreed to pay herein. In addition, for VA
81. loans, Seller agrees to pay the escrow fee. All other costs of obtaining the loan shall be paid by the Buyer.

2j. 82. **Changes:** Buyer shall immediately notify Seller of any changes in the loan program, financing terms, or lender described in
83. the LSR and shall only make any such changes without the prior written consent of Seller if such changes do not adversely
84. affect Buyer's ability to obtain loan approval without conditions, increase Seller's closing costs, or delay COE.

2k. 85. **FHA Notice (FHABuyer Initials Required):** HUD does not warrant the condition of the property. By initialing below, Buyer acknowl-
86. edges receipt of Form **HUD-92564-CN, "For Your Protection: Get a Home Inspection."** Buyer further acknowledges that such
87. form was signed at or before the Contract date. Signed HUD-92564-CN is attached and made a part of this Purchase Contract.

88.   **(FHA BUYER'S INITIALS REQUIRED)**   SAMPLE   SAMPLE
                                                                  BUYER   BUYER

3. TITLE AND ESCROW

3a. 89. **Escrow:** This Contract shall be used as escrow instructions. The Escrow Company employed by the parties to carry out the
90. terms of this Contract shall be:

91. _____   _____
             "ESCROW/TITLE COMPANY"   PHONE/FAX

3b. 92. **Title and Vesting:** Buyer will take title as determined before COE. Taking title may have significant legal, estate planning
93. and tax consequences. Buyer should obtain legal and tax advice.

3c. 94. **Title Commitment and Title Insurance:** Escrow Company is hereby instructed to obtain and deliver to Buyer and Seller
95. directly, addressed pursuant to 8t and 9c or as otherwise provided, a Commitment for Title Insurance together with
96. complete and legible copies of all documents that will remain as exceptions to Buyer's policy of Title Insurance ("Title
97. Commitment"), including but not limited to Conditions, Covenants and Restrictions ("CC&Rs"); deed restrictions; and
98. easements. Buyer shall have five (5) days after receipt of the Title Commitment and after receipt of notice of any
99. subsequent exceptions to Seller of any items disapproved. Seller shall convey title by general warranty
100. deed. Buyer shall be provided at Seller's expense an American Land Title Association ("ALTA") Homeowner's Title
101. Insurance Policy, or if not available, an ALTA Residential Title Insurance Policy ("Plain Language"/"1-4 units") or, if not
102. available, a Standard Owner's Title Insurance Policy, showing title vested in Buyer. Buyer may acquire extended coverage
103. at Buyer's own additional expense.

3d. 104. **Additional Instructions:** (i) Escrow Company shall promptly furnish notice of pending sale that contains the name and
105. address of the Buyer to any homeowner's association in which the Premises are located. (ii) If the Escrow Company is also
106. acting as the title agency but is not the title insurer issuing the title insurance policy, Escrow Company shall deliver to the
107. Buyer and Seller, upon deposit of funds, a closing protection letter from the title insurer indemnifying the Buyer and Seller for
108. any losses due to fraudulent acts or breach of escrow instructions by the Escrow Company. (iii) All documents necessary to
109. close this transaction shall be executed promptly by Seller and Buyer in the standard form used by Escrow Company. Escrow
110. Company shall modify such documents to the extent necessary to be consistent with this Contract. (iv) Escrow Company
111. fees, unless otherwise stated herein, shall be allocated equally between Seller and Buyer. (v) Escrow Company shall send
112. to all parties and Broker(s) copies of all notices and communications directed to Seller, Buyer and Broker(s). (vi) Escrow
113. Company shall provide Broker(s) access to escrowed materials and information regarding the escrow. (vii) If an Affidavit of
114. Disclosure is provided, Escrow Company shall record the Affidavit at COE.

3e. 115. **Tax Prorations:** Real property taxes payable by the Seller shall be prorated to COE based upon the latest tax information available.

3f. 116. **Release of Earnest Money:** In the event of a dispute between Buyer and Seller regarding any Earnest Money deposited with Escrow
117. Company, Buyer and Seller authorize Escrow Company to release Earnest Money pursuant to the terms and conditions of this Contract
118. in its sole and absolute discretion. Buyer and Seller agree to hold harmless and indemnify Escrow Company against any claim, action
119. or lawsuit of any kind, and from any loss, judgment, or expense, including costs and attorney fees, arising from or relating in any way to
120. the release of Earnest Money.

3g. 121. **Prorations of Assessments and Fees:** All assessments and fees that are not a lien as of the COE, including homeowner's
122. association fees, rents, irrigation fees, and, if assumed, insurance premiums, interest on assessments, interest on
123. encumbrances, and service contracts, shall be prorated as of COE or [] Other:_____

3h. 124. **Assessment Liens:** The amount of any assessment, other than homeowner's association assessments, that is a lien as of
125. the COE, shall be [] paid in full by Seller [] prorated and assumed by Buyer. Any assessment that becomes a lien after
126. COE is the Buyer's responsibility.

3i. 127. **IRS and FIRPTA Reporting:** Seller agrees to comply with IRS reporting requirements. If applicable, Seller agrees to
128. complete, sign, and deliver to Escrow Company a certificate indicating whether Seller is a foreign person or a non-resident
129. alien pursuant to the Foreign Investment in Real Property Tax Act ("FIRPTA"). Buyer and Seller acknowledge that if the Seller
130. is a foreign person, the Buyer must withhold a tax equal to 10% of the purchase price, unless an exemption applies.

Initials:_____ SAMPLE/SAMPLE   Initials:_____ SAMPLE/SAMPLE
       SELLER   SELLER   ©ARIZONA ASSOCIATION OF REALTORS® Form RPC 5/05   BUYER   BUYER

4. DISCLOSURES

4a. 131. **Seller Property Disclosure Statement ("SPDS"):** Seller shall deliver a completed AAR SPDS form to the Buyer within five
132. (5) days after Contract acceptance. Buyer shall provide notice of any SPDS items disapproved within the Inspection Period
133. or five (5) days after receipt of the SPDS, whichever is later.

4b. 134. **Insurance Claims History:** Seller shall deliver to Buyer a written five-year insurance claims history regarding Premises (or
135. a claims history for the length of time Seller has owned the Premises if less than five years) from Seller's insurance
136. company or an insurance support organization or consumer reporting agency, or if unavailable from these sources, from
137. Seller, within five (5) days after Contract acceptance. (Seller may obscure any reference to date of birth or social
138. security number from the document). Buyer shall provide notice of any items disapproved within the Inspection Period or
139. five (5) days after receipt of the claims history, whichever is later.

4c. 140. **Lead-Based Paint Disclosure:** If the Premises were built prior to 1978, the Seller shall: (i) notify the Buyer of any known
141. lead-based paint ("LBP") or LBP hazards in the Premises; (ii) provide the Buyer with any LBP risk assessments or
142. inspections of the Premises in the Seller's possession; (iii) provide the Buyer with the Disclosure of Information on
143. Lead-based Paint and Lead-based Paint Hazards, and any report, records, pamphlets, and/or other materials referenced
144. therein, including the pamphlet "Protect Your Family from Lead in Your Home" (collectively "LBP Information"). Buyer shall return
145. a signed copy of the Disclosure of Information on Lead-Based Paint and Lead-Based Paint Hazards to Seller prior to COE.

146. [] LBP Information was provided prior to Contract acceptance and Buyer acknowledges the opportunity to conduct LBP risk
147. assessments or inspections during Inspection Period.
148. [] Seller shall provide LBP Information within five (5) days after Contract acceptance. Buyer may within ten (10) days or
149. _____ days after receipt of the LBP Information conduct or obtain a risk assessment or inspection of the Premises for
150. the presence of LBP or LBP hazards ("Assessment Period"). Buyer may within five (5) days after receipt of the LBP
151. Information or five (5) days after expiration of the Assessment Period cancel this Contract.

152. If Premises were constructed prior to 1978, **BUYER'S INITIALS REQUIRED**   <u>SAMPLE</u> <u>SAMPLE</u>
                                                                                        BUYER   BUYER

153. If Premises were constructed in 1978 or later, **BUYER'S INITIALS REQUIRED**   <u>SAMPLE</u> <u>SAMPLE</u>
                                                                                        BUYER   BUYER

4d. 154. **Affidavit of Disclosure:** If the Premises is located in an unincorporated area of the county, and five or fewer parcels of
155. property other than subdivided property are being transferred, the Seller shall deliver a completed Affidavit of Disclosure in
156. the form required by law to the Buyer within five (5) days after Contract acceptance. Buyer shall provide notice of any Affidavit
157. of Disclosure items disapproved within the Inspection Period or five (5) days after receipt of the Affidavit of Disclosure,
158. whichever is later.

4e. 159. **Changes During Escrow:** Seller shall immediately notify Buyer of any changes in the Premises or disclosures made
160. herein, in the SPDS, or otherwise. Such notice shall be considered an update of the SPDS. Unless Seller is already
161. obligated by Section 5a or otherwise by this Contract or any amendments hereto, to correct or repair the changed item
162. disclosed, Buyer shall be allowed five (5) days after delivery of such notice to provide notice of disapproval to Seller.

5. WARRANTIES

5a. 163. **Seller Warranties:** Seller warrants and shall maintain and repair the Premises so that at the earlier of possession or COE: (i) all
164. heating, cooling, mechanical, plumbing, and electrical systems (including swimming pool and/or spa, motors, filter
165. systems, cleaning systems, and heaters, if any), free-standing range/oven, and built-in appliances will be in working
166. condition; (ii) all other agreed upon repairs and corrections will be completed pursuant to Section 6j; (iii) the Premises,
167. including all additional existing personal property included in the sale, will be in substantially the same condition as on the date of
168. Contract acceptance; and (iv) all personal property not included in the sale and all debris will be removed from the Premises.

5b. 169. **Warranties that Survive Closing:** Seller warrants that Seller has disclosed to Buyer and Broker(s) all material latent defects
170. and any information concerning the Premises known to Seller, excluding opinions of value, which materially and adversely
171. affect the consideration to be paid by Buyer. Prior to the COE, Seller warrants that payment in full will have been made for
172. all labor, professional services, materials, machinery, fixtures, or tools furnished within the 150 days immediately preceding
173. the COE in connection with the construction, alteration, or repair of any structure on or improvement to the Premises. Seller
174. warrants that the information regarding connection to a sewer system or on-site wastewater treatment facility (conventional
175. septic or alternative) is correct to the best of Seller's knowledge.

5c. 176. **Buyer Warranties:** Buyer warrants that Buyer has disclosed to Seller any information that may materially and adversely affect
177. the Buyer's ability to close escrow or complete the obligations of this Contract. At the earlier of possession of the Premises or
178. COE, Buyer warrants to Seller that Buyer has conducted all desired independent inspections and investigations and accepts
179. the Premises. **Buyer warrants that Buyer is not relying on any verbal representations concerning the Premises**
180. **except disclosed as follows:** _____
181. _____

6. DUE DILIGENCE

6a. 182. **Inspection Period:** Buyer's Inspection Period shall be ten (10) days or _____ days after Contract
183. acceptance. During the Inspection Period Buyer, at Buyer's expense, shall: (i) conduct all desired physical, environmental,
184. and other types of inspections and investigations to determine the value and condition of the Premises; (ii) make inquiries
185. and consult government agencies, lenders, insurance agents, architects, and other appropriate persons and entities
186. concerning the suitability of the Premises and the surrounding area; (iii) investigate applicable building, zoning, fire, health,
187. and safety codes to determine any potential hazards, violations or defects in the Premises; and (iv) verify any material multiple
188. listing service ("MLS") information. If the presence of sex offenders in the vicinity or the occurrence of a disease, natural death,
189. suicide, homicide or other crime on or in the vicinity is a material matter to the Buyer, it must be investigated by the Buyer
190. during the Inspection Period. Buyer shall keep the Premises free and clear of liens, shall indemnify and hold Seller
191. harmless from all liability, claims, demands, damages, and costs, and shall repair all damages arising from the inspections.
192. Buyer shall provide Seller and Broker(s) upon receipt, at no cost, copies of all inspection reports concerning the Premises
193. obtained by Buyer. Buyer is advised to consult the Arizona Department of Real Estate *Buyer Advisory* provided by AAR to
194. assist in Buyer's due diligence inspections and investigations.

6b. 195. **Square Footage: BUYER IS AWARE THAT ANY REFERENCE TO THE SQUARE FOOTAGE OF THE PREMISES, BOTH**
196. **THE REAL PROPERTY (LAND) AND IMPROVEMENTS THEREON, IS APPROXIMATE. IF SQUARE FOOTAGE IS A**
197. **MATERIAL MATTER TO THE BUYER, IT MUST BE INVESTIGATED DURING THE INSPECTION PERIOD.**

6c. 198. **Wood-Destroying Organism or Insect Inspection: IF CURRENT OR PAST WOOD-DESTROYING ORGANISMS OR**
199. **INSECTS (SUCH AS TERMITES) ARE A MATERIAL MATTER TO THE BUYER, THESE ISSUES MUST BE**
200. **INVESTIGATED DURING THE INSPECTION PERIOD.** The Buyer shall order and pay for all wood-destroying organism or
201. insect inspections performed during the Inspection Period. If the lender requires an updated Wood-Destroying Organism or
202. Insect Inspection Report prior to COE, it will be performed at Buyer's expense.

6d. 203. **Flood Hazard:** Flood hazard designations or the cost of flood hazard insurance shall be determined by Buyer during the
204. Inspection Period. If the Premises are situated in an area identified as having any special flood hazards by any
205. governmental entity, the lender may require the purchase of flood hazard insurance. Special flood hazards may also affect
206. the ability to encumber or improve the Premises.

6e. 207. **Insurance: IF HOMEOWNER'S INSURANCE IS A MATERIAL MATTER TO THE BUYER, BUYER SHALL APPLY FOR**
208. **AND OBTAIN WRITTEN CONFIRMATION OF THE AVAILABILITY AND COST OF HOMEOWNER'S INSURANCE FOR**
209. **THE PREMISES FROM BUYER'S INSURANCE COMPANY DURING THE INSPECTION PERIOD.** Buyer understands that
210. any homeowner's, fire, casualty, or other insurance desired by Buyer or required by lender should be in place at COE.

6f. 211. **Sewer or On-site Wastewater Treatment System:** The Premises are connected to a:
212. [] sewer system [] septic system [] alternative system.

213. **IF A SEWER CONNECTION IS A MATERIAL MATTER TO THE BUYER, IT MUST BE INVESTIGATED DURING THE**
214. **INSPECTION PERIOD.** If the Premises are served by a septic or alternative system, the AAR On-site Wastewater Treatment
215. Facility Addendum is incorporated herein by reference.
216.   (BUYER'S INITIALS REQUIRED)   **SAMPLE SAMPLE**
                                                   BUYER   BUYER

6g. 217. **Swimming Pool Barrier Regulations:** During the Inspection Period, Buyer agrees to investigate all applicable state,
218. county, and municipal Swimming Pool barrier regulations and agrees to comply with and pay all costs of compliance
219. with said regulations prior to occupying the Premises, unless otherwise agreed in writing. If the Premises contains a Swimming
220. Pool, Buyer acknowledges receipt of the Arizona Department of Health Services approved private pool safety notice.
221.   (BUYER'S INITIALS REQUIRED)   **SAMPLE SAMPLE**
                                                   BUYER   BUYER

6h. 222. **BUYER ACKNOWLEDGMENT: BUYER RECOGNIZES, ACKNOWLEDGES, AND AGREES THAT BROKER(S) ARE NOT**
223. **QUALIFIED, NOR LICENSED, TO CONDUCT DUE DILIGENCE WITH RESPECT TO THE PREMISES OR THE**
224. **SURROUNDING AREA. BUYER IS INSTRUCTED TO CONSULT WITH QUALIFIED LICENSED PROFESSIONALS TO**
225. **ASSIST IN BUYER'S DUE DILIGENCE EFFORTS. BECAUSE CONDUCTING DUE DILIGENCE WITH RESPECT TO THE**
226. **PREMISES AND THE SURROUNDING AREA IS BEYOND THE SCOPE OF THE BROKER'S EXPERTISE AND**
227. **LICENSING, BUYER EXPRESSLY RELEASES AND HOLDS HARMLESS BROKER(S) FROM LIABILITY FOR ANY**
228. **DEFECTS OR CONDITIONS THAT COULD HAVE BEEN DISCOVERED BY INSPECTION OR INVESTIGATION.**

229.   **(BUYER'S INITIALS REQUIRED)**   **SAMPLE**   **SAMPLE**
                                                               BUYER   BUYER

6i. 230. **Inspection Period Notice:** Prior to expiration of the Inspection Period, Buyer shall deliver to Seller a signed notice of any
231. items disapproved. AAR's Buyer's Inspection Notice and Seller's Response form is available for this purpose. Buyer shall
232. conduct all desired inspections and investigations prior to delivering such notice to Seller and all Inspection Period items
233. disapproved shall be provided in a single notice.

6j. 234. **Buyer Disapproval:** If Buyer, in Buyer's sole discretion, disapproves of items as allowed herein, Buyer shall deliver to Seller
235. notice of the items disapproved and state in the notice that Buyer elects to either:
236.   (1) immediately cancel this Contract and all Earnest Money shall be released to Buyer, or
237.   (2) provide the Seller an opportunity to correct the items disapproved, in which case:
238.   (a) Seller shall respond in writing within five (5) days or _____ days after delivery to Seller of Buyer's notice of
239.   items disapproved. Seller's failure to respond to Buyer in writing within the specified time period shall
240.   conclusively be deemed Seller's refusal to correct any of the items disapproved.
241.   **(b) If Seller agrees in writing to correct items disapproved, Seller shall correct the items, complete any**
242.   **repairs in a workmanlike manner and deliver any paid receipts evidencing the corrections and repairs**
243.   **to Buyer three (3) days or _____ days prior to COE Date.**
244.   (c) If Seller is unwilling or unable to correct any of the items disapproved, Buyer may cancel
245.   this Contract within five (5) days after delivery of Seller's response or after expiration of the time for
246.   Seller's response, whichever occurs first, and all Earnest Money shall be released to Buyer. If Buyer does
247.   not cancel this Contract within the five (5) days as provided, Buyer shall close escrow without correction
248.   of those items that Seller has not agreed in writing to correct.

249. VERBAL DISCUSSIONS WILL NOT EXTEND THESE TIME PERIODS. Only a written agreement signed by both parties will
250. extend response times or cancellation rights.

251. BUYER'S FAILURE TO GIVE NOTICE OF DISAPPROVAL OF ITEMS OR CANCELLATION OF THIS CONTRACT WITHIN
252. THE SPECIFIED TIME PERIOD SHALL CONCLUSIVELY BE DEEMED BUYER'S ELECTION TO PROCEED WITH THE
253. TRANSACTION WITHOUT CORRECTION OF ANY DISAPPROVED ITEMS.

6k. 254. **Notice of Non-Working Warranted Items:** Buyer shall provide Seller with notice of any non-working warranted item(s) of
255. which Buyer becomes aware during the Inspection Period or the Seller warranty for that item(s) shall be waived. Delivery of
256. such notice shall not affect Seller's obligation to maintain or repair the warranted item(s).

6l. 257. **Home Warranty Plan:** Buyer and Seller are advised to investigate the various home warranty plans available for purchase.
258. The parties acknowledge that different home warranty plans have different coverage options, exclusions, limitations, service
259. fees and most plans exclude pre-existing conditions.

260.   ☐ A Home Warranty Plan will be ordered by ☐ Buyer or ☐ Seller with the following optional coverage
261.   _____, to be issued by _____ at a cost not to exceed
262. $ _____, to be paid for by ☐ Buyer ☐ Seller
263.   ☐ Buyer declines the purchase of a Home Warranty Plan.

6m. 264. **Walkthrough(s):** Seller grants Buyer and Buyer's inspector(s) reasonable access to conduct walkthrough(s) of the Premises for the
265. purpose of satisfying Buyer that any corrections or repairs agreed to by the Seller have been completed, warranted items are in
266. working condition and that the Premises is in substantially the same condition as of the date of Contract acceptance. If Buyer does
267. not conduct such walkthrough(s), Buyer releases Seller and Broker(s) from liability for any defects that could have been discovered.

6n. 268. **Seller's Responsibility Regarding Inspections and Walkthrough(s):** Seller shall make the Premises available for all
269. inspections and walkthrough(s) upon reasonable notice by Buyer. Seller shall, at Seller's expense, have all utilities on,
270. including any propane, until COE to enable Buyer to conduct these inspections and walkthrough(s).

7. REMEDIES

7a. 271. **Cure Period:** A party shall have an opportunity to cure a potential breach of this Contract. If a party fails to comply with any
272. provision of this Contract, the other party shall deliver a notice to the non-complying party specifying the non-compliance. If
273. the non-compliance is not cured within three (3) days after delivery of such notice ("Cure Period"), the failure to comply shall
274. become a breach of Contract.

7b. 275. **Breach**: In the event of a breach of Contract, the non-breaching party may cancel this Contract and/or proceed against the
276. breaching party in any claim or remedy that the non-breaching party may have in law or equity, subject to the Alternative
277. Dispute Resolution obligations set forth herein. In the case of the Seller, because it would be difficult to fix actual damages
278. in the event of Buyer's breach, the Earnest Money may be deemed a reasonable estimate of damages and Seller may, at
279. Seller's option, accept the Earnest Money as Seller's sole right to damages; and in the event of Buyer's breach arising from
280. Buyer's failure to deliver the notice required by Section 2a, or Buyer's inability to obtain loan approval due to the waiver of
281. the appraisal contingency pursuant to Section 2c, Seller shall exercise this option and accept the Earnest Money as Seller's
282. sole right to damages. An unfulfilled contingency is not a breach of Contract.

7c. 283. **Alternative Dispute Resolution ("ADR"):** Buyer and Seller agree to mediate any dispute or claim arising out of or relating
284. to this Contract in accordance with the REALTORS® Dispute Resolution System, or as otherwise agreed. All mediation costs
285. shall be paid equally by the parties. In the event that mediation does not resolve all disputes or claims, the unresolved
286. disputes or claims shall be submitted for binding arbitration. In such event, the parties shall agree upon an arbitrator and
287. cooperate in the scheduling of an arbitration hearing. If the parties are unable to agree on an arbitrator, the dispute shall be
288. submitted to the American Arbitration Association ("AAA") in accordance with the AAA Arbitration Rules for the Real Estate
289. Industry. The decision of the arbitrator shall be final and nonappealable. Judgment on the award rendered by the arbitrator
290. may be entered in any court of competent jurisdiction. Notwithstanding the foregoing, either party may opt out of binding
291. arbitration within thirty (30) days after the conclusion of the mediation conference by notice to the other and in such event
292. either party shall have the right to resort to court action.

7d. 293. **Exclusions from ADR:** The following matters are excluded from the requirement for ADR hereunder: (i) any action brought
294. in the Small Claims Division of an Arizona Justice Court (up to $2,500) so long as the matter is not thereafter transferred or
295. removed from the small claims division; (ii) judicial or nonjudicial foreclosure or other action or proceeding to enforce a deed
296. of trust, mortgage, or agreement for sale; (iii) an unlawful entry or detainer action; (iv) the filing or enforcement of a
297. mechanic's lien; or (v) any matter that is within the jurisdiction of a probate court. Further, the filing of a judicial action to
298. enable the recording of a notice of pending action ("lis pendens"), or order of attachment, receivership, injunction, or other
299. provisional remedies shall not constitute a waiver of the obligation to submit the claim to ADR, nor shall such action
300. constitute a breach of the duty to mediate or arbitrate.

7e. 301. **Attorney Fees and Costs:** The prevailing party in any dispute or claim between Buyer and Seller arising out of or relating
302. to this Contract shall be awarded their reasonable attorney fees and costs. Costs shall include, without limitation, attorney
303. fees, expert witness fees, fees paid to investigators, and arbitration costs.

8. ADDITIONAL TERMS AND CONDITIONS

8a. 304. _____
305. _____
306. _____
307. _____
308. _____
309. _____
310. _____
311. _____
312. _____
313. _____
314. _____
315. _____

Initials: **SAMPLE/ SAMPLE**   ©ARIZONA ASSOCIATION OF REALTORS® Form RPC 5/05   Initials: **SAMPLE/ SAMPLE**
      SELLER   SELLER   BUYER   BUYER

AAR Residential Resale Purchase Contract

8b. 316. **Risk of Loss:** If there is any loss or damage to the Premises between the date of Contract acceptance and COE or
317. possession, whichever is earlier, by reason of fire, vandalism, flood, earthquake, or act of God, the risk of loss shall be on
318. the Seller, provided, however, that if the cost of repairing such loss or damage would exceed ten percent (10%) of the
319. purchase price, either Seller or Buyer may elect to cancel the Contract.

8c. 320. **Permission:** Buyer and Seller grant Broker(s) permission to advise the public of this Contract.

8d. 321. **Arizona Law:** This Contract shall be governed by Arizona law and jurisdiction is exclusively conferred on the State of Arizona.

8e. 322. **Time is of the Essence:** The parties acknowledge that time is of the essence in the performance of the obligations
323. described herein.

8f. 324. **Compensation:** Seller and Buyer acknowledge that Broker(s) shall be compensated for services rendered as previously agreed by
325. separate written agreement(s), which shall be delivered by Broker(s) to Escrow Company for payment at COE, if not previously paid.
326. If Seller is obligated to pay Broker(s), this Contract shall constitute an irrevocable assignment of Seller's proceeds at COE. If Buyer
327. is obligated to pay Broker(s), payment shall be collected from Buyer as a condition of COE. COMMISSIONS PAYABLE FOR THE
328. SALE, LEASING, OR MANAGEMENT OF PROPERTY ARE NOT SET BY ANY BOARD OR ASSOCIATION OF REALTORS®, OR
329. MULTIPLE LISTING SERVICE, OR IN ANY MANNER OTHER THAN BETWEEN THE BROKER AND CLIENT.

8g. 330. **Copies and Counterparts:** A fully executed facsimile or electronic copy of the Contract shall be treated as an original Contract. This Contract
331. and any other documents required by this Contract may be executed by facsimile or other electronic means and in any number of counterparts,
332. which shall become effective upon delivery as provided for herein, except that the Lead-Based Paint Disclosure Statement may not be signed
333. in counterpart. All counterparts shall be deemed to constitute one instrument, and each counterpart shall be deemed an original.

8h. 334. **Days:** All references to days in this Contract shall be construed as calendar days and a day shall begin at 12:00 a.m. and end at 11:59 p.m.

8i. 335. **Calculating Time Periods:** In computing any time period prescribed or allowed by this Contract, the day of the act or event
336. from which the time period begins to run is not included and the last day of the time period is included. Contract acceptance
337. occurs on the date that the signed Contract (and any incorporated counter offer) is delivered to and received by the
338. appropriate Broker. Acts that must be performed three days prior to the COE Date must be performed three full days prior
339. (i.e., if COE Date is Friday the act must be performed by 11:59 p.m. on Monday).

8j. 340. **Entire Agreement:** This Contract, and any addenda and attachments, shall constitute the entire agreement between Seller and
341. Buyer, shall supersede any other written or oral agreements between Seller and Buyer and can be modified only by a writing
342. signed by Seller and Buyer. The failure to initial any page of this Contract shall not affect the validity or terms of this Contract.

8k. 343. **Subsequent Offers:** Buyer acknowledges that Seller has the right to accept subsequent offers until COE. Seller understands that
344. any subsequent offer accepted by the Seller must be a backup offer contingent on the cancellation of this Contract.

8l. 345. **Cancellation:** A party who wishes to exercise the right of cancellation as allowed herein may cancel this Contract by
346. delivering notice stating the reason for cancellation to the other party or to the Escrow Company. Cancellation shall become
347. effective immediately upon delivery of the cancellation notice.

8m. 348. **Notice:** Unless otherwise provided, delivery of all notices and documentation required or permitted hereunder shall be in
349. writing and deemed delivered and received when: (i) hand-delivered; (ii) sent via facsimile transmission; (iii) sent via
350. electronic mail, if email addresses are provided herein; or (iv) sent by recognized overnight courier service, and addressed
351. to Buyer as indicated in Section 8r, to Seller as indicated in Section 9a and to the Escrow Company indicated in Section 3a.

8n. 352. **Earnest Money:** Earnest Money is in the form of: [] Personal Check [] Other _____
353. If applicable, Earnest Money has been received by Broker named in Section 8r and upon acceptance of this offer will be
354. deposited with: [] Escrow Company [] Broker's Trust Account

8o. 355. **Release of Broker(s): Seller and Buyer hereby expressly release, hold harmless and indemnify Broker(s) in this**
356. **transaction from any and all liability and responsibility regarding financing, the condition, square footage, lot lines,**
357. **boundaries, value, rent rolls, environmental problems, sanitation systems, roof, wood infestation, building codes,**
358. **governmental regulations, insurance or any other matter relating to the value or condition of the Premises.**

359. **(BUYER'S INITIALS REQUIRED)** <u>SAMPLE</u> <u>SAMPLE</u>
BUYER   BUYER

8p. 360. **Terms of Acceptance:** This offer will become a binding Contract when acceptance is signed by Seller and
361. a signed copy delivered in person, by mail, facsimile or electronically, and received by Broker named in Section 8r
362. by _____, _____ at _____ a.m./p.m., Mountain Standard Time. Buyer
363. may withdraw this offer at any time prior to receipt of Seller's signed acceptance. If no signed acceptance is received by this
364. date and time, this offer shall be deemed withdrawn and the Buyer's Earnest Money shall be returned.

8q. 365. THIS CONTRACT CONTAINS NINE PAGES EXCLUSIVE OF ANY ADDENDA AND ATTACHMENTS. PLEASE ENSURE THAT
366. YOU HAVE RECEIVED AND READ ALL NINE PAGES OF THIS OFFER AS WELL AS ANY ADDENDA AND ATTACHMENTS.

Initials: <u>SAMPLE/ SAMPLE</u>	©ARIZONA ASSOCIATION OF REALTORS® Form RPC 5/05	Initials: <u>SAMPLE/ SAMPLE</u>
SELLER SELLER		BUYER BUYER

8r. 367. **Broker on behalf of Buyer:**

368. _____
PRINT SALESPERSON'S NAME   AGENT CODE   PRINT FIRM NAME   FIRM CODE

369. _____
FIRM ADDRESS   STATE   ZIP CODE

370. _____
TELEPHONE   FAX   EMAIL

8s. 371. **Agency Confirmation:** The Broker named in Section 8r above is the agent of (check one):
372. ▢ the Buyer ▢ the Seller or ▢ both the Buyer and Seller

8t. 373. **The undersigned agree to purchase the Premises on the terms and conditions herein stated and acknowledge receipt of a**
374. **copy hereof including the Buyer Attachment.**

375. **SAMPLE**   **SAMPLE**
_____   _____
BUYER'S SIGNATURE   MO/DA/YR   BUYER'S SIGNATURE   MO/DA/YR

376. _____   _____
ADDRESS   ADDRESS

377. _____   _____
CITY, STATE, ZIPCODE   CITY, STATE, ZIPCODE

9. SELLER ACCEPTANCE

9a. 378. **Broker on behalf of Seller:**

379. _____
PRINT SALESPERSON'S NAME   AGENT CODE   PRINT FIRM NAME   FIRM CODE

380. _____
FIRM ADDRESS   STATE   ZIP CODE

381. _____
TELEPHONE   FAX   EMAIL

9b. 382. **Agency Confirmation:** The Broker named in Section 9a above is the agent of (check one):
383. ▢ the Seller; or ▢ both the Buyer and Seller

9c. 384. **The undersigned agree to sell the Premises on the terms and conditions herein stated, acknowledge receipt of a**
385. **copy hereof and grant permission to Broker named on Section 9a to deliver a copy to Buyer.**

386. Counter Offer is attached, and is incorporated herein by reference. Seller should sign both this offer and the Counter Offer. If there
387. is a conflict between this offer and the Counter Offer, the provisions of the Counter Offer shall be controlling.

388. **SAMPLE**   **SAMPLE**
_____   _____
SELLER'S SIGNATURE   MO/DA/YR   SELLER'S SIGNATURE   MO/DA/YR

389. _____   _____
SELLER'S NAME PRINTED   SELLER'S NAME PRINTED

390. _____   _____
ADDRESS   ADDRESS

391. _____   _____
CITY, STATE, ZIPCODE   CITY, STATE, ZIPCODE

392. ▢ **OFFER REJECTED BY SELLER:** _____ _____, 20 _____   **SAMPLE**
MONTH   DAY   YEAR   (SELLER'S INITIALS)

For Broker Use Only:

Brokerage File/Log No._____ Manager's Initials_____ Broker's Initials_____ Date _____
MO/DA/YR

Initials: **SAMPLE/ SAMPLE**   Initials: **SAMPLE/ SAMPLE**
        SELLER   SELLER   ©ARIZONA ASSOCIATION OF REALTORS® Form RPC 5/05   BUYER   BUYER

PAGE 9 of 9

Index

About The Author

K. Michelle Lind is General Counsel to the Arizona Association of REALTORS® (AAR). She serves as the primary legal advisor to the association, provides legal direction in the development of standard real estate forms, is involved in legislative advocacy, and assists in the Association's educational efforts.

She received her undergraduate degree from Arizona State University (ASU), graduating *summa cum laude*, and her *Juris Doctor* degree, graduating *cum laude*, from ASU College of Law (now the Sandra Day O'Connor College of Law). She is a State Bar of Arizona board-certified real estate specialist.

Michelle began her legal career at the Phoenix law firm of *Jennings, Strouss & Salmon, P.L.C.* Thereafter, she joined Christopher A. Combs and Richard V. Mack and they became partners at *Combs, Mack & Lind, P.C.*, a law firm focusing on real estate and commercial litigation, transactions and brokerage defense.

Michelle has served on numerous Arizona Department of Real Estate committees, as Chair and Journal Editor for the Arizona State Bar Real Property Section Executive Council and on the Central/Northern Arizona Better Business Bureau Arizona Mortgage Advisory Council. Michelle is a guest lecturer for the College of Business MBA Real Estate Strategies class and has also served as an adjunct professor at ASU College of Law. She continues to be a frequent speaker on real estate issues at real estate and legal continuing education courses, firms and local REALTOR® associations. She is a regular author for the *Arizona REALTOR® Digest* and the *Arizona Journal of Real Estate & Business*.

Prior to attending law school, Michelle worked for five years as a registered nurse in obstetrics and out-patient surgery. She has two adult sons, Eric and Ryan.

Arizona Association of REALTORS®
255 East Osborn Road, Suite 200
Phoenix, AZ 85012-2327
Phone: (602) 248-7787
(800) 426-7274
Fax: (602) 351-2474